THREE
BULLETS
SEALED
HIS LIPS

THREE BULLETS SEALED HIS LIPS

by
Bruce A. Rubenstein
and
Lawrence E. Ziewacz

Michigan State University Press
1987

Design & Production: Julie L. Loehr
Typeset: Infinity, Okemos, MI
Cover: Lynne A. Brown, Media Graphics

Printed in the United States of America

The paper used in this publication meets the miniumum requirements of American National Standard for
Information Sciences — Permanence of Paper for Printed Library Materials ANSI Z39.48-1984

Michigan State University Press
East Lansing, Michigan 48823-5202

Library of Congress Catolging-in-Publication Data
Rubenstein, Bruce A. (Bruce Alan)
Three bullets sealed his lips.

Bibliography: p.205
1. Abramowitz, Sam — Trials, litigation, etc.
2. Trials (Murder) — Michigan — Detroit.
3. Hooper, Warren G. — Assassination.
I. Ziewacz, Lawrence E. (Lawrence Edward).
II. Title.
KF 224.A33R8 1987   345.73'02523   87-42552
ISBN 0-87013-252-0

To Harry J. Brown
Mentor, Scholar, and Friend

CONTENTS

ACKNOWLEDGMENTS

We are indebted to many organizations and individuals for helping make this project a reality. Special thanks go to Colonel Gerald Hough, Director of the Michigan State Police, and his staff, for greatly facilitating our task by graciously meeting every request for access to State Police files and photographs concerning the investigation into the assassination of Warren G. Hooper. The officers, detectives, and troopers who devoted thousands of man-hours in a quest to apprehend the killers, only to be denied the rewards of their diligent professionalism, are the heroes of this story, and it is to them that we dedicate this book.

Gratitude also goes to LeRoy Barnett and John Curry of the Michigan History Division of the Michigan Department of State. Their expertise and willingness to comply with our requests for source materials and photographs proved invaluable. Additional thanks go to Morris O. Thomas for his excellent maps; Michigan Department of Corrections for furnishing prison and parole records; Jeanne Bryden and the staff of the *Albion Evening Recorder* for their assistance during our visits to Albion; Richard Hathaway, Joann Frankena, and the staff of the State of Michigan Library who guided us to several useful sources, especially the clippings file; staff members of the Bentley Historical Library which houses the Michigan Historical Collections of The University of Michigan, and the Waldo Library of Western Michigan University; the Calhoun County Clerk's Office for unearthing the murder conspiracy examination and trial records; the Ingham County Clerk's Office for transcripts of cases brought to trial by the Carr-Sigler grand jury; Robert Ianni, of the Criminal Division of the Michigan Attorney General's Office, for permitting us to examine the sole remaining box of grand jury records concerning the Hooper case; Mrs. Betty Holloway, Administrative Secretary for the History Department of The University of Michigan-Flint, for helping type the manuscript; and Professor Henry Silverman, Chairman of the Department of American Thought and Language at Michigan State University, for his constant efforts on our behalf.

Don Gardner, Al Kaufman, Victor C. Anderson, Richard B. Foster, Sr., Eugene F. Black, Marvin J. Salmon, George V. Mather, Betty Keyes, Janet Pierson, and Gertrude Ludwick gave hours of interviews, either in person, by telephone, and/or in writing, which afforded us an insight not only into the politics surrounding the grand jury and the murder of Senator Hooper, but also of the personal characteristics of many of the key figures in this drama.

Dr. Richard Chapin, Ms. Ellen Link, and Ms. Julie Loehr of the Michigan State University Press have been uniformly supportive and helpful. We also appreciate comments made by reviewers of our manuscript. The book was enhanced by their observations and criticisms.

Finally, heartfelt appreciation and affection go to our friends, colleagues, and especially our families, for enduring our idiosyncrasies while this book was being researched and written. Usually willingly, but occasionally under duress, they served as our sounding boards, and their comments and questions kept us on course. In many respects, this project became an object of enthusiasm and excitement for them as well as for us, and we are grateful beyond words for their patient understanding and encouragement.

Bruce A. Rubenstein
Lawrence E. Ziewacz
May 1987

AUTHORS' NOTE

All quotations in this book were taken directly from published accounts, private correspondence, personal interviews, trial transcripts, or sworn statements made before either the Michigan State Police or members of the Ingham County Grand Jury. The only liberty assumed was the deletion of certain questions posed by attorneys during the examination and trial so that the witness response would read as a coherent story; the quotations themselves, however, were altered in no way from the original source. Likewise, all descriptions of individuals, events, or places were taken from published accounts, trial transcripts, sworn testimony, or interviews with persons well acquainted with the individuals, events, or places involved. Multiple citations were required before descriptions were considered for inclusion.

CAST OF MAJOR CHARACTERS

SAM ABRAMOWITZ
a three time loser who was willing to do anything, including murder, to achieve status in Detroit's underworld

VICTOR C. ANDERSON
Kim Sigler's chief legal advisor and confidante

LOUIS BROWN
a convict whose version of the Hooper murder captivated Sigler's imagination

LELAND W. CARR
respected mid-Michigan judge who hoped his one man grand jury probe into legislative corruption would earn him promotion to the state's Supreme Court

LOUIS COASH
Carr's successor, who clashed with Sigler over grand jury procedure

JOHN R. DETHMERS
Michigan's Attorney General whose report on prison scandals infuriated Sigler by suggesting a possible method by which Hooper's murder could have been accomplished

FLOYD FITZSIMMONS
Michigan sports promoter and business associate of Frank D. McKay

HARRY FLEISHER
Detroit mobster who ascended to prominence in the Purple Gang when its leaders, Raymond Bernstein and Harry Keywell, were imprisoned for murder

SAM FLEISHER
Harry's younger brother who had served time in Alcatraz for armed robbery and prohibition violations

CALLIENETTA HOOPER
the statuesque wife who resented living in the Senator's shadow

WARREN G. HOOPER
an admitted bribe taker who was brutally murdered before he could testify who was behind the pay-off schemes

ALFRED KURNER
the youthful armed robber who furnished authorities with their best lead on those involved in the conspiracy to slay Hooper

DONALD S. LEONARD
veteran State Police officer who replaced Oscar G. Olander as Commissioner in 1947

HENRY LUKS
a convicted safe cracker who would do almost anything for easy money

PETE MAHONEY
a small-time gambler who sought importance through his friendship with Harry Fleisher

FRANK D. McKAY
the oft charged, but never convicted, millionaire former "Boss" of Michigan's Republican party who was targeted by Sigler as the person who bankrolled Hooper's assassination

MYRON (MIKE) SELIK
the dapper chief lieutenant of Harry Fleisher

KIM SIGLER
a flamboyant clotheshorse who expected that his role as grand jury special prosecutor would catapult him into the governorship and possibly the White House

OTHER CHARACTERS

MURL K. ATEN
Jackson County prosecutor who assisted Sigler's investigation into Hooper's murder

EDWARD N. BARNARD
political associate of Frank D. McKay

RAYMOND BERNSTEIN
imprisoned head of the Purple Gang

WILLIAM H. BIBBINGS
Justice of the Peace who presided over the pre-trial examination of the Fleishers, Selik, and Mahoney

EUGENE F. BLACK
Michigan Attorney General (1947-48)

MITCHELL BONKOWSKI
convict at Southern Michigan Prison

WILLIAM E. BRACEY
witness near the scene of the Hooper slaying

GEORGE BRANTON
Detective Inspector in the Detroit Police Department

EVELYN IRIS BROWN
Albion barmaid who testified against Mahoney

VERNON J. BROWN
Lieutenant Governor of Michigan (1946-47) and unsuccessful candidate in the 1946 Republican gubernatorial primary

DAVID BUTLER
robbery accomplice of Al Kurner

SAM CHIVAS
ex-boxer and small-time hoodlum

CHARLES E. COBB
brother of Callienetta Hooper

EDWARD COOPER
Michigan State Police detective

MAURICE CUYLER
Albion service station owner

JAMES DADAS
owner of the Aristocrat Club

JOHN DALTON
grand jury staff member

HUGH DALY
Detroit Times Washington correspondent

WILLIAM DAVIDSON
armed robber and alleged Purple Gang gunman

MAX DAVIS
Flint jeweler

HERMAN FAUBERT
convict at Southern Michigan Prison

FRANK FITZGERALD
Governor of Michigan (1935-36, 1939)

RICHARD B. FOSTER
Sigler's successor as grand jury prosecutor

DON GARDNER
Detroit Times political writer

GORDON GILLIS
private detective associated with Leo Wendell

EDWIN GOODWIN
editor of the *Michigan State Digest*

WILLIAM GREEN
co-defendant with Floyd Fitzsimmons and Frank D. McKay

WILLIAM HANSEN
Michigan State Police captain

GEORGE B. HARTRICK
Oakland County Circuit Judge

BLAINE W. HATCH
Circuit Judge who presided over the murder conspiracy trial of the
Fleishers, Selik, and Mahoney

CHARLES F. HEMANS
debonnaire Lansing lobbyist who was a key witness before the grand
jury

ERNEST HENRY
convict at Southern Michigan Prison

BION HOEG
Michigan State Police detective

MERVYN B. HOWARD
witness at the scene of the Hooper slaying

HARRY JACKSON
Warden of the Southern Michigan Prison

HAROLD JOHNSON
convict at Southern Michigan Prison

IVAN A. JOHNSTON
chair of the Michigan Senate Committee investigation into Sigler's conduct as special prosecutor

AL KAUFMAN
Detroit Times political writer

HARRY F. KELLY
Governor of Michigan (1943-47)

EDWARD H. KENNEDY, JR.
defense counsel for Harry Fleisher and Mike Selik

HARRY KEYWELL
imprisoned Purple Gang leader

PHIL KEYWELL
imprisoned Purple Gang leader

ROBERT G. LEITCH
defense counsel for Sam Fleisher

CHARLES LEITER
former Purple Gang member and bodyguard for Frank D. McKay

JOHN LINSEY
initial grand jury special prosecutor

IRA H. MARMON
former head of the Michigan State Police Detective Bureau and associate of Edwin Goodwin

GEORGE V. MATHER
editor of the *Albion Evening Recorder*

DAVID MAZROFF
former Purple Gang member

KENNETH McCORMICK
Detroit Free Press reporter who won a Pulitzer Prize for his coverage of the grand jury proceedings

WILLIAM H. McKEIGHAN
former mayor of Flint who was McKay's chief political aide

JAMES MELTON
crime reporter for the *Detroit Times*

FLOYD MODJESKA
witness at the scene of the Hooper slaying

RALPH MOREHOUSE
the Hoopers' family physician

LYLE MORSE
Michigan State Police detective

HAROLD V. MULBAR
Michigan State Police Chief of Detectives

VINCENT NEERING
Michigan State Police investigator

ALLEN J. NIEBER
crime reporter for the *Detroit News*

DONALD C. NOGGLE
Oakland County Prosecutor

OSCAR G. OLANDER
Michigan State Police Commissioner at the time of Hooper's murder

WILBER H. PETERMANN
Michigan State Police polygraph expert

D. C. PETTIT
Deputy Warden of the Southern Michigan Prison

MORRIS RAIDER
former member of the Purple Gang

HARRY RICHARDS
Albion automobile dealer

LOUIS ROBINSON
owner of the Buick Garage in Albion

THEODORE RODGERS
defense counsel for Pete Mahoney

ABE ROSENBERG
former Purple Gang member

VITA ROSENBERG
wife of Abe Rosenberg

STEPHEN J. ROTH
Michigan Attorney General (1949-50)

HERBERT J. RUSHTON
Michigan Attorney General (1941-44)

ISADORE SCHWARTZ
former Purple Gang member and bodyguard for Frank D. McKay

NAOMI SELIK
wife of Mike Selik

JOSEPH SHERIDAN
Michigan State Police detective

JOHN SIMPSON
Circuit Judge who presided over the liquor conspiracy trial of Frank D. McKay

HARRY SNYDER
witness at the scene of the Hooper slaying

CLARE SPEARS
Sam Abramowitz's parole officer

HARRY S. TOY
Detroit Police Commissioner (1947-48)

KYLE VAN AUKER
witness at the scene of the Hooper slaying

FRED A. VAN CAMPEN
Michigan State Police trooper

LEO VAN CONANT
chief of Sigler's Michigan State Police detail

THEODORE VAN DELLEN
attorney for Callienetta Hooper

MURRAY D. VAN WAGONER
Governor of Michigan (1941-43) and unsuccessful Democratic gubernatorial candidate in 1946

TOMMY VIOLA
alleged Purple Gang gunman

GUY VROMAN
Albion area farmer

FRED WALKER
attorney for Floyd Fitzsimmons

MAURICE WALSH
defense counsel for Harry Fleisher, Selik, and Mahoney

JEANETTE WELKER
girlfriend of Harry Fleisher

LEO WENDELL
initial grand jury investigator for Leland W. Carr

AGNES WICKENS
Senator Hooper's personal secretary and confidante

WALTER B. WILLIAMS
Michigan State Police detective

ROBERT WILSON
Southern Michigan Prison Inspector

STANLEY WROBEL
convict at Southern Michigan Prison

MURRAY YOUNG
Michigan State Police detective

CHAPTER ONE

KINGS, KNIGHTS AND KNAVES

I Nothing so disrupts tranquil, complacent societies as the sight of husbands, fathers, and sons leaving for military service. Like most Americans during the years following the United States' entry into World War II, Michiganians preoccupied themselves with domestic sacrifices and vicarious involvement in ·actual combat through printed tales of Allied encounters with the Axis powers. By late summer of 1943, however, state residents were disquieted still further when battlefield accounts were suddenly forced to share headlines in local newspapers with reports of a grand jury investigation into alleged corruption in their government. More serious than anyone first imagined, this probe eventually would result in indictments against, and the successful prosecution of, a former lieutenant governor, twelve state senators, eleven state representatives, and scores of prosecuting attorneys, police officials, and lobbyists.[1] A total of 130 arrests were made, including three for perjury and five for contempt of court, and 62 convictions were garnered. Of the remaining cases, eleven were dismissed, nine brought acquittals, three ended with hung juries, and the others never came to trial. During the course of the nearly six-year investigation, a state police task force put in 5,780 man hours, nearly 1,300 subpeonas were served, and one witness was murdered.[2]

Although this inquiry did not begin until 1943, rumors long had persisted that malfeasance ran rampant through the not-so-hallowed halls of the Michigan legislature. A favorite story of Guy Jenkins, veteran Booth newspaper capitol correspondent, was how Fred Green, an austere rural Republican who served as governor during the last years of prosperity in the 1920s, stood with correspondents viewing group portraits of the members of the state house and senate. One reporter happened to remark that they were "fine pictures,"

1

to which the governor replied without a smile, "Yes, sir. There's one of the finest legislatures money can buy."[3] Stories spread about the lobbyist with a black bag filled with cash who sought out legislators to pass a bill placing the natural ice industry under the sway of the Public Service Commission, and of another man with a similar valise who chased a reluctant lawmaker through the capitol hallways in an effort to solicit his opposition to a small loan company proposal. In 1933 a novice solon complained to the attorney general about such blatant vote buying, but the subsequent investigation was aborted when the complainant announced that he must have been "hallucinating" when he made his allegation.[4]

Unfortunately, these incidents were not isolated. For two decades, rumors swept Michigan's capital city of Lansing of lawmakers who had accepted money and gifts in return for votes on sausage manufacturing, commercial fishing, barber and beautician regulation, naturopathy, chain banking, taxation, kerosene inspection, legalizing of dog racing and slot machines, horse racing, small loan company interest rates, the manufacture of oleomargarine, and the size of bakery bread pans.[5] By 1943, those in the know knew the newly dubbed "Arsenal of Democracy" was mired in a cesspool of undemocratic political behavior.

II Silver-haired, 66-year-old Michigan Attorney General Herbert J. Rushton, himself a former member of the state senate during the period of purported corruption, turned a deaf ear to pleas from William P. Lovett, executive secretary of the influential Detroit Citizens' League, to establish a grand jury to examine evidence of graft which his organization had assembled following a six-month independent investigation. However, when William C. Stenson, who represented Rushton's home district in the state house, blurted to reporters that a man in a gray suit had placed $1,350 and a note of instruction in his overcoat pocket as it hung in the capitol cloakroom to ensure his vote against an impending anti-chain bank measure, the attorney general was forced, albeit reluctantly, to petition the Circuit Court of Ingham County (where the alleged bribe occurred) to convene a grand jury to look into not only Stenson's story, but also any other reputed wrongdoings which fell within the state's six-year statute of limitation. The court members then selected their senior judge, Leland W. Carr, to serve as a one-man panel.[6]

A member of the circuit court since 1921, the 60-year-old jurist was a legend in Ingham County. A hulking, grey-haired, pachydermatous man who was so careless of his personal appearance that he

2

earned the sobriquet "Old Gravy Vest" from the local press corps, Carr operated a law school as a hobby and was renowned among his constituents for a strict adherence to the letter of the law.[7] This policy, while popular with the masses, caused consternation among certain Lansing newsmen. Al Kaufman, then a reporter for the *Detroit Times*, recalled that Carr, although personally cordial, was "Mr. Jurisprudence...a jurist who wore blinders. If the law said you shall get fifty years for killing a man, you went to prison, notwithstanding the fact that he had raped your mother, your grandmother, and your three sisters. The law was the law and you should have called the police."[8] Don Gardner, another youthful member of the capitol press at that time, remembered Carr as a man who "spent his whole life aiming for the Supreme Court and he didn't care how he got there."[9] Despite these reservations, neither man questioned his integrity, and they concurred with every newspaper editorial in the state that Carr was the best man to ferret out grafters who were in the taxpayers' employ.

Upon authorization from the Emergency Appropriation Committee on September 1 of an initial allocation of $150,000, Carr launched his crusade.[10] During the first two weeks of September, the grand juror was a black-robed dynamo, hearing testimony from nearly one hundred witnesses in his small city hall office. By the end of the month two warrants had been issued. The first charged Francis P. Slattery, a vice president of the Michigan National Bank in Grand Rapids, with attempted bribery on a banking bill. The second alleged that William Burns, executive secretary of the Michigan Medical Society, had offered a California vacation to Warren G. Hooper, the chairman of the House Public Health Committee if he would quash a measure favorable to osteopaths.[11]

As the probe progressed, Carr insisted on as much secrecy as possible, telling newsmen that "a grand jury always functions best when its witnesses are not stirred up by headlines."[12] However, by early December a rift between the jurist and the attorney general threatened to undermine or possibly even destroy the entire investigation. On December 7, without prior consultation with Carr, Rushton appointed Jay W. Linsey, a prominent Grand Rapids lawyer, to be chief grand jury prosecutor. The next morning's *Detroit Free Press* assailed the selection as an attempt by the attorney general to sabotage the inquiry before it could uncover the roots of legislative corruption.

The crux of the tirade was not Linsey's legal prowess, but rather his one-time association with fellow townsman Frank D. McKay, whom the *Free Press* had railed against for years because of his domi-

3

nation of Republican state politics.[13] So intent was the *Free Press* on impugning McKay at every opportunity, that before the first warrant was served by the grand jury, it ran a story predicting the imminent arrest of a prominent Grand Rapids financier — an obvious implication of McKay rather than the obscure Slattery.[14]

III McKay, a self-made banker, real estate magnate, and general entrepreneur whose estimated wealth at the time of his death in 1965 was $50,000,000, truly deserved the title of political czar. After serving three terms as State Treasurer, he left office in 1931 under the cloud of a grand jury inquiring into his handling of state funds.

During his stint in office, McKay claimed to have "smartened up" as a politician, driving across the entire state to gain support, especially in the often neglected Upper Peninsula.[15] At this time, he also mastered the art of political revenge by leading an intraparty revolt against three-term liberal governor Alex Groesbeck, who had opposed the conservative McKay's nomination for treasurer. Consequently, in the 1926 gubernatorial primary the incumbent was upset by little-known Fred Green.[16]

Governor Green thanked his benefactor by appointing him chief legislative lobbyist and chairman of the highway and finance committees on the State Administrative Board. To further increase his influence, McKay used his ties with Green to manipulate Republican politics through control of party conventions. Joining with GOP kingpins Edward Barnard of Detroit and William McKeighan of Flint, the three formed a triumvirate which dictated Republican fortunes for nearly two decades. So absolute was their authority that McKay could boast with complete truth: "Reporters who covered those conventions had an easy time of it. I would tell them the night before the convention what the ticket was going to be and they could play cards all night."[17]

His ever expanding power was accompanied by insinuations of corruption from foes in both parties. It was charged that McKay, as the guiding force behind Republican Governor Frank Fitzgerald (1935-37, 1939), had urged his affable fellow Irishman to ignore widespread illegal gambling operations in several of the largest, and most Republican, counties, and that Fitzgerald had instructed the state police to curtail their investigations into such crimes.[18] Moreover, reports circulated that "The Boss" had used his clout to have friends appointed to such key positions as state purchasing director, chairman of the State Liquor Control Commission, and chairman of the State Corrections Commission, and that he was extorting business from banks and private companies for his surety bond company through the use of state contracts. Furthermore, as founder of the General Tire Company, McKay made certain that all state vehicles were fitted with his product. Worse than the obvious conflict of interest, however, was the discovery that, while state treasurer, he had purchased from his own company — with state funds — hundreds of obsolete, flawed, and otherwise unusable tires which he then stored — also at state expense — in a local warehouse.[19]

Beginning in 1940, McKay was the subject of three federal grand jury probes charging him with receiving money from distillers in exchange for his influence in getting their products on the shelves of state liquor stores; using the mails to defraud the City of Grand Rapids with fraudulent bids on municipal bonds; and extorting $9,918 from Edsel Ford, president of the Ford Motor Company, on the pretense that the sum was necessary to defray party campaign debts. In each instance he was acquitted as his attorneys argued, with probable validity, that their client was the target of a political vendetta by United States Attorney General Frank Murphy, whose defeat for re-election as Michigan's governor in 1938 had been orchestrated by McKay.[20]

His reputation greatly soiled, McKay managed to remain as the state's Republican national committeeman until 1944, when he was ousted by reformers led by his former protege, Governor Harry F. Kelly. McKay steadfastly proclaimed his innocence of any wrongdoing, explaining to reporters: "I always played politics hard. We gave appointments to those who were loyal. That's the way you stay on top and those are the rules of the game. But I never took anything from the state. I never gave money to a legislator in my life. Why should I have? I was doing pretty well for myself outside of politics."[21] This disclaimer notwithstanding, by 1944 McKay was perceived by many Michiganians as an evil genius, and political fame and national acclaim would belong to the man who put him behind bars.

IV Following the appointment of Linsey as chief grand jury prosecutor, Carr silently seethed for three days over what he considered an unwarranted intrusion by Rushton into grand jury affairs, before announcing on December 11 his intention to select another special prosecutor. In a carefully phrased release, the jurist set forth in icy terms his perception of the situation. "I shall, within a few days," the proclamation read, "appoint counsel to assist in the grand jury investigation. This is entirely satisfactory to Attorney General Rushton, and also has the approval of Governor Kelly. This arrangement will give Mr. Rushton more time for the regular work of his department, which is particularly heavy at this time.... He has given a large part of his time to the grand jury and, of course, will continue to take part in proceedings as much as possible. We worked together in close cooperation and our relations have been at all times friendly and congenial. I respect his ability and integrity and capacity for hard work...."[22]

Piqued, Rushton responded with resentment to what he thought was a blatant invitation to divorce himself from the probe. In a formal written reply, the attorney general was noble, saying that "if my not being too prominent in these proceedings will help the court to gain its objective, then I feel I should not appear very often."[23] He added, again without apparent rancor, that "in view of the attitudes of some of the newspapers and unfounded accusations made, I believe it is just as well for you to take full charge of the money, the unspent $24,126.23 from the legislative appropriation of $40,000. This will prevent those people who are trying to sabotage the grand jury from going any further."[24] To newsmen, however, Rushton vented his true emotions. "I'll be delighted to step aside if that is the court's wish," he began, his eyes unable to hide the pain and fury welling within his outward composure. "Remember, I receive no additional compensation for serving with the grand jury. My payment has been hard work, unjustified criticism for some of my decisions, and slanders upon my character by persons outside the grand jury. I have the highest respect and deep affection for Judge Carr, whom I know to be an able judge. But it now seems that my presence in the grand jury room is embarrassing because of the attacks that have been made upon me. This seems clear from the language in the judge's statement.... Rather than embarrass the grand jury investigation, especially one as important as this one, I'll be tickled to death to step aside and once more devote full time to the job of being attorney general. Of course, I shall continue to cooperate in every way I can with the grand jury and the conduct of any resulting trials."[25]

For his part, Carr elected to ignore Rushton's verbal insincerities, and replied with an equal lack of candor that he appreciated the attorney general's promise of assistance and that he never intended to do anything to alter the "wholly congenial and harmonious" relations between the two men in the past.[26] He then met with several prominent attorneys, including Burrit Hamilton of Battle Creek, to discuss possible choices for special prosecutor. Hamilton, one of the most respected legal minds in the state, urged consideration of his junior partner, Kimber Sigler. In deference to his old friend, Carr agreed to interview Sigler, and was so impressed by the dapper 49-year-old barrister's enthusiasm and knowledge that on December 14 his selection was made official.[27]

Kimber Cornellus Sigler, whose name had been shortened in his youth as a reflection of the popularity of Rudyard Kipling's *Kim*, was the complete opposite of his new employer. Carr viewed the law as his entire life, whereas Sigler, the son of a wealthy Nebraska cattle rancher, had pursued a variety of careers as a cowboy, boxer, football player, and factory worker before settling into the legal profession. Carr was humorless and stern, while Sigler was a garrulous, flamboyant, astute courtroom technician who reveled in "putting on a good show" for juries. The massive Carr wore clothes merely to cover his frame; the handsome Sigler chose clothing to adorn his broad-shouldered, trim-waisted physique. Possessing 47 suits, a typical Sigler ensemble would be a wide-billed coal black hat, light gray fitted Chesterfield topcoat with a black velvet collar, blue pinstripe suit, starched white shirt, flaming maroon tie and matching pocket handkerchief, pearl gray vest with white piping, ruby cuff links, two-tone gloves, spats, and a walking stick. Thus garbed, and with his Barrymore-like profile and iron gray hair, Sigler cut a dashing figure. It was for these differences that Ingham County Prosecutor Victor C. Anderson, a protege of Carr, expressed reservations to his mentor concerning the new special prosecutor. The judge urged patience, and soon Anderson was echoing Carr's admiration for Sigler's diligence and skill.[28]

Always confident to the point of arrogance, Sigler harbored no doubts as to his mission. Judge Carr informed the new special prosecutor that the reason for his appointment was that the Lansing jurist distrusted the Rushton-Linsey intimacy with Frank McKay. Sigler, who already thought of the Grand Rapids politico as a personification of every evil which plagued American government, correctly interpreted the judge's remarks to mean that the ultimate target of the grand jury probe was to be McKay. Invigorated by the thought of eradicating evil, Sigler threw himself into his work, writing his longtime friend and political advisor William R. Cook, editor and publisher of the *Hastings Banner*, that the job was terrific and "so completely all-absorbing that it demands and receives every second of my time from awakening in the morning until falling asleep."[29] In other correspondence with Cook, Sigler had expressed the awesomeness of his duties in different terms, saying: "I've gone into this job with a feeling inside of me that I've never had before. It seems as if from somewhere there comes an impelling force that leads me on with greater political strength and determination than I've ever known before. Political considerations seem as nothing. Publicity seems infinitesimal. Somehow I feel obsessed with but one ambition, and that is to go down through the middle of this thing with all I've got, without the slightest regard for whom it may hit. I want to so conduct the affairs of this grand jury so that you, Cook, and the other friends who believe in me, will always be proud of it."[30] As to the contrast with Carr, Sigler wrote: "In many ways he [Carr] is a great big, wonderful man. He has the greatest knowledge of fundamental law of any judge or lawyer I've ever come in contact with. He is so stalwart and strong, patient, conservative, kind, and somehow seems to possess those qualities which I need. I guess it is generally being understood that he and I make a team and I suppose this is because we are so entirely different. I know what 'my mission' is and it seems as if every expression of my entire life has been training me to accomplish that mission."[31] When Cook cautioned Sigler that, as a former Democrat, he ought to go easy on assailing McKay and other prominent Republicans if he hoped to advance within that party, Sigler dismissed any fears and explained his strategy to his friend airily: "You spoke of Frank McKay and some other big shots. Don't worry, Old Top. I have my heavy artillery constantly trained on them, and one of these days I expect to blow them out of the water. It may take some time and there may be a number of other indictments in the meantime, but you can rest assured that I'm going to give them all I've got, and the funny thing about it, Bill, is that they all know it."[32]

VI Less than a week after Sigler's appointment, the grand jury was racked again by dissension as Rushton proclaimed that he stood by his intention to employ Linsey. When asked if he had conferred with Carr on the decision, the crusty attorney general snarled: "Oh, sure. I asked everybody, including the Supreme Court. It doesn't make any difference what Judge Carr thinks. After the grand jury is finished and some people are indicted, then the attorney general takes charge and begins prosecution. The two phases are separate and distinct."[33] Carr differed, contending logic dictated that the man who did the detail work on the investigation would be best suited to direct the prosecution. The only way to settle the dispute, the judge suggested, was to seek an opinion from Governor Kelly.[34]

While the question was pending, Sigler sought to influence the chief executive's decision by making public his recommendation to Carr that John Dalton, a 40-year-old grand jury investigator who had been hired by Rushton at a salary of $400 per month, be removed because he had chauffeured Frank McKay from Lansing to Grand

Rapids in the attorney general's state-owned Buick on grand jury time. Sigler related that Dalton had admitted making the trip on orders from Rushton, and that McKay had asked him about the grand jury probe. According to the special prosecutor, Dalton recalled that the Grand Rapids boss stated he "didn't like grand juries because you never know where they're going to stop, and they are a lot of trouble to people."[35]

Acting upon Sigler's evidence, Carr released Dalton from duty but refused to be quoted as to the specific reasons for his action. When reached by reporters, the portly Dalton, who carried more than 250 pounds on his rather squat frame, said only that he had been taken to the grand jury "hideout" at Jackson on December 18 and had been questioned at length that night about the McKay incident. Wavering between anger and tears, he shouted that he was "tired of being bullied, questioned, and interviewed." Defensively, he added that he had not disclosed any secrets, because he did not know any, and that the car was not Rushton's, but a "borrowed red Pontiac."[36] Rushton denied giving any such order to Dalton, saying his position had been merely to suggest to his employee that if he were going to Grand Rapids it would be a kind gesture to invite McKay. He further reiterated his intention to employ Linsey, despite the grand juror's objections, at the prearranged stipend of $2,000 per month. The funds, he added pointedly, would come from the grand jury appropriation because his budget could not bear the extra expenditure.[37] As newspapers blared the controversy across the state, it seemed that Lansing was treating the citizens to an expensive pre-Christmas farce. Yet, behind the scenes, Sigler was working at a furious pace, often putting in twenty-hour days in an effort to centralize and coordinate grand jury power within his control.[38]

During the Carr-Rushton-Linsey-Dalton imbroglio, Sigler spent hours quizzing legislators to uncover details of alleged corruption. Despite the mandatory cloak of secrecy surrounding grand jury proceedings, astute observers predicted an impending explosion. Red-eyed, sullen, stooped-shouldered lawmakers, both Democrat and Republican, emerged from Sigler's office suite in a seemingly endless succession. An "official leak," possibly from Sigler, relayed that even Judge Carr, who had been holding court across the street from the Capitol for twenty-five years, was amazed to find that more than half of the senators and representatives interviewed admitted to accepting bribes and that, if the trend continued, by the time the legislature convened on January 31, 1944 more than one-third of its members could be under indictment.[39]

Despite bipartisan involvement in wrongdoings, it was also forecast that Republicans would gain from the grand jury revelations. Frank Morris, veteran *Detroit Times* Lansing correspondent who was reputed to be on the payroll of McKay, predicted that the grand jury would elevate Carr to his long-coveted seat on the state supreme court, and Sigler, described as a man with the "homely philosophy of the small town, the glamor of brightly lighted streets, the self assurance of a Texas cowboy, the meekness of a guy checking his hat at an expensive hotel, and the emphatic honesty of a mirror," would be the successor to Harry Kelly as governor.[40] Neither man cast a frown or issued a disclaimer to the prognostication.

VII The December furor faded softly when Linsey quit, citing a need to devote more time to his private practice, and Rushton, having penned a lengthy defense of his actions to the governor, proclaimed his intention to leave the grand jury entirely in Carr's hands.[41] While this had been a "tempest in a teapot," the anticipated explosion rocked the state on January 22, 1944 when Carr issued indictments against six finance company officials and twenty past and current members of the state legislature, fifteen of whom came from Detroit, alleging participation in a $25,000 bribery plot to influence passage of a 1939 automobile financing bill.[42]

Events appeared rosy for the grand jury when one of the accused financiers pleaded guilty the day after his indictment and agreed to become a state witness without benefit of immunity. Soon afterward, he was joined by one of the indicted Republicans — 77-year-old Miles Callaghan, a fifteen-year veteran legislator, who accepted Sigler's offer of immunity plus $100 a month to serve as an informant.[43] On February 1, however, Carr and Sigler were confronted with yet another potential disaster. The celebrated New York columnist Walter Winchell reported that Charles "Nightshirt" Spare, a grand jury investigator hired by Rushton and paid under the alias of Charles Allen, was a former Ku Klux Klan and Black Legion organizer. In the state senate, Democrats unsuccessfully urged their colleagues to delay passage of a $150,000 grand jury appropriation until Carr explained Spare's employment. Stanley Nowak, a Detroit labor organizer, recounted Spare's role in instigating factory strikes among disgruntled whites, causing the loss of millions of man-hours of war production, while his fellow senator, Charles C. Diggs, a black, expressed doubt whether he or any of his Roman Catholic codefendants could expect justice from an account submitted by a Klansman.[44] Both Carr and Sigler refused comment, but within the week they announced that Spare had been released. Six months later, without any reason cited, Sigler rehired – secretly – the alleged racist and during the following nearly seven months paid him $3,947.32 in salary and expenses under the pseudonym of "Mary Duke."[45]

Having weathered this crisis, Sigler devoted the next two months to the examination of those indicted in the finance conspiracy warrant. The hearing began on February 28 in Judge Carr's court. One by one, defendants were forced to peer into Sigler's cold eyes and listen to him state in a harsh, bitter voice: "Come clean, fellow. You might as well confess. I'm going to convict you anyway, because you're guilty. I'm going to send you to prison."[46] Moreover, the accused knew the truth of those words when Sigler brought forth his prize witness, Charlie Hemans.

VIII

Debonair, witty, and charming, 47-year-old Charles Fitch Hemans was an attorney by profession and lobbyist by avocation. A former regent of the University of Michigan, Hemans plied his lobbying trade first out of his Detroit law office and then from a suite in the Olds Hotel in Lansing. Because he had so many employers, he meticulously recorded all payments made to legislators in a little black book, which he never showed anyone. Enlisting in the army in 1943, he used his legal training and past service in World War I to secure a position on the provost's marshal's staff in Washington, D.C. with the rank of major.[47]

When the Ingham County grand jury convened, Carr assigned his chief sleuth, Leo Wendell, to determine if the lobbyist's long-rumored, but never seen, ledger actually existed. Hemans denied having made any payments to lawmakers, but when his former secretary was located in Fort Wayne, Indiana, she stated that her boss had moved all his business material to his family's farm near Lansing. Wendell braved a pitchfork-wielding caretaker and, in the hayloft, uncovered cardboard boxes filled with yellowing papers and the black book. Sigler then accompanied Wendell to Washington, D.C. and induced the lobbyist to return to Michigan and testify.[48]

Over the course of the next two years, Sigler and Hemans developed an unusual relationship. The special prosecutor knew that Hemans was the key to unlocking the anti-chain bank bill intrigue, the task for which the grand jury had been established. The witness was equally aware of his importance and made a series of escalating demands upon the grand jury, threatening to turn mute if his conditions were not met. Despite the crudeness of such extortion, Sigler continually acquiesced and, immediately upon the major's arrival in Lansing, put him on the grand jury payroll under the assumed names of R. Millard and F. Benson. Through February 1945, Hemans received $150 monthly, with Sigler laundering the money by authorizing checks to the chief of his state police detail, Sergeant Leo Van Conant, who cashed them and delivered the money to the witness. In March 1945, the ante was upped to $450, and then for the following eleven months the lobbyist was given $600 per month from grand jury funds.[49]

In addition, Sigler, who honestly enjoyed Hemans' company and urbanity, approved expenditures of $1,337.10 to house the witness in an Olds Hotel suite; $601.04 for meals, valet service, and long distance telephone calls; $2,000 for travel to such diverse places as Washington, D.C., Cleveland, Texas and Mexico; and unspecified amounts to provide "high-priced Scotch whiskey" and equally expensive prostitutes, and $16 to replace a mattress ruined when Hemans, in a drunken stupor, urinated.[50] By contrast, the legal state expenditure for witnesses was $2 per day plus meals in the jail dining room, the same as was given jurors. Moreover, since Michigan law forbade use of paid testimony, Sigler felt compelled to conceal the payments to his witness.[51]

Unfortunately, the more than $15,500 spent on the major did not bring about the desired results.[52] Although his testimony did convict all but two of the defendants in the nine-week trial of the finance company conspiracy which culminated on August 14, 1944, Hemans refused to take the stand against his wealthy friends in the anti-chain bank case. He became even more intransigent by March 1946, when both Carr and Sigler had been replaced on the grand jury by Judge Louis Coash and Richard B. Foster, respectively. As Foster recalled: "One of the first things that Coash did was cut Hemans from the payroll and throw him out of the hotel. He told the state police to take his clothes to his house. In hindsight, that wasn't the smartest thing to do."[53]

Hemans subsequently fled to Washington, D.C., and he was sentenced to a year and a half in federal prison for unlawful flight from Michigan. After he was released, his silence was rewarded with a high paying position in a company owned by one of the bankers against whom he had refused to testify.[54] More than anyone else, Charlie Hemans symbolized what was wrong with Sigler's operation of the grand jury, and his spectre haunted the special prosecutor throughout the remainder of his public career.

IX In the evening following the verdict in the finance company case, Sigler held a victory party, complete with champagne, in his suite. Present were his staff, Charlie Hemans, and two reporters, Kenneth McCormick of the *Detroit Free Press* and Al Nieber of the *Detroit News,* who had earned the special prosecutor's favor through their stories lionizing him as "Sir Kim," the state's foremost crime fighter. In later years, co-workers of the two newsmen recalled that McCormick and Nieber had boasted to Sigler that their articles could make him governor, and that Sigler held them to their pledge.[55]

Throughout the autumn, there appeared to be little grand jury activity, and critics questioned the wisdom of further funding. Sigler urged patience and intimated that he was interviewing witnesses in preparation for the issuance of warrants in the long-awaited anti-chain bank bill case. In anticipation of that event, several newspapers ran stories recounting the history of the case, how an anti-chain bank bill had been passed in 1941 only to be vetoed by then-Governor Murray D. Van Wagoner on the advice of his chief legal aide, who also was a vice president of the state's largest chain bank, and how the bill would have saved smaller banks from being devoured by large institutions with branches across the state.[56] The *Detroit Free Press* and *Detroit News* abstained from these articles, however, as McCormick and Nieber knew that Sigler's real target was not the bankers, but Frank D. McKay.

During his individual interrogation of every state legislator, Sigler had a stroke of exceptional good fortune. State Senator Warren G. Hooper cracked under the pressure and admitted to being on McKay's payroll. In 1943, the Senator confessed, McKay had summoned him to his room at the Olds Hotel and said: "[State Representative William] Green, [sports promotor Floyd] Fitzsimmons, and I don't want that pending horse racing bill out of committee. You get busy on it. Bill or Fitz were supposed to see you on it. They have some money for you. You keep the bill in committee and don't worry about the money. You'll get it when the bill is killed."[57] In November, Sigler, for reasons known only to himself, assembled Green, Fitzsimmons, and McKay, and confronted them with Hooper. Visibly shaken, the senator repeated his accusations in their presence.[58] Moreover, Hooper claimed that McKay had attempted to bribe legislators to prevent passage of the anti-chain bank bill.[59]

Armed with Hooper's testimony, Sigler realized perhaps for the first time that he had an opportunity to do what no person had ever accomplished — convict Frank McKay. If that occurred, it might be possible for the special prosecutor to follow Thomas E. Dewey's path to prominence: crimefighter to governor to a bid for the White House. Warren Hooper would be Sigler's ticket to fame.[60]

On December 2, 1944, conspiracy warrants were served on Green, Fitzsimmons, and McKay.[61] The battle lines were drawn and, once again, the eyes of the nation were focused on Michigan's grand jury.

CHAPTER TWO

THE GUISE OF SUCCESS

I Bright rays of sunlight bursting through the early morning clouds on Thursday, January 11, 1945 were a welcome sight to residents of Lansing. The state capital, along with the rest of mid-Michigan, was in the grips of a near-record cold wave which had brought daily snowfalls and single-digit temperatures. The frigid conditions had replaced both news of World War II and the local Ingham County grand jury investigation into legislative graft as the primary topics of conversation. However, the promise of warming temperatures and the imminent reconvening of the state legislature promised to restore politics to its place of prominence in the capitol city.

On that icy morning, newly elected 9th District State Senator Warren G. Hooper of Albion sat alone in his capitol office, nervously chain smoking cigarettes, pondering his fate, and wondering how many more times he would return there. This desolate, disconsolate figure, from all external appearances, seemed to be an upwardly mobile politician with a rosy future. At 40, he was considered by the military too old to be fighting for freedom against Axis tyranny, but he was trying to do his duty for democracy at home as a public servant. A family man married to a statuesque beauty and the father of two young sons aged six and four, this slim, balding, bulging-eyed lawmaker had recently purchased a large new home in Albion. In the eyes of those who knew him best, he was the epitome of the American success story.

II A native of Alhambra, California, not far from Los Angeles, Warren Green Hooper was a fourth generation descendant of William Hooper, a North Carolinian signer of the Declaration of Independence. He had attended the University of California and

DePauw University, but did not receive a degree. After leaving DePauw, he moved to Los Angeles, became a member of the California Stock Exchange and married a school teacher. In 1931, amidst the throes of the Great Depression, he lost his job and abandoned his wife, who subsequently gained a divorce on the grounds of desertion.[1]

He then journeyed to Tacoma, Washington, where he edited a weekly newspaper — the *Outlook* — for a year and a half. In the latter part of 1932, he left to become editor of the weekly *Herald* in Sequim, Washington. Another year and a half found him in Chicago where he worked at the copy desk of the *Herald-Examiner*.[2]

In 1935, Hooper took his journalistic talents to Albion, Michigan, where he became advertising manager for the *Albion Evening Recorder*. While there, he enrolled at Albion College, taking courses primarily in the humanities. It was in college that he met, and married, a tall, attractive, musically-inclined brunette coed named Callienetta Cobb. Although high-strung and flighty, "Callie" worked hard as a music teacher, took in college students as boarders, and helped finance her new husband's trip to Berlin, where he covered the 1936 Olympics as a free-lance writer.[3]

Upon his return, Hooper found that he had been replaced at the *Evening Recorder*, and so he purchased a service station, which he operated for eleven months. Capitalizing on the acquaintances he had made in his business endeavors, he ran for the state legislature in 1938 and was elected.[4] He sold his gasoline station and prepared for a new career, which would earn him the princely sum of $3 per day while the legislature was in session. After three terms he was elevated to the state senate — basically, as his critics were quick to point out, because many voters believed he was related to a popular senator of the same surname from a neighboring district.[5]

III As Hooper gazed out his office window, he may have reflected pensively on his immediate future. Normally on the eve of the Republican State Convention he would be packing his bags to attend and join his fellow lawmakers in three days of drinking, story-swapping, and the general ribald camaraderie which surrounded the annual assemblage. This year's gathering was to be in Grand Rapids, however, and there was no way he would show his face in that city, which was the home of Frank D. McKay, Republican national committeeman and titular head of the state party. True, he and McKay had been political allies in the past, but next Monday Hooper was scheduled to appear before the state graft grand jury and put on record testimony which the prosecution believed would send McKay to prison. Lighting another cigarette, Hooper probably thought, "Frank will hear enough from me on Monday. No need to bring the sheep to the wolf."

What a mess his life had become. His fragilely structured career was beginning to tumble around him like a tower of cards facing a cyclone. Once his testimony became public and his constituents learned that he, too, had taken bribes, his brief senate tenure would be over, his reputation demolished, and, unless grand jury special prosecutor Kim Sigler kept his promise of immunity, a prison cell rather than the senate chamber would be his next address.[6] On top of that, Callie was running around Albion spreading rumors and trying to secure a divorce. "It's a good thing she shot her mouth off to Agnes," he doubtless thought, "so I could get over to her attorney and quash it in time. Thank goodness for Agnes Wickens. More bosses need loyal secretaries like her."[7]

It had all seemed so good. In the house, he had determined to find an area of legislation in which to specialize. Becoming chair of the Public Health Committee was deemed a just reward for his diligence. In addition, serving as the executive secretary of the Michigan Association of Osteopathic Physicians and Surgeons, despite being a conflict of interest, brought in much needed extra income. Hooper could have reflected to 1939 when William Burns, of the Michigan Medical Society, had offered him a free trip to California if he would support a bill excluding osteopaths from certain medical practices, and how he had refused. Of course, he should not have waited until 1943 to report the bribe, but it was an unwritten law among his colleagues to look the other way at such practices.[8] Besides there was no way that any bill discriminating against osteopaths would get through his committee. They had always treated him as a child; he liked them; and, most of all, there was no way he would ever risk his extra income from them for a mere vacation trip.[9]

It could have been so perfect, if only he had not become involved with Frank McKay; but it was next to impossible to avoid "The Boss" if you were a Republican in Michigan. The Grand Rapids financier bankrolled major political campaigns, manipulated the State Liquor Control Commission, and controlled the selection of Republican candidates. Of course, being in McKay's pocket had had its advantages also. There was a ready supply of cash to be earned as a reward for legislative favors, and the money came in handy, especially when Callie began complaining about needing more clothes and items for the house. Moreover, there was the prestige of being able to stay in the finest hotels without ever having to pay for anything. He felt so

17

important, and it was all because of his friendship with McKay.[10] However, after Monday it would all be gone.

If only he had been stronger when he first went before the grand jury, none of this would have happened. He had tried to lie, but Sigler ignored his protestations of innocence.[11] Fidgeting with a pack of cigarettes, Hooper possibly remembered grimly how Sigler's eyes had bored right into his; how he had called him such a liar that he would break a lie detector machine; and how he had broken down and told the truth.[12] If only he had been stronger, but his world was made up of "ifs."

The shrill ringing of his telephone roused him from his reverie. It was his wife. For days she had been receiving a series of mysterious calls from a foreign-sounding man asking for her husband. Shortly before noon she had received another and, fearing for her husband's safety, wanted to warn him. He assured her that there was no danger and that he would be home for dinner. Then he left his office to have his customary lunch of a sandwich and a bowl of soup at the senate cafeteria.[13]

IV Callienetta Hooper was no more satisfied with her life than was her husband. Despite extensive schooling at several colleges, she had never earned a degree. Then she had married Warren and had to work to support him and his expensive hobbies, especially his penchant for antiques. Now she had two children to care for. Her talents were being wasted and, besides, she was not well liked in Albion, as most of the local residents thought she acted as if she was too good for their community. She resented her husband's popularity and his freedom to travel across the state on political and osteopathic business while she had to stay home. Moreover, she distrusted Warren. He was, in her mind, obsessed with flirting and being in the company of other women. Why, she wondered, did he want to be with that gangster Harry Rosenberg's prostitute wife Vita? Why had he not made love to her in more than a month? She was glad she had threatened to get a divorce. That would be the leverage she needed to force her wayward husband to move his family to Lansing, where she could meet new people and earn some money of her own as a music teacher.[14]

All this, of course, might change after Monday. She wondered if McKay knew what Warren had said to the grand jury. If he did, had he hired that strange sounding man to harass her and keep asking the time and route of her husband's trip home? Worse yet, did McKay think that Warren had told *her* his testimony, placing her life in danger also? All these concerns probably crossed her mind as she prepared to greet her husband that evening. She determined to fix him a nice meal and then, after the children were in bed, she would ask him if he had signed a lease for a house in Lansing as he had promised.

V Shortly after 2:30, Senator Hooper left his office and went to his car, a 1939 green Mercury, parked in the capitol lot. He carelessly tossed an overnight bag into the front seat, lit a cigarette, and drove to the McLaughlin Osteopathic Hospital, where he kept a room while in Lansing. Having picked up some literature there, at 3:45 he left and went to the nearby Porter Hotel, where he made reservations for eight osteopathic physicians who were coming to Lansing Saturday for a convention. As he left the desk, two young men about thirty years old, wearing top coats and hats, stopped Hooper. The two men engaged in animated and jovial conversation for about five minutes, repeatedly drawing the attention of the two desk clerks. They then walked out to the parking lot, where the senator's car was waiting to take him along that familiar stretch of rural M-99 to his home.[15] It would be the last restful weekend he could expect for a long time, and he was looking forward to it.

CHAPTER THREE

THREE BULLETS SEALED HIS LIPS

Occasionally, extraordinary events lead individuals to discover an inner strength which lifts them from their mundane existence to heroic proportions. Floyd Modjeska, however, was not one of those people. Stout to the point of obesity, with thin lips forming an almost invisible line over his double chin, and wearing a polka dot bow tie which was nearly lost under the flesh, the graying Springport grain elevator operator was engaged in a slow, routine drive home south along M-99 when, approximately 3½ miles north of his home-town, he spied what seemed to be smoke seeping from the windows of an automobile parked on the east shoulder of the road. Pulling over, he left his vehicle and approached the smouldering sedan, noticing first footprints in the snow leading from the driver's door around the front of the car to the pavement. The imprints were so small, he thought that they must have been made by a woman, per-haps wearing galoshes. Cautiously circling this object of curiosity, but never daring to come within several feet of it, he drew back suddenly when he caught sight of the bullet hole in the right rear window.[1]

Horror stricken, Modjeska frantically peered up and down the highway. Within minutes, a car appeared on the crest of the small hill just to the north. Arms flailing within his dark blue overcoat, Modjeska dejectedly watched the car pass. His heart leapt again when the car suddenly stopped and the driver, Kyle Van Auker, an Eaton Rapids clothing salesman, stuck out his head and asked what was wrong.

"Come back here a minute," pleaded Modjeska, and Van Auker, accompanied by his dog, obliged.

Pointing to the rear window, Modjeska whispered, "What do you think about that bullet hole there?"

"God, I don't know what to think."

"Shall we open the door?"

"No!" blurted the new arrival, obviously cut from the same nonheroic cloth as Modjeska.

"Are you afraid?"

"Yes, aren't you?"

"I sure am," whispered Modjeska.[2]

The two men huddled in fearful indecision for nearly fifteen minutes, when another car approached from the north. "Look," exclaimed Modjeska excitedly, "we'll stop this car and see if he'll help."[3]

Driving this third car was Mervyn B. Howard, a 42-year-old representative of the Greyhound Bus Company, who was en route to Albion from his Lansing home. Having parked behind the smoking vehicle, Howard peered through his dark-rimmed round glasses, donned his hat to protect his black crewcut hair, and inquired as to the problem. Saying that something looked queer, Van Auker timidly pointed to the bullet hole, admitting, "We've been afraid to open the door."[4]

"Why? What are you afraid of?" demanded Howard.

"Well, that bullet hole there," replied Van Auker, adding that the thick smoke precluded any glimpse into the car's interior.

"God, we ought to see if there's anybody inside," offered Howard, inching forward to listen for any signs of life. Hearing no coughing or voices, he tried to open the right rear door, but finding it locked, unlatched the front one. Black smoke billowed out, momentarily blinding him. Van Auker moved in and began to fan the smoke away, causing small flames to spit out from under the seat. Through the haze, they saw the body of a man, head down, right arm dangling between his legs, slumped forward in the passenger's seat.[5]

"I guess we'd better go call the state police," stammered Modjeska, quickly volunteering to leave and find a telephone.

"While you're gone," said Howard in disgust, "we'll take the body out."[6]

Just as they were about to begin, three women — who obviously had been viewing the proceedings from a nearby house — raced to the scene and pleaded with the men not to touch the car lest it explode. While not disclosing the presence of a body, Howard impatiently explained that since there was no odor of gasoline or kerosene, nor a raging inferno, there was no immediate danger. As a precaution, however, he urged them to return home and notify the Springport Fire Department. Thus mollified, they departed.[7]

"My God," gasped Howard, as he reached for the corpse, which by now had six-to-seven inch flames rising between its legs, "the fingers on his right hand are burned nearly off. And his arm — it looks like it's popped open just like a cooked wienie!" Nauseated by the combination of the grisly sight, the smell of burning flesh, and his companion's colorful description, Van Auker turned away, leaving Howard to drag the remains by the overcoat from the car. Only when he heard Howard's command — "Hey, grab his legs, will you — they're catching on the door jamb" — did he force himself to reface morbid reality. As they placed the body along the pavement near the right rear of the automobile, Howard noticed that the man's trousers were smouldering at the crotch. They tossed snow on him and then turned their attention to the fire within the car.[8]

At 6:05 p.m., Eastern War Time, Dispatcher Lawrence J. Baril of the state police post at Jackson received Modjeska's call concerning his discovery, approximately a half hour earlier, of a burning car containing both a bullet hole and a body. Detective Bion Hoeg and another trooper arrived at the scene twenty minutes later. They saw Modjeska, Howard, and Van Auker heaving snow into the parked car in a futile effort to douse the flames. Rushing in with fire extinguishers, the troopers joined in the attempt but also failed. Much to the relief of the police, the Springport Fire Department got to the site before the car, replete with any possible evidence and clues, had its gas tank ignite.[9]

A cursory examination of the body by Hoeg revealed three bullet holes — one in the left cheek near the corner of the eye, one behind the left ear near the base of the skull, and yet another near the top of the head above the left ear. The right arm and hand were severely seared, as were the insides of both legs and the stomach. It appeared to the homocide expert that any of the wounds could have caused instantaneous death.[10]

Before the excitement of flashing lights and shrieking sirens lured the entire countryside to the scene, Hoeg questioned Howard, Modjeska, and Van Auker. They escorted him to the two footprints in the inch-deep snow and proudly proclaimed they had saved them by cordoning off the area with the rear seat of the deceased's car, which they had ripped out. All agreed a woman might have made them. Quickly measuring, Hoeg noted the length of the impressions as $10^{7}/_{8}''$ and the width of the heel as $2^{15}/_{16}''$, with a $1'\ 8^{1}/_{2}''$ stride. Each print was smooth, indicating the person was wearing either shoes or well-worn galoshes. Plaster molds were ordered. A small man, Hoeg thought, was a more likely suspect than a woman, but he was willing to remain open-minded on the matter.[11]

Modjeska interrupted the detective's thoughts with the revelation that, while urinating near the rear of the deceased's car, he accidentally found a lone skid mark, perhaps as long as 24 feet. The mark on the ice and snow of both the pavement and shoulder led Hoeg to believe the vehicle had slid gradually in a straight line from the west side to the east in a southeasterly direction. It did not seem to be a panic stop.[12]

The detectives then began to search the possessions found in the car and on the body. A black leather zipper bag, with no identification, contained a white shirt, blue pajamas, a straight razor, talcum powder, and two neckties. In the glove compartment was a list of names, later found to be those of osteopaths throughout the country. As Hoeg was itemizing the contents of the decedent's wallet, he received information on the car. The 1939 green Mercury, license number JD4848, had not been reported stolen or missing. This, coupled with the campaign literature found in the trunk and identification in the wallet, led Hoeg to conclude his fears must be true. He instructed his partner to notify State Police Commissioner Oscar G. Olander that the body which Hoeg had just ordered removed to a Springport undertaking parlor was that of Republican State Senator Warren G. Hooper.[13]

II At 7:45 p.m., "Ole" Olander received news of the assassination and immediately notified his chief of detectives, Captain Harold V. Mulbar, and the Associated Press, United Press, Booth newspaper service, *Detroit Free Press, Detroit News, Detroit Times*, and the *Lansing State Journal*. Lieutenant Lyle Morse, a seasoned veteran, and Detective Fred Van Campen were sent to the murder scene to assist in the investigation. Van Campen took five flash pictures of Hooper's car, and at 10:23 p.m. Morse instructed Stewart's Wrecker Service to haul the vehicle to the Jackson State Police Post where it would undergo a thorough search for fingerprints. Morse and Van Campen then sped to the Hoffman Funeral Home in Springport where the autopsy was to be performed. Van Campen took three pictures of Hooper's body, two of his head wounds, and one each of his charred abdomen and the autopsy.[14]

III Warren Hooper had told his wife when he left for Lansing on Tuesday, January 9 that he would be home for dinner on Thursday, thus she had spent much of the afternoon preparing a meal and dessert.[15] Warren always got home before dark, she knew, because he never traveled after nightfall.[16] Thus, when he had not arrived by 5:30, the high-strung, unpredictable wife — despite her fears expressed earlier in the day for the safety of both her husband and herself — inexplicably became piqued, left the dinner on the table, bundled her two small sons in heavy coats and scarves, put them on a sled, and pulled them eight blocks in near single-digit temperatures to have a meal at The Coffee Cup, a downtown restaurant.[17]

Deputy Sheriff George Lewis was new to Albion and did not know the Hoopers, so he asked George Mather, editor of the *Albion Evening Recorder* and former co-worker with Senator Hooper, to accompany him to the Hooper home to break the news to Mrs. Hooper.[18] When they arrived they found the house empty, with a lone lamp burning in the living room. While they sat in the patrol car pondering what to do, Mrs. Hooper, her children in tow, came along the dimly lit street.[19] Lewis introduced himself, and Mather, known by Mrs. Hooper, offered his greetings. The deputy slowly said that he had some bad news and asked if she would accompany them to Springport to meet with Kim Sigler. Saying that she had received threats on her life and was suspicious of strangers — even though Mather was well known to her — she refused, unless her close personal friend Dr. Ralph Morehouse, a local osteopath, could join her. Lewis departed to locate the doctor, and an obviously pleased Mrs. Hooper telephoned her babysitter.[20]

During the journey, Mather and Lewis tried to keep the details of her husband's "accident" from her, but since there was no hospital in Springport, she concluded that Warren was dead. Mather, who knew her to be an extremely emotional person, thought it was unusual that she took the realization quite calmly, almost without surprise. Perhaps, he thought, the expected hysteria would set in later.[21]

IV Kim Sigler was questioning grand jury witnesses in Lansing when he was interrupted and told of the slaying. He finished his interrogation and was driven to the scene, arriving at nearly 9:00 p.m.[22] Dapper as ever in a dark double-breasted overcoat and light Homburg with matching gloves and scarf, the special grand jury prosecutor surveyed the gruesome surroundings, examined the car, and predictably held a press conference. "I am convinced," he intoned grimly, "that whoever shot Hooper was riding in the automobile with him. This would indicate that the murderer was known to the victim. Two of the bullets entered Hooper's head through the hat, which was badly powder burned. One bullet went into the back of the head, traveled a downward course, and came out through the chin. Another bullet went in near the left ear, continued down through the neck, and then came out through the lung. A third bullet penetrated Hooper's face at the left cheekbone, took a downward course, and remained in his body. The direction of the bullets would seem to indicate that the murderer was towering over Hooper. Hooper may have been slugged by a blackjack so his body slumped sideways in the seat and then was shot from above."[23] Amazing deductions, especially since Sigler had not seen the body and the autopsy had not yet been performed. Clearly, despite his initial contention that the killing was not necessarily linked to the grand jury, the special prosecutor was setting the stage for future news releases with this initial observation and theory. After departing the scene, Sigler was taken to Springport to meet with Mrs. Hooper, detectives, and doctors performing the autopsy. Exhausted but strangely exhilarated, he returned to his Lansing hotel suite shortly after 3:00 a.m.[24]

Six hours later, a totally refreshed Sigler held a conference with his fifteen state police grand jury investigators and instructed them to carry sidearms at all times. Ironically, a few weeks earlier he had told them to shed their weapons because the grand jury "wasn't dealing with gangsters."[25] After a hastily arranged meeting with Judge Leland W. Carr, Sigler called another press conference and revealed, for the first time, that the slain senator was to have been a state witness against Frank D. McKay, Floyd Fitzsimmons, and William Green at Monday's scheduled pretrial examination of the three on a graft conspiracy charge.[26] When the indictment had been issued in December, Sigler had promised: "There are going to be prominent men as surprise witnesses and they will have an amazing tale to tell. Their testimony will be a neat little package of dynamite."[27] Now he solemnly said, "Hooper made a complete confession involving McKay, Fitzsimmons, and Green before the grand jury and was granted immunity to testify against them. He was to be our chief witness. His death is a serious blow to our case against McKay and the others."[28] His dynamite would never explode because grand jury testimony is not perpetuating, which means that it is not binding unless the accuser is present at the examination to be cross-examined. Because of this, Sigler issued a thirty-day postponement of the examination.[29]

Sigler further proclaimed that the state police had ordered a constant guard over the special prosecutor and, smiling, added that Sergeant Leo Van Conant, head of the grand jury detail, had promised that his men "would not leave me alone for a minute." Waving to the reporters, he left, soon to be joined by Olander and Mulbar on a trip to Jackson, where he planned to establish a command headquarters to coordinate the investigation.[30]

V While Sigler was holding forth in Lansing, Springport — a small rural community of a few hundred residents — teemed with activity. Police officers and scores of newspaper reporters from throughout the nation had come to examine and report on the sensational crime. The local telephone exchange, operated by an elderly couple on the second floor of an old building, became the hub of local action as reporters fought to possess one of the two lines leading out of town.[31]

The funeral home where the bullet-riddled, charred remains of Senator Hooper had been taken was the object of an all-night and early morning vigil for both police and media personnel. Restaurants and taverns were swamped with customers Friday morning and overwhelmed in the afternoon, as hundreds of curious sightseers jammed the town seeking gossip.[32] Like the man lying on the coroner's table, Springport had gained momentary fame.

VI Frank McKay, tanned and smiling, had arrived in Grand Rapids from his Miami residence on Thursday. Friday morning he was sitting, still clad in bright paisley pajamas, in his suite in the Morton Hotel, swapping stories with political cronies attending the State Republican Convention, when a *Detroit Times* reporter entered and broke the news about Hooper's murder. McKay took it calmly, but leaped to his feet in shock and amazement when the reporter added that Sigler had publicly identified Hooper as "the fingerman" in the upcoming graft conspiracy trial.[33]

Pacing the floor, an obviously troubled McKay offered his informant a scoop. He said that the slaying was "a terrible thing" and urged that all "law enforcement agencies should be relentless in their search for those responsible." Then he related his version of his dealings with Hooper. "The first time I saw him," he began, "was about two years ago when he came to my office and said the osteopaths of Michigan wanted to open a hospital in Grand Rapids. He asked me for $2,000 as a contribution toward buying the home of the late Bishop Plagens. I told him I had a lot of physician friends and couldn't contribute because of my friendship with physicians who opposed the project. The second time was about a year ago at the Book-Cadillac Hotel in Detroit. I had just come back from Florida and had just checked in my room. There was a knock at my door and it was Mr. Hooper. He apparently had been in the lobby and had followed me to the room. I said to him: 'Mr. Hooper, how is your hospital in Grand Rapids?' Hooper said it was coming all right, but he needed money to equip it. Hooper said: 'If you would give $500 it would be very helpful.' But I again told him I could not do it and he did not press the issue as he had done the first time in Grand Rapids. Then we made a little casual conversation about Republican politics and he left. The last time was when I shook hands and exchanged greetings with him in the waiting room of the Lansing grand jury headquarters where we both had been called to appear. Hooper was a total stranger to me before that first visit."[34]

McKay knew that Sigler was plotting to link him to the murder, and the Grand Rapids political boss realized that he would have to employ all his considerable skills to squelch that scheme. Given his lengthy background as a wheeler-dealer, his gangster connections and his bodyguards from the Purple Gang — one of Detroit's most notorious organized crime syndicates — that would be no easy task; but this article, filled with half-truths and total fabrications, seemed to be a promising beginning.[35]

His co-defendants, after hasty consultations with their lawyers, also came out on the side of the angels. Floyd Fitzsimmons, with Bill Green at his side, told reporters: "This is once that we are rooting for Kim Sigler and the Carr grand jury, and hoping that they will clear this thing up quick. We know what a lot of people are probably saying or thinking. Nobody who knows any of us would think such a thing for even a minute, but the other people are different. It's an awful thing and the quicker the killer is found, the quicker this silly talk about us will stop. On this one, we're in Sigler's corner." Green concurred, adding: "We are both family men and it's tough on our families, too."[36]

VII While the murder of the key witness was, as Judge Carr noted, a "severe loss, but not necessarily a fatal blow" to the prosecution's case against McKay and the other defendants, ironically it also brought significant benefits to the grand jury probe.[37] Until that fateful Thursday afternoon, many politicians and newspaper editors had come to the conclusion that while convictions for petty graft were important in a moral and symbolic sense, they did not warrant the additional legislative grant of $250,000 requested by Carr to maintain its operation.[38] After the assassination, however, more credence was given to the seriousness of the grand jury's investigations.

Across the state, editorials echoed the words of Judge Carr that "this terrible, terrible thing cannot stop the work of the grand jury" but rather should "spur our citizens onward."[39] The politically influential *Lansing State Journal* expressed the sentiment of the state's populace when it editorialized: "There must be no more rumors in the legislative halls as to possible rebellion against provision of funds with which to begin the inquiry being conducted by Judge Leland W. Carr.... The legislature has no alternative to prompt action financing continuation of the important work which is under way."[40] Lieutenant Governor Vernon J. Brown, stating he shared the view that Hooper had been slain to prevent him from providing grand jury testimony, agreed, asserting: "Many persons will realize now for the first time that the grand jury is dealing with something pretty sinister. There was a time around here that some people thought the grand jury was somewhat inept and that it might not get too far. Now any ideas like that are gone. The killing really brought the people of Michigan to their feet."[41]

To emphasize their sincerity, members of the state senate and house passed without dissent not only the grand jury appropriation but also a $25,000 reward for information leading to the capture and conviction of their colleague's slayer.[42] Originally a $10,000 figure was proposed, but Governor Harry F. Kelly, after conferring with his legal and law enforcement advisors, urged the senate to increase the amount in an effort to stimulate a tipster's greed. "In my opinion," successfully argued the Governor, himself a former prosecuting attorney, "the number one test of the adequacy of a reward is whether it is sufficient to induce those who have information to make that information known. Because the investigators are virtually convinced that the killers were hired professionals, if any information as to their identities is to be gained, the most likely source is the underworld."[43] Senator Ben Carpenter, sponsor of the measure, concurred, pointing out that everyone, including policemen, would be eligible for the reward, and he pledged that "the money will be on the barrelhead in a very short time."[44]

In a spate of emotionalism, two other measures were introduced. One was an unsuccessful attempt to reinstate the death penalty for murder, with the bill's sponsor pleading, "There's no sense in keeping such killers alive and living off the fat of the land in prison after they've been convicted."[45] The other was a resolution to give Mrs. Hooper the remainder of her husband's full term salary of $2,190, despite the fact that he had served but eleven days, plus $500 to help defray funeral expenses. After a heated debate which elicited much sympathy for the late senator's family but little for him, the resolution was sent, without recommendation, to committee. One Republican lawmaker acidly remarked that "if the senate knew what it knows now and Hooper was alive, the order of business would be a resolution to remove him from the Senate."[46] In the senate's view, the murder of their colleague was most foul — but so was the victim. However, continuation of the grand jury was now assured.

VIII A burly, dark-haired man, looking older than his actual forty-seven years, sat troubled behind his cluttered desk. In his eighteenth year with the Michigan State Police, Harold V. Mulbar was a nationally recognized figure in law enforcement. An early exponent of the use of lie detectors, he had rapidly risen to be chief of detectives. With the outbreak of World War II in Europe, he had been named head of the State Police Subversive Activity Squad, which maintained surveillance on more than 50,000 suspected traitors in Michigan.[47] Now, with the war nearing its inevitable climax, a new challenge, replete with the opportunity for additional renown, faced him: the apprehension of those persons responsible for the assassination of Warren G. Hooper.

Less than thirty-six hours after the discovery of the corpse, Mulbar, having conferred with Captain William Hansen, who was in charge of sifting through the meager evidence and hundreds of tips pouring in from concerned citizens and notoriety seekers, ushered in reporters and held his initial press briefing on the case. Cupping a fist in his hand and saying that he would not entertain questions because he refused to offer "blind guesses," he somberly began reading a brief statement.[48]

"Although it's impossible to tell exactly what happened — this is one of the most difficult cases I've ever had to reconstruct — and although we are working on the case with no preconceived notions, we believe the killer was riding in Hooper's car. The skid marks indicate the car was stopped hurriedly, but that it was under control. There are no indications it was forced to the side of the highway by another vehicle. However, there is the possibility that a second car followed Hooper's car to the scene and picked up the killer or killers after the crime was committed. The slayer may have been riding in that other car in Lansing and transferred to Hooper's car after shouting from one vehicle to the other that he wanted to talk with Hooper."[49]

"What about a hitchhiker, Harold?" shouted a voice from the crowd. Glaring at the sea of would-be sleuths, Mulbar coolly replied that friends and relatives of the senator were all in agreement that he never picked up riders. "Moreover," he continued, assuming an air of professional superiority, "if he had picked up someone he knew or a hitchhiker, Hooper would have been in the driver's seat, which he was not."[50]

"Chief — "

Ignoring the plea for recognition, Mulbar plodded along with his remarks. "I believe the killer had his gun trained on Hooper as they sat there and told him to keep looking straight ahead. Normally, as you know, when two persons sit together in the seat of an automobile and talk, they turn toward each other. The angle at which the bullets entered Hooper's head indicate that the first was fired squarely into the side of his head, and the second and third were fired as Hooper's body slumped toward his slayer."[51]

"Any news on the fingerprint check?"

"How about the *Chicago Herald Examiner* article that three professional gunmen did the job for $25,000?"

"No more today, fellows," he smiled, adding "we have absolutely no information to substantiate that Chicago report."[52]

There was also serious doubt in his mind whether there would be anything of substance to tell in the near future. The around-the-clock, house-to-house investigations near the murder site by more than fifty officers had not yet shed any light, nor had the results of a five-hour examination of the senator's car. Partial prints of three fingers of a left hand on the driver's door just beneath the handle, a partial palm print on the left rear door, and the impression of a knit glove on the left front window frame would be grist for the crime reporters' rumor mills, but were not likely to help trace the killers, Mulbar feared. Furthermore, he was dismayed by the report that the car's interior revealed nothing of significance except for an ashtray crammed with crushed cigarette butts. This merely reinforced his belief that the fire in the automobile was caused not by the assassins in an effort to incinerate the evidence, but rather by the senator's own lifeless hand involuntarily releasing a clutched lighted cigarette when the impact of the three bullets smashed his skull. The only potentially useful news was the six-inch scrape of maroon paint on the right fender. If the murderers' car was that color perhaps Hooper's car was forced off the road, after all.[53]

Meanwhile, at his desk at the Jackson State Police Post, Captain Hansen, a greying, heavyset, thick-handed man who looked as though he belonged in a James Cagney script, shared his superior's gloom. Before speaking to the ever-present horde of reporters who hung on every word spoken inside or outside of the building, he mulled over what had been his most promising lead.

At the Springport funeral parlor, Mrs. Hooper had related to Sergeant Van Conant that for nearly three months a man — using what she now thought was an alias of Alex Nippincock — had telephoned her several times seeking to learn where her husband was, when he was coming to Albion, and by what route. Knowing that her husband's friends and business associates never asked brusquely for "Hooper" as did this gruff, thickly-accented voice, she never relayed any information to him, instead offering some excuse for ignorance of her husband's itinerary. Nor did she tell her husband of the calls, explaining to the sergeant that she did not want to worry him. On the morning of the crime, however, she received another call asking the same questions, but for some reason unknown to her she "forgot to lie" and stated that she expected the senator home before nightfall. Convinced that she might have erred, she then telephoned her husband and inquired if he knew anyone by the name of Alex Nippincock. He laughed and said no, and that she should not worry about the call.[54]

Her moods alternating between anguish and an uneasy serenity, she had sworn to Van Conant and the assembled reporters: "I think I'll never forget that voice. If I ever hear it again I will recognize it. My vocal training has taught me to remember voices, and if I do hear it again, my husband's death will be avenged. I'll see to that!" Lapsing into self-recrimination, she wailed, "If only I had not told the man that my husband was coming home on Thursday night, he might still be alive today. I blame myself, for Warren was the kindest, most gentle man in the world. He thought only of the children and me." Suddenly composed again, she announced, "Half of my life is now gone, but I have to try to live for my children."[55]

After this impressive performance, she was driven by state troopers to Albion, accompanied by the ever-present Dr. Morehead. Her physician then ordered her to remain in isolation, and even refused entry to state police who were assigned to protect her.[56] Answering her door, Morehouse stated that his patient wanted the officers nearby to protect her from prying newspaper correspondents, but did not wish them at, or inside, her home, as she did not believe she was in any danger — a view which was not shared by any of her immediate family, all of whom argued with the doctor, in vain, for police protection.[57]

Unfortunately, Mrs. Hooper's professed desire for vengeance would have to be redirected. On Saturday morning, January 13, after reading the widow's account in a newspaper, Alex Mymachod of Albion appeared at the Jackson State Police Post and, in an Austrian accent, notified authorities that he had placed the calls on behalf of his father to find out if the senator had met with success in his promise to obtain a liquor license for their new restaurant.[58] "Some trained ear," Hansen probably thought to himself, "she couldn't even get his name right!" His lead had turned to dust.

Even though he had just returned from his conference with Mulbar, Hansen wearily summoned forth his interrogators and set out two scenarios for the murder. "It is possible," he sighed with resignation, "that Senator Hooper may have been abducted by two or more gunmen in his own car and executed in gangland fashion. It is also possible, based on the same evidence, that he may have fallen into a coldly, carefully prepared death trap, baited by a companion of whom he felt no fear or distrust, unaware almost to the last that he was being taken for a ride. All the police officers are agreed that the slayer was driving the car. They believe that it was either someone he trusted or who forced him to let him drive."[59]

Reluctantly, he admitted that not all the investigators shared his contention that the car was brought to a skidding halt during an altercation between Hooper and the driver. "Of course," he explained defiantly, "it's still supposition, but it appears to me that the driver stopped the car, jerked the brim of Hooper's gray felt hat down over his eyes, and killed him. The hat brim was torn as though it had been jerked hard. It was, by all indications, a paid killer job."[60] Furthermore, he contended, the validity of his theory was strengthened by the footprints which led away from the left front door, around the front of the car, and onto the road. Because none led toward the driver's door, he solemnly proclaimed it was "highly unlikely that anyone approached Hooper's car after it had stopped and forced him into the passenger's seat."[61]

Placing the time of death at between 5:15 and 5:30 Eastern War Time, based on testimony of passersby who saw no parked car at the site before 5:10 and the discovery of the body at 5:30, Hansen left his coterie with the expectation that little would unfold during the next few days. "Our job now," he said authoritatively, hoping to mask his own uncertainties, "is to learn what happened during that important hour and twenty minutes from the time Senator Hooper left Lansing until he met his death. We are continuing our extensive inquiry along the twenty-four mile stretch from Lansing to the spot of the killing to determine whether anyone along that route saw something which would help us."[62]

Despite this dreary prognosis, within hours the entire complexion of the case was suddenly transformed. Shortly after 3:00 p.m., Sigler, Jackson County Prosecutor Murl K. Aten, Olander, Mulbar, Hansen, and Morse crowded into a small interrogation room on the fourth floor of the Jackson County Building. Their objective was to hear an account from Harry Snyder, a 48-year-old Jackson grocery salesman, who claimed to have seen the murderers at the scene.

Guided by Sigler, he recounted leaving Springport for Lansing shortly after 5 o'clock. As he drove north along M-99, which was speckled with patches of ice, he reduced his speed to below 40 miles per hour. Rounding a curve, he spied a dark green car on the side of the highway with a shiny maroon-colored sedan, possibly a Hudson because of its "torpedo-shaped nose," sitting crossways in front of it, forming a T. To clarify his story, the stenographer drew a map on which Snyder could place the correct positions.[63]

"Did you slow down as you approached the scene?" asked Sigler with an accentuated grimness in his voice.

"Yes, and the fellow in the maroon car pulled out when he seen me right here," he said, pointing to a spot which Sigler had labeled "A" on the map. "Now, this bird slowed up, see," continued Snyder, assuming what he perceived to be proper gangster parlance, "and, of course, I am always watching for a holdup. I carry quite a lot of the company's money all the time, see, and I am always on the alert if somebody blocks the way. He came across here so slow I thought he was going to stop, so I slowed down. But he pulled across the road and right down this way he headed south. He parked right there, and I got a good look at him."

"Wait a minute," ordered Sigler. "We'll call this position "B" where he parked. Now, as he came out from in front of the Hooper car, did he hesitate at all?"

"Yes, right in the road there. I thought he was going to block the highway. I got a good look at him. If I could see his picture, I believe I could identify him."

"Well, could you describe him for us?" requested Sigler in a tone of skepticism.

"Sure. He had on a light overcoat, sort of grayish — salt and pepper color — and a soft gray hat. He was very white, light-complected [sic]. He was a pretty good looking fellow. Well dressed. Weighed, from what I could see of him sitting in the car there, about 150 pounds. He looked right at me, and I looked at him," Snyder repeated, perhaps expecting to be shown volumes of "mug shots" as he had seen done so often in movies.

"Was his window closed or open?"

"Closed."

"Was it free from frost?" probed Sigler, doing his best to unsettle the witness.

"I couldn't notice no frost," Snyder snorted, adding indignantly in anticipation of the next question, "and there was no frost on mine either."

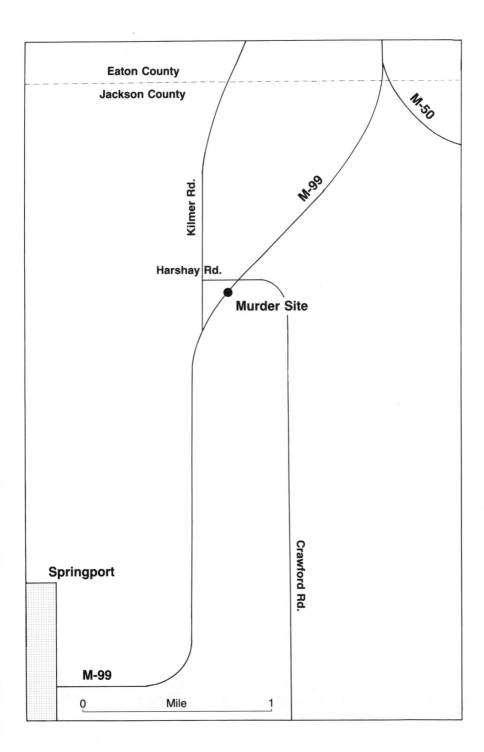

Eaton County

Jackson County

M-50

Kilmer Rd.

M-99

Harshay Rd.

Murder Site

Crawford Rd.

Springport

M-99

0   Mile   1

"All right," Sigler proceeded acidly, "what was your next observation?"

"Well, this here fellow stood on the side of the green car — "

"That is another man?" interposed Aten.

"Yes, but the top of this car came right to his head, and I couldn't see him, see," he said apologetically. "You could see he had no hat on and he had dark hair, but you couldn't see his face. He had on a dark overcoat, and one of his hands was on the door." Then, leaning forward, he startled the policemen by asking if they had bothered to check the door itself, in addition to the frame, for fingerprints.

Before the bemused officers could reply, Sigler fired another salvo at the witness. "Which way was he facing, Mr. Snyder?"

"Oh," came the calm response, "he was as if he was talking to this fellow setting in the car, which afterwards I found out was the dead fellow, see. The dead fellow sat with his head down like a drunk would."

"Was there any evidence of smoke?"

"No." Scratching his head, Snyder added thoughtfully, "That is why I can't figure out how he got burned so bad in such a short time."[64]

Again nipping the witness in mid-thought, Sigler inquired if he made any further observations. "No, not there. To tell the truth, I just figured there was something damn phoney, but I didn't know what. My idea was this was a drunk in the car and them fellows was trying to help him or something, see. Then I thought, the way they backed this car off the road — at least it looked to me as if it had been backed off the road — and this maroon car was backed in front of it, that it was intentional so that nobody could see their license plates."[65]

Becoming impatient, Sigler paced the limited space between the walls and long table. "Then what happened, Mr. Snyder?" he snapped.

"I kept driving by, real slow, and kept looking in my mirror. Then when I got to here," which was designated "C" on the sketch, "I saw this bird here leave the green car and went across the road and ran down this way. I took it he went toward that other car, see. He ran all the way. Then an old, dilapidated Chevy went by with this old fossil and his wife in it. He wore a cap and she had a shawl over her head. He was going south. Then another two-door car went by with one fellow in it — a small fellow who wore glasses."[66]

The special prosecutor, who did not share the mirth expressed by everyone else in the room at these remarks, somberly notified them that "D" would mark the meeting with the elderly couple's car and

"E" would be the second vehicle. Glowering, he urged the grinning witness to finish his tale.

"Well, right about here," he continued, pausing while Aten quickly inserted an "F" at the spot at the tip of Snyder's index finger, "this same maroon car passes me." Becoming animated, he implored his audience to believe him. "It was the same driver. I seen him, see. I positively know it was the same fellow. And this other bird was with him in the car, in the seat with his hat over his face like this," he pantomimed, "with the back of his head on the back of the seat. The boy — the younger fellow — was still driving. That is the reason I knew it was the same red car that was now heading back toward Lansing."[67]

After having Snyder ushered from the building unseen, Sigler hastily notified the media that he would hold a news conference later that afternoon in Lansing. As reporters jostled for position in his grand jury office in the Olds Hotel, a smiling, ebullient Sigler paraphrased everything he had just learned, omitting only the name of the witness. In his exuberance, he embellished the facts by implying strongly that the license number of the maroon car was known, although prudence mandated that it not be disclosed "until we're more certain about it." Noting a perceptible look of displeasure on the faces of Mulbar and Hansen, who were seated at his side during this masterful blending of fact and fancy, the special prosecutor concluded with the warning that "this may still develop into a long drawn-out manhunt. The search is nationwide. Officials have thrown out a dragnet all over the country for suspects and for the maroon car."[68]

Waving as he strode confidently toward the door, Sigler abruptly halted and told the milling newspeople, as if in afterthought, that he and Commissioner Olander expected, within the week, to meet with law enforcement officials in Chicago. Turning a deaf ear to cries about the validity of the *Chicago Herald American* theory, he concluded his exit, pleased with the prospect of the next day's laudatory headlines.[69] Moreover, he was anxious to keep his scheduled appointment with Kenneth McCormick, the crime reporter for the *Detroit Free Press* and Sigler's most ardent supporter in the press.

Perhaps as a result of this closed-door conference, the Sunday edition of the *Free Press* ran a feature by McCormick entitled "How Hooper Was Murdered" which, in many respects, bore an unmistakable similarity to the views of the special prosecutor. Claiming to be an "official" reconstruction based on contacts with police officials, McCormick effectively put forth, in the style that would earn him a Pulitzer Prize for his grand jury coverage, a gripping account:

Senator Hooper was 'hot'.... No outsider knew what Hooper had told the grand jury. They only knew he was talking. If his lips were sealed his 'confession' would be just a scrap of paper.

His killers were professionals. The crime had the customary superficial gangland stamp of crudity — but it was carefully plotted and timed.

The pair studied their victim's habits. One may even have won Hooper's friendship, not an unknown trick in the killer's trade. They knew he went home to Albion on weekends. They knew his route. They may even have known a stop.

The pair drove over M-99 looking for a likely spot for a slaying. They picked one 1/4 of a mile from any house. They may even have rehearsed the method by which they would assassinate him. They were ready.

When Senator Hooper drove out of Lansing last Thursday he picked up the small footed gunman. Their meeting was probably prearranged — 'business' or a 'lift.' There was no mistrust that this was a death ride. Hooper let the other man drive. He was found on the right side of the car, a weekend bag to his left. They probably chatted — Hooper smoking a cigarette — as they drew nearer and nearer to the selected spot.

The maroon sedan, the getaway car, fell in behind. It was to serve several purposes. The accomplice watched in the rearview mirror until he saw the road behind was clear of cars. The maroon car squeezed in ahead, swerved Hooper's car to a sudden, skidding stop on the left side of the road, both blockading it and offering a shield from cars approaching from the south.

Hooper was on the spot. His attention was caught by the car forcing them off the road. His killer then had time to get out his .38 calibre Colt. The Albion Senator may never have realized that his 'friend' was his assassin. The gun — with the thoroughness of the mobster — was put only eight inches from his head. Three bullets went through his head from the left side. He hadn't turned around. The killer's work was done. Hooper was through talking.

The small footed gunman stepped out from behind the wheel of Hooper's car and ran to the getaway car, now pulled back on the highway. They drove away and — if the old pattern is the same — probably in a stolen car.[70]

Monday morning bestowed more blessings on the authorities. William E. Bracey, a 65-year-old farmer and former guard at Jackson Prison who resided not far from the murder scene, met with Murl

Aten to make a statement on his observations during the early afternoon of January 11.

"Between 1 and 2 o'clock — I didn't think I would have to know it exactly then," he drawled through a slight smile, "I saw a maroon sedan parked along Bradford Road, a side street about forty rods from my house, and which intersects M-99. I saw a man and a woman out behind the car when I first looked out my window, and I was curious enough to watch because I thought it was funny."[71]

"What was the size of the man?"

"I'd say he weighed 135-140 pounds. Maybe 5'7" or 5'9" — I can't tell, of course, but he wasn't a large man. I'm sure of that."

"How about the woman?" asked Aten.

"She was very large," answered Bracey, his voice giving emphasis to the visual impression. "God, she looked like a haystack standing down there. Anyway, she wore a dark coat and a dark hat. Not a fur coat. The man had on a dark overcoat, with a belt, and a dark hat. You know, forty rods is a long ways, but it was a clear day and I could see pretty good."[72]

"Then what happened, Mr. Bracey?" urged Aten, amused at his mental image of the woman and also relieved that neither Sigler nor Judge Carr, under whom the Jackson County prosecutor had studied law, were present to discourage his momentary levity.[73]

"Well, a snow plow came along behind them and moved them away. They parked along the right-hand side of M-99 going south towards Springport. I guess they stayed there about 45 minutes. Didn't pay any attention," he said nonchalantly, not wishing to appear abnormally inquisitive, "but it was quite a while with the motor never shut off while they stood there."[74]

Smiling again at this likeable man, the usually dour Aten felt totally at ease. Perhaps it was because Sigler was not in attendance, but for whatever reason, the bespectacled, double-chinned prosecutor was enjoying himself for the first time in days. Running his hand across his slicked black hair, he inquired leisurely, "So, what else did you see?"

"Well, the man got out once — out of the car. Came around back. They seemed to be doing something, or at least he did. She was just standing there watching him. Struck me right straight out," he said firmly, "that they were possibly removing license plates." Pausing, he rubbed his chin, and with twinkling eyes confessed, "Well, at first, I guess I thought they might be changing a tire, but they couldn't have done it in that snowbank. Anyway, then they threw something in the trunk and slapped it right down again. The woman just stood there a minute — kind of thinking, maybe — and then walked through the

39

snowbank to get into the right hand door. Then they left. That's all I seen."[75]

Aten excused the witness and thanked him for his assistance. As he reached the door, Bracey wheeled and asked softly, "I understand, Mr. Aten, that they found tracks of a small-footed person around the car in the snow?"

"Yes."

"Well, did it ever strike you," Bracey pondered thoughtfully, "that it could have been a woman's tracks? That same woman that was in that car? I have had that on my mind every damn minute since this fellow was killed!"[76]

Thanking him again, Aten politely escorted the witness to the main lobby of the Jackson County Building and bid him farewell without responding to his query. Standing alone, Aten was momentarily lost in thought. Like every police officer who viewed those footprints, he had believed a woman could have made them. Yet Sigler steadfastly refused to admit that that possibility existed. As he slowly trudged back to his office, he likely kept wondering why.

After Sigler received Aten's telephone call relating his new findings, he notified his cadre of newspaper sycophants — to no one's surprise. Indulging in his typical self-aggrandizement, during the press conference he neglected to utter Aten's name and asserted, without reservation, that the occupants of the maroon car had changed the vehicle's license plates. Most significant, however, was his statement that the latest witness had observed two *men* in the suspect automobile, and that the witness's positive identification of them agreed in every detail with that offered by Saturday's eyewitness.[77]

Only Aten knew that Sigler was willfully misleading the press — and the people of Michigan — again on the implication of a woman participant in the crime; yet, either from loyalty, respect, or, more likely, fear of recrimination, he never challenged the special prosecutor. Consequently, newspaper accounts soon spoke of only male suspects. Not entirely by coincidence, Aten's silence was rewarded the following year when Republican gubernatorial candidate Kim Sigler dubbed the obscure Jackson County prosecutor to run on his ticket for auditor general. Despite published speculation that this selection was a payoff for his behavior in the Hooper case, Aten triumphed and was re-elected in 1948.[78] Gratitude to Sigler for making him a statewide influence in Republican politics sealed Aten's lips as effectively as the three .38 calibre slugs silenced Hooper. Sigler's crusade to use the Hooper murder to further his own career could continue, at least for the present, unabated.

CHAPTER FOUR

I'M AFRAID OF YOU, KIM

I Flowers formed a half-circle around Warren G. Hooper's final resting place in Albion's Riverside Cemetery. Knights Templar conducted a Masonic ritual for their fallen comrade, a final prayer was offered by Reverend Victor Dowdell, rector of St. James Episcopal Church, and then the body was committed to its wintry grave.[1]

Earlier on the snowy, blustery, bitterly cold Monday, a simple service consisting merely of the Episcopal rites for the dead had been held at the church. No reference was made as to the manner by which the state senator had met his death.[2]

Anticipating that hundreds of his townspeople and legislative colleagues would overflow the church's limited seating capacity, a network of loudspeakers was installed in the adjoining church house and a funeral parlor across the street to broadcast the burial litany to those unable to find space within the main building. However, it was not necessary, as fewer than two hundred mourners — primarily relatives of Mrs. Hooper, family friends, seven state legislators, osteopaths, and plainclothes state police detectives — were present. Interestingly, no one from the senator's family came to the services. His parents and two sisters claimed it was too far to travel from their California homes, and his only brother, living in Ohio, steadfastly declined to divulge the motivation behind his absence.[3] In death, as in life, Warren Hooper was a pathetically lonely man.

The flower-draped bier was led into the church through a line of plumed Knights Templar, their swords drawn, by a black cassocked altar boy, a crucifix bearer, and two boys holding lighted candles. Behind the casket strode the strikingly attractive widow, escorted by her brother, Charles Cobb. Garbed in a black dress, black gloves, and a black hat with a white flower, Mrs. Hooper, clutching a small white prayer book, certainly appeared funereal. Yet her black veil, worn at a jaunty angle to reveal one eye, and her heavy make-up with flaming red lipstick, offered a contrasting, almost theatrical, demeanor.[4] Although all eyes were on her, she never looked up, apparently lost in thoughts and grief.[5] Perhaps she was pondering the truth of the words she would later have inscribed on her husband's tombstone: "With honesty he lived, for honesty he was taken."

II Shortly after 6:00 p.m., January 16, Sigler, Aten, and Olander escorted Mrs. Hooper into the oft-used Room 438 of the Jackson County Building for interrogation. In response to preliminary probing, she admitted having been married in her youth to a wealthy man whom she described, without elaboration, as a "sex pervert," how she had left him, returned to live with her parents in Battle Creek, and had never sought employment while residing there.[6]

Nervously crossing and uncrossing her long legs, she fidgeted in the wooden armchair and finally became indignant. "Why is all this necessary, Kim? I can't understand it. What bearing does my past have on all this? Are you trying to establish *my* character?"[7]

"Not in the least," cooed Sigler, with a reassuring smile masking his intent to unveil the lies which he knew she had spewed to reporters concerning her dedication to the late senator. "I'm simply trying to find out all the background of you and Senator Hooper. And you certainly do not want it said that Mrs. Hooper is not cooperating with the officers trying to find the man who murdered her husband, do you?"[8]

Without acknowledging this transparent threat, she glared malevolently into his eyes as he continued. "You certainly ought to realize that there isn't any disposition to do anything other than treat you with the utmost courtesy and kindness, but we must insist — "

"I'm afraid of you, Kim," she interrupted. "I used to think you were grand, but I'm afraid of you now."

"Because of Dr. Morehouse, I suppose," he sneered. Regaining his composure, he airily dismissed it with a wave of his hand. "Well, let's not go into that. There isn't any reason under the sun why you should be afraid of me."[9]

More silence.

"I came to your house, as you must remember. I talked with you and your husband. We sat on a settee. I told him and you that I didn't think there was anything to worry about, but we didn't want to take any chances. I offered him police protection at the time and told him we had officers that I wanted to send to be with him to protect him, but he refused, saying that their presence would embarrass him. I said — "

"Of course, I didn't hear any of the conversation. I left for the seamstress," she interjected, doubtless mindful of her diatribe against Sergeant Van Conant at Springport the night of the murder, which earned headlines in the next day's newspapers, that the state police and grand jury had repeatedly refused her husband's pleas for guards — an insensitivity which cost them a witness but deprived her of "half of my life."[10]

"We are going to have to insist that you cooperate and let us have all the facts about everything in this matter," warned Sigler, rapidly losing patience with her disdainfulness. "If you'll just sit back and relax and answer these questions, we'll get along very beautifully and there won't be any arguments or discussion."[11]

"Well," came her haughty reply, "I don't see how anything I did from the time I was born until I met Warren has anything to do with this case."

"Listen, lady," he thundered, with a fury that surprised even his co-inquisitors, "the father of your children has been murdered. Don't you want to try to find out about that? Maybe you know a lot more than you realize. I don't care whether you think my questions are immaterial. We owe a duty to the people of Michigan and we're going to perform it!"

"I want my attorney."[12]

No doubt Sigler's thoughts reverted to his questioning of her attorney, Theodore Van Dellen, the previous evening at the Olds Hotel in Lansing. He had expressed an interest in Dr. Morehouse and was not startled in the least to learn that, in the lawyer's opinion, the doctor was "second rate" and had a reputation for being a "ladies' man."[13] Probing more deeply, he had inquired: "Would it surprise you to find that there was a relationship beyond that of doctor and patient between Dr. Morehouse and Mrs. Hooper?" and was told matter-of-factly, "No, that wouldn't surprise me."[14] He recalled how, after he had mentioned to Van Dellen that Mrs. Hooper had "not in any sense been cooperative as a woman should have been whose husband has been murdered," the lawyer had shrugged and said simply that he had informed Captain Hansen the night of the murder that, despite the Hoopers' marital difficulties, he did not think she would cause his death but "he could take that into consideration in his questioning of her."[15] Clearly she was hiding something — but why?

Snapping out of his momentary reverie, his bright eyes ablaze, Sigler pointed his finger menacingly toward his adversary. "If that's your attitude," he threatened, "I will have the officers serve a subpoena to have you appear before Judge Carr and the grand jury, where your attorneys cannot be present. You can't imagine for one moment, Mrs. Hooper, that when a great subject like the murder of a man is involved that you can proceed along this line. All I'm asking you is for some sensible cooperation on your part, and we are entitled to that, and you should give it to us. You do not think we are doing this for fun or because we like it, do you?"[16]

Seeking solace from the others present but finding none, the widow reiterated, although this time with cause, "I'm afraid of you, Kim."[17]

Knowing that he had sufficiently shaken her confidence, a suddenly soothing Sigler resumed his examination, eliciting innocuous facts about her early married life with Hooper. Then, striking without warning, he unnerved his prey by asking why, on several occasions, she had sought a divorce. Caught off guard by this unexpected thrust into what she hitherto had thought was a confidential matter, she warily claimed it was because they did not experience what she considered a normal home life because of his legislative and osteopathic-related travels.[18]

"Did you think your husband was running around with other women on these trips?"

"Well," she stammered, moistening her lips, "there was gossip. No, I don't think he ever did."

"But didn't you hire a former sheriff, Moon French, to check up on your husband?"

"No," she bristled, straightening in the chair and puffing smoke from a cigarette offered her by Commissioner Olander. "I confronted Warren with the gossip and he hired the man to find out who started it. We traced it down to a taxi cab driver in Albion. He admitted it was all lies. Warren was cross enough to have him arrested, but I didn't want that because he had three little children and a wife at home."[19]

Leaving several obvious questions unanswered for the moment, the special prosecutor informed her that he had heard several stories in Albion regarding her infidelity. Smug in his knowledge that few persons cared for Mrs. Hooper because of her perceived snobbishness toward those she considered her social inferiors, he eagerly awaited her response.[20]

"I don't know about the stories," she replied indignantly. Following an uneasy pause, she reflected: "Well, there was one time I went to a show alone and someone called Warren and said they had seen me with a man, but there wasn't any man at all. Then, once someone called Warren and said I was at a party with a man named Lloyd Cush. Well, he's a nice person, but I'd never think of it — " Noticing

Sigler's head cock, she hastily added, "Well, I would never think of going out with anybody," before continuing. "Anyway, they said I was out with him and that I was so drunk that he carried me home. Warren was very upset about it, but it was just small-town gossip. There was no truth in it."[21]

"There has been quite a bit of gossip around Albion, hasn't there?" he prodded, hoping she might volunteer something his investigators had not yet uncovered.

"Oh, I don't know. If there was, I didn't hear it," she stated innocently, unmindful of the contradiction to her previous utterances.[22]

On a happier note, she bubbled excitedly about how her husband had found for them a house to rent for $90 a month in East Lansing; how she would have a music room in which to instruct pupils in the piano; how her youngest son would be enrolled in pre-kindergarten; and how she would earn money of her own as a hostess in a Lansing hotel. They would have been a family again, and all their domestic troubles would vanish.[23]

"Is there anything else that you and he had trouble about during the last year except the fact that he was away from home so much?" probed the prosecutor, once again preparing to disrupt her brief respite into tranquility.

"No."

"Are you sure about that? You see, Mrs. Hooper, someday a man is going to be apprehended who murdered your husband. There will be a trial. Now, it is so much better for you to tell us about the facts now."

"There is nothing I can tell you," she insisted. "We had no more troubles than other married couples. Warren was quite a dreamer, you know. He loved lovely things and he had to go down and borrow money on the furniture in order to pay. I didn't like that. He had antiques, 450. I didn't have any money. When we went to California, we were offered money to go by that man Burns of the Medical Association, but Warren turned it down, and we had to go down and borrow again. That's the thing I didn't like. But, other than that, there wasn't any trouble at all."[24]

Sigler's heart leapt, as once again his thoughts honed in on Agnes Wickens' remarks in this very room three days earlier that the senator was "happy enough" with his marriage, but that his wife was "always nagging, always sputtering, and always fussing" at him; that she had sworn at him, screamed, and caused scenes in public places, usually berating him for not earning enough money; that she had confided that Hooper's credit was so bad he no longer could get a loan in Albion; that he had told his secretary less than a week before his death that things were so bad at home "Callie is going to throw my clothes in the office." Simultaneously he recalled how his own probe had revealed that Hooper could not even afford to pay his property taxes and that, in 1943, the title of the property at 1001 East Porter Street had reverted to his wife's parents.[25] Hooper needed money — in large amounts — to pacify his wife, and who better to turn to than Frank McKay?

Snapping back, the prosecutor asked if Mrs. Hooper knew all of the people her husband met.

"Oh, yes. I knew all of them. They were at the funeral yesterday." Beaming with Pearl Mesta pride, she added, "There was over a hundred in my house."

"Who were his closest friends?"

"Well, Warren didn't have many friends," she asserted flatly, and then began to engage in rambling self-pity. "You see, that's why I didn't like his job. In Albion, I didn't feel that I belonged anywhere. I didn't feel that I belonged to the osteopaths professionally because I was the wife of a paid employee. And I would never associate with his friends. And his work wasn't in Albion, so I couldn't, you know, go with a group there. Oh, we had a lot of acquaintances — but I meant the kind of friends that come back to the back door and say, 'How are you?'"

"Yes," reassured the disinterested barrister, "but who were his closest friends?"

"Well, members of his Masonic lodge, I'd say. You know, Warren was kind of a lone wolf. I mean he didn't have time for friendship or for his family. He had the — "

"Well," injected Sigler, "I tried to help."

"I don't know," Mrs. Hooper shot back. "That's what you told Warren and now he's gone!"

His face reddened, Sigler barked, "If you were afraid for his safety on the day of his death, why didn't you call me?"

"I'll tell you why. I was going downtown that day to save $1.50 to get my bills paid before noon. It was the 11th and my bills were due on the 10th."

Taken aback by the apparent inanity of her statement, Sigler murmured, "Well, it wouldn't have cost you anything to call me."

"The point is," she continued, "that I had John ready on the sled and it was already 11 o'clock."

"Well," intoned the prosecutor, verbalizing the harsh truth which had to be inferred from her testimony, "you can't blame me for his death then, Mrs. Hooper. If there's anyone to blame, you don't want to blame me. You knew what the situation was, and you didn't call me."

Seemingly oblivious to the implications of that remark, Mrs. Hooper whispered, as if for dramatic impact, "Well, it was just a premonition. You would have thought I was silly."

"No," came the honest reply, "I wouldn't have."

Smiling at Olander, she requested another cigarette. Inhaling deeply, she chided, "No, Kim. If I had called you and said, 'I'm afraid. I think something's going to happen,' you would have said, 'Why?' and I would have had to say it was just a feeling. You would have thought I was silly. You and your cold, legalistic mind."[26]

"That is silly, Mrs. Hooper," he bristled, brushing aside any thoughts that her observation might contain a trace of validity, "and let me tell you something. If you are going to keep on talking like that, there is only one thing we can do and that is to tell the people of Michigan that Mrs. Hooper does not want to cooperate with the police in discovering the murderer of her husband. Now, where did he stay the Tuesday night before his murder?"[27]

Chastened by the verbal onslaught, Mrs. Hooper replied meekly, "He always stayed at the hospital when he was in Lansing. He was afraid to stay anywhere else."

"Did he ever tell you he was afraid?"

"Oh, no, no, no!" rang through the dimly lit room like an echo.

"Well, then, how do you know he was afraid?"

"By his behavior. He never walked in anymore with his head in the air. He was always with sunken shoulders. I used to tell him 'Daddy, straighten up. You're too young a man to walk that way.' And he was jumpy. Whenever the telephone rang, he wouldn't answer it. And we never went out at night."

"Yes," urged Sigler, "but did he ever say anything to you that led you to think he was afraid?"

"Oh, he was afraid ever since the day Fitzsimmons went to his office and offered him money."

"What did he tell you Fitzsimmons said?"

"I don't remember."

Eyes widening and fist clenched, Sigler drew near her chair and bellowed, "Yes, you do! Go ahead and tell us about it! Why do you act like this?"

"Because I'm afraid they'll get me next," she trembled. "I have two little boys at home and they need me. Even if I told you, it would just be hearsay."

"How much money did he say Fitzsimmons offered him?" came the barked reiteration.

"I don't know!"

"Mrs. Hooper, he told you!"

"He did not," her voice now choked with gasps, "because he wasn't offered money. I shouldn't have said money. He was offered protection of attorneys."

"But what did he say?" coaxed Sigler, desperate to learn what, if any, of his dead informant's testimony lived on in his spouse.

"I don't remember," she sighed, slumping in her chair under the emotional strain, "I don't remember if Warren ever talked. We never had any time to talk together. Maybe I just put facts together. He didn't tell me 'This is the way it went.' Before he went to Lansing on Tuesday, I said: 'Please keep out of it. We're just getting started. Let's not get anywhere near it.' Then he said something to do with you, Kim. Oh, I don't want to think any more. I've thought enough. Please."

Like a hunter pursuing a weakened prey, Sigler pressed on relentlessly. "What did he say?"

Exhausted, Mrs. Hooper unburdened herself of her secret. "He said: 'I don't know about this now. I might better be a state witness and be for the right and have the protection of the state, than to be a little man outside of McKay's pie.'"[28]

At last, that name. All that remained was for the special prosecutor to develop the fears of the Hoopers for this man and the trap could be sprung. Instant fame was within his grasp.

Glancing at her watch and seeing that it was nearly 8 o'clock, Mrs. Hooper asked if she might be allowed to go home and put her children to bed and hear their nightly prayers. His adrenaline flowing, Sigler refused. "Let's go over a few more things before we call it a day. Now tell me, wouldn't you like to see us find the man who did this terrible thing?"[29]

"Oh, yes, but I'm afraid. If only it didn't mean giving up my life. My boys need me. My dad is 65. I've been afraid — I don't know — a long time," she sobbed, dabbing at the corner of her eyes with a handkerchief. Then, suddenly composed, she asked the startled lawyer, "Do you remember the night in Lansing that Bill Green was in your office?"

"Yes."

"And you called in Warren and you said: 'Bill Green gave you that money, didn't he, Warren?' and Warren said 'Yes.' Well, when he got home that night and told me, I said: 'Warren, your life isn't worth a penny. Not a penny.' From then on I've been dreadfully afraid. I haven't let the children play in the yard. When I've gone out at night, I've gone in taxis. I've only been out once. I went to one show. That's all. That was the night that settled everything for Warren."[30]

"Of whom are you afraid, Mrs. Hooper? Tell me."

"I don't dare say the name, Kim. You say it," she trembled.

"Say it! Say it!"

"There is only one — possibly one man that would have wanted Warren out of the way."

"Who is that?" he pleaded, wanting to hear the name of Frank McKay ring in his ears once again.

"I'm not going to say. I'm afraid of $10,000,000. I'm afraid of these people that were afraid of Warren, not because I know anything, but just because I happen to be Mrs. Hooper," was the adamant response.

Irate with her intransigence, Sigler determined to leave her with a discomforting thought to mull over until the next interview. "Have you ever talked with Dr. Morehouse about these matters?"

"No."

"Then why did he come here with you and your brother tonight?"

"Because I feel very safe when he is around." Eyes widening, she snapped, "Why? What makes you say a thing like that? There is nothing at all between Ralph and I, if that is what you mean!"

"Not at all," smiled Sigler, noting the familiar first-name description of the physician. "I just wondered why he was always with you, that's all."[31] With that, the nearly two-hour session ended, and Sigler summoned Charles Cobb into the room.

"Your sister, Mr. Cobb," he stated soberly, "has not been very cooperative with the officials in this matter. It seems to me that she, above all other people, should be cooperative because her husband has been murdered. Some day the guilty person is going to be brought before the bar of justice and above everything else it certainly doesn't want to appear publically or otherwise that she isn't giving all the aid and assistance that she might in tracking down the person who murdered her husband. Isn't that logical?"

"That's right," came the solemn reply.

"Now, it may be due to the nearness of the event — it may be fear on her part — but whatever it is, the time is coming very, very soon when we must insist, and we are entitled to expect, that she is going to help and do what she can to assist us. Do you think that that is asking for any more than is fair?"

"No, that's right."

"Now, we've been very considerate of her, Mr. Cobb," he said in a soothing, yet firm, tone. "No one has bothered her. Ordinarily, the average law-enforcing agency would have been over there long before this and would have been taking statements from her and grilling her on facts and all that sort of thing, and we haven't done that. We've respected the situation in which she found herself and have stayed away from her. But here's the situation. Someday there is going to be a murder trial on this case. The defense is going to cast all the aspersions they can at everybody connected with the murder. They always do, don't they? And the more facts she can tell us about their marital affairs and about their personal life, the more it places her in a position where we can protect her against those things, don't you see?"[32]

Despite the paternalistic demeanor of the prosecutor, a stony silence met his query. "Does Mrs. Hooper plan on remaining in Albion?" he continued.

"Well, eventually, but now we'd like to get her away to Milwaukee or Madison as soon as possible. Perhaps tomorrow or the next day for a month or two."

"In the meantime, you expect things here to just go the best they can, do you? She has not given us all she can! Don't try to deny it! I'm telling you! I now learn that she would have left here without ever saying a word to us either tomorrow or the next day had it not been for the fact that we just happened today to send the officers over to see her."

"Well, I — "

"Now, don't misunderstand me," Sigler raged on, "I don't want to hold the woman here one minute longer than is absolutely necessary, but we would like to have her not leave until we are through ascertaining all the facts we can, as far as she is concerned."

"I understand, Mr. Sigler," the young man responded in a curious mixture of contempt and awe, "but we are concerned about her health and the two boys."

"True, Mr. Cobb," he nodded, "but at the same time the people of Michigan are concerned with apprehending the man who murdered her husband. To make a long story short, and to make it very plain, if you persist in her leaving immediately, we'll have to take legal action to see that she does not."

"She'll leave when her lawyer says she can."

"Not unless we agree, Mr. Cobb. You may go," Sigler commanded.[33]

Packing his briefcase, Sigler mentally reviewed the evening. While he had learned little of value, his badgering, he believed, had planted seeds which would bear fruit at his next encounter with Mrs. Hooper. Donning his Chesterfield, he strode confidently into the frigid night air to be driven home.

III The second week of the probe was highlighted by an examination into a different "woman angle" in the case. Satisfied that they knew how the professional assassins had earned their blood money, state police investigators turned their attention to possible motives, other than prevention of Hooper's grand jury appearance, which might have precipitated the slaying. Several rumors quickly surfaced regarding numerous sexual peccadillos on the part of the late Albion legislator. Agnes Wickens, the matronly secretary who also was the senator's business associate in his patent medicine company, mentioned to Detective Vincent Neering that Hooper had hidden "quite a few sex books around the office" in downtown Albion.[34] When Neering and another detective arrived to search the premises several days later, no such literature was present.[35] Recalling that shortly after the murder, Dr. Morehouse had requested permission to enter the building to remove a typewriter belonging to the Michigan Osteopathic Association, the officers surmised that the physician, as an act of gallantry toward the widow, had rifled the office and committed the petty larceny.[36] Another allegation was made by a state representative who piously denounced Hooper for degrading the character of all public officials by "carrying and displaying dirty pictures."[37] Along similar lines, a woman informed the state police that the senator had made lewd advances toward a female Battle Creek attorney at a dinner party at which she was in attendance and had engaged in what she described, without detail, as "acts of gross indecency."[38]

None of these stories were deemed relevant by Sigler. At one of his daily press briefings, he snapped at reporters who had asked about the "not for publication" gossip they had heard around state police headquarters: "Lest there be any misunderstanding, from all the evidence coming to me, there is nothing to indicate there was a woman angle to this case. And, in the investigation of Hooper's life, whatever we discover will remain secret unless it was connected with his death."[39] This subtle disclaimer, while apparently innocuous, was inserted deliberately, because the special prosecutor's curiosity had been whetted by one, and only one, of these state police accounts: that Hooper's life had been threatened by former Purple Gang mobster "Buffalo Harry" Rosenberg, whose prostitute wife Vita reputedly had been "laying up" with the senator.[40]

Sigler's attention initially had been drawn toward the Detroit-based mob as early as January 13, when the *Detroit News* ran an interview with an Albion businessman who claimed that Sam Fleisher, a former "Purple," had visited his automobile repair shop two or three days prior to Hooper's death.[41] Even though in the 1930s Sam and his brothers Harry and Louis had operated a junkyard in Albion which served as a front for their criminal activities, they no longer resided there.[42] Consequently, after the senator's murder, recollections of Fleisher's sudden reappearance caused much speculation among the city's residents.[43] Captain Hansen issued a low-keyed announcement that the report was "interesting" and would be investigated but cautioned that, to his knowledge, Fleisher was still incarcerated, and that even if he had been recently released, "his presence in Albion in itself would not be incriminating."[44] With the Rosenberg story, however, the possible Purple Gang aspect could not be summarily dismissed. Moreover, Sigler knew that Frank McKay's chief bodyguard, Charles Leiter, was a former "Purple," and any guilt-by-association could prove beneficial in his plot to tie "The Boss" to the crime in the public's mind.[45]

Making the accusation against Rosenberg — a slim, bushy eyebrowed, pug-nosed, 44-year-old mobster — was John Widmer, whose reputation for honesty was not considered above reproach by his fellow citizens of Bay City. According to Widmer, who had lived with Vita Rosenberg during the early months of 1940 while her husband was serving a ninety-day sentence in Detroit, Vita had told him that she had spent several nights with Senator Hooper of Albion at a Saginaw Hotel and, implying blackmail, that she could get money from him at any time. During the last week of October 1944, he met Vita and Hooper at a Bay City restaurant, where the three had a lively conversation, dinner, and drinks. While the senator was in the restroom, Widmer and Vita spied her husband brandishing a pistol outside the front window of the bar. Remembering that the extremely jealous Harry had threatened at one time to kill him, Widmer fled, but he heard Rosenberg scream, "I'll kill the son of a bitch," referring to Hooper.[46]

While Widmer's story was being verified, Murl Aten interviewed Stella Kalenchick. Mrs. Kalenchick lived across the street from the Streetcar Tavern in Albion, one of several roadhouses owned by Rosenberg and his brother Louis, and let out a room in which Vita could ply her trade. She positively identified Hooper as the man she had seen with Vita in the tavern sometimes two or three times a week, and who had visited Vita's bedroom at least three times.[47] She was quick to point out, however, that she also had seen Hooper talk with both Harry and Louis at their private table several times and that only "their friends used to sit there with them."[48] When Aten inquired if she had ever seen the Rosenbergs angry or disgusted when Hooper fawned on Vita, she said no, but explained: 'If they were, they probably wouldn't show it. They were that kind. Probably talk it over later, but not at that time. When they got mad, they'd talk in Jewish, anyway, so I didn't know what they said."[49]

On the strength of these accounts, Abe (alias "Buffalo Harry") Rosenberg, then employed as a tobacco salesman in Detroit, was arrested but was released within hours after passing a lie detector test.[50] Before Rosenberg left the East Lansing State Police Post, Sigler inexplicably confronted the oft-arrested criminal with his accuser. Not unexpectedly, the terrified Widmer, as a laughing Sigler later recalled, "promptly folded up" and denied that Rosenberg was the man he had seen threaten Hooper.[51]

At a Lansing press conference, Sigler related how the unfounded Rosenberg rumor had been circulated. "At one time this man was in trouble with the Liquor Control Commission because he had been selling to minors. On two occasions, Senator Hooper had accompanied the hoodlum's wife to Lansing and appeared before the liquor commission on their behalf. The place did not lose its license. But the hoodlum insists he did not pay Hooper money. Neither had he reason to suspect an affair between the senator and his wife. Apparently attracted by the reward of $25,000 offered for information, a man in Bay City told us he had heard this hoodlum threaten Hooper in a restaurant in that town last October. As a matter of fact, the hoodlum, no longer in the saloon business, proved to us by his trip sheets that he was at work in Detroit the day of the alleged threat. Moreover, he has been divorced from his wife, who is supposed to have been present when the threat was made. We have found that the wife has since remarried a sailor and was out of the state at the time."[52] Having made certain that even though Rosenberg was innocent, he was unsavory, Sigler announced that he and Commissioner Olander were leaving for Chicago to enlist the aid of that city's police in combing their underworld haunts for clues.[53]

State police continued their probing into a possible Hooper-Rosenberg-mob connection and on January 24 Rosenberg was arrested again, booked for "investigation of murder," and held incommunicado "somewhere in Lansing."[54] Captain Mulbar, the portly chief of detectives who made the apprehension, told reporters cryptically that authorities "were not satisfied with everything he told us the first time he was questioned and because we want to be sure he is available if we need him for anything."[55] Cynics sneered that the arrest was staged because the murder investigation no longer commanded front page coverage and the special prosecutor required at least one story and photograph daily to satisfy his ego. Sigler's defenders rebuffed such slander and predicted that after the Chicago junket there would be a definite connection between Rosenberg and the hired gunmen who slew Hooper.[56] Unfortunately, the former proved nearer the truth and Rosenberg, having been fired from his job because of the notoriety, was set free again, never to be further implicated in any way with the case."[57]

IV Upon his return from Chicago late Thursday night, January 25, Sigler prepared for his scheduled encounter the next day with Mrs. Hooper by studying two state police files. The first concerned revelations by Dr. Hubert G. Moore, a Bay City osteopath and personal friend of the late senator, that on the night before the murder, he had dined with Hooper at a Chinese restaurant near the Capitol. During the meal, the doctor recounted, Hooper had constantly complained about his wife's incessant nagging at him for being away from home so often and for the infrequency of their sexual intercourse.[58] The second folio contained a summary by Detective Neering of an interview he, along with Captain Hansen and Lieutenant Morse, had had the preceding day with Mrs. Hooper at her home. Neering enumerated several items he thought significant: First, she believed her husband was to have been "bumped off" in December on his way to an osteopathic conference in Bay City. Second, a man claiming to be a grand jury investigator had come to her house in early 1944 requesting, and receiving, from her the senator's check stubs. Third, in September 1944, Floyd Fitzsimmons had offered her husband funds to retain an attorney. Finally, Frank McKay was lying when he told the press that he did not know Hooper well.[59] Putting down the folders, Sigler glanced at his wristwatch and began readying himself for bed, his mind reeling with possible tactics in Friday's confrontation.

Shortly after three o'clock in the afternoon, Sigler, Mulbar, and Olander rose to greet Callienetta Hooper as she entered the grand jury room in the Olds Hotel. Gliding through the usual amenities, Sigler launched into a stern reproach. "Well, I suppose you've seen the attempts in the press to involve some woman angle in this case?" he grunted, leaving unsaid that he had forecast that eventuality in his earlier meeting with her.

"Yes," agreed the pert witness, her fair complexion accentuated by her dark dress, "I suppose they always come up with this sort of thing."

"Perhaps," Sigler intimated, "those who did the crime will try to fix up a smokescreen — to throw out some camouflage to throw everybody off the track. We are, of course, in a much better position to meet that sort of thing if we know exactly what the facts are." Putting his hands on the arm rests of her chair, he stared into her eyes and demanded: "Tell us fully and frankly about your marital situation, Mrs. Hooper."

"I think I discussed that with Captain Hansen, Mr. Neering, and Lieutenant Morse the other night. We talked about Rosenberg. There wasn't any notes taken, of course, but — "

"I'm not referring to that," interrupted Sigler. "I just don't want us left rather defenseless when the other side attempts to claim a lot of things about you and Warren. We must know the full story."

"Well, there was some gossip about Warren chasing with that girl Vita," volunteered the widow, intent on discussing an occurrence whose publication had obviously distressed her. "I went out there to the Streetcar with Warren. He went so often, I thought if it was a good enough place for Warren, maybe I could get used to it. I saw her there, but I never did know her name. Warren was alarmed, but I told him, 'If this is the type of place you want to go to, I will go, too!'"[60]

"Wouldn't you say that Warren started going out there about the time Harry Rosenberg came to take over that Streetcar business?" came the leading question.

"No," was the innocent reply, "it was just that Rosenberg needed a liquor license."

"Did either Louis or Harry Rosenberg pay Warren anything for it?"

"No," she shot, her eyes ablaze with fury. "Warren never accepted money. Not a penny for any of his legislative work!"

"Did you know that Vita went with Warren to Lansing to try to straighten things out?" asked the unruffled special prosecutor.

"No," she replied, either telling a falsehood or naively admitting ignorance of Sigler's press release, "but I personally don't see anything wrong with it. However, I did get alarmed about her at Christmas time in 1941 when I found out Warren had bought her an electric clock. I said to him, 'What on earth was the idea of buying a present like that? I can't understand you doing a thing like that. We don't know them socially.' I was very upset about it. I even went down to the store where he bought it. The man there told me he bought it there." Reliving her old rage, she paused and drew a deep breath. "Well, then, after I found out his attitude towards places like that, I went out there. I used to take taxi cabs out there. I went alone, just to be mean." Her eyes sparkled at the memory, as she continued, "It was a horrid place, and I thought my going along might cure him of going out there."

"Did it?"

"No," she snapped, lighting a cigarette.

"Is that when you first saw Van Dellen about a divorce?" pressed Sigler, never removing his eyes from hers.

"No, that wasn't that far back. Besides, our trouble was always over finances and me being alone. I wasn't a very good sport about it," she confessed with a wry grin, "because I didn't feel I had to get married for my room and board. I had my own way of making a living, but I just didn't like being alone all the time. That's why."

"Well," continued the staring face, "when — "

"Oh, I've wanted to leave him for the last two years," she stated in a very matter-of-fact tone, "because he had no interest at home, in the children, or myself. I had all the work and worry. But that's all the trouble we had. I mean, there wasn't anything else than this financial trouble."[61]

Shaking his silver locks in apparent disbelief, Sigler replied in mock exasperation, "See, here's the thing, Mrs. Hooper. Your husband's been murdered."

Nonplused, she babbled, "Well, I know that — but — goodness me — I know it — every night — "

"The thing that the captain and the commissioner and I are trying to do here," he went on, "is to solve the situation. Don't you see? The thing you should do is tell us the story, the whole story, without attempting to color it."

"Yes," came the curt retort, "that's what Warren did and look where he is today."

"Well," chided Sigler, "that is not the right way to look at it. Why don't you tell us what you know so we can piece all the evidence together. I was so in hopes this time when you came in you would tell us the whole story without reservation — without trying to hold anything back."

"I would rather not say some things, that's all."

"In other words, you would rather have it said that the officials cannot get wholehearted cooperation from you?" he asked, reviving the threat which had served him so well in their previous session.

"Yes," was her firm response.[62]

After frustrating Sigler with a series of monosyllabic replies, she suddenly whispered, as if in a trance, "I know who killed McKay — I mean who killed Warren."

"Who?"

"If I could shoot, I would go and kill him and you would go and get me," she proceeded, still staring vacantly past her audience.

"Who do you think killed Warren?" Sigler reiterated.

"McKay killed him! she exploded venomously.

"Now what makes you say that? What makes you think that?" prompted Sigler, hoping to learn the extent of her knowledge of her husband's involvement with the Republican boss.

"There isn't anybody else in the world who would want to do it. There isn't anybody else who is powerful enough to have it done," she explained, as though she were describing an omnipotent, fearsome god.

"Do you have any idea how?"

"Yes, I do, but — " Her voice trailed off, and she began to violently shake her head from side to side. "I don't believe he was ever mixed up with another woman," she sobbed, remembering Sigler's admonition that the actual killers might try to use the Vita Rosenberg story as a red herring, "I don't believe he was."

Not wishing her to lapse into hysterics, Sigler eased his attack and calmly reassured her. "Well, let's assume that is true. The important thing is to give us all the facts you can now."[63]

While asking a series of insignificant questions aimed primarily at restoring her emotional stability, Sigler's thoughts may have drifted to a recently published editorial in the unabashedly partisan *Wayne County Democrat* which criticized his "smearing of McKay." It had blasted the special prosecutor also for announcing that Hooper was to have been the main witness against McKay and for casting "unjust suspicion" on him before his case even went to trial. Moreover, it had come painfully close to scoring a bull's eye in its bold type allegation: **If Sigler does not win his case against McKay he has an alibi for his failure in the murder of his star witness. And, in making the statement, he lays a murder charge on the doorstep of the pet enemy and goat of the current Republican State Machine, Frank McKay."**[64]

Sensing that Mrs. Hooper had regained her composure, he returned to his primary line of inquiry. With another cudgel-like blow, he asked, "Did you ever stay at the Otsego Hotel in downtown Jackson, Michigan, with a man other than your husband?"

"No," she replied slowly and carefully, giving the impression of wanting to have every thought exact, "I went there alone. I registered under a fictitious name. I took the bus over. I went to a jewelry store, bought a vanity case, went back to the hotel, had dinner alone, went up to my room and mended sixteen pairs of socks, and went home the next day. I did it just to show Warren how it is to come home and not find someone there once in a while. I was only like a picture on the wall to Warren."

"You mean that you did that just to show Warren — "

"Yes," she boasted, "and, by the way, when he called the State Police to try and find me that night, it made me madder than a wet hen!"[65]

"Can you think of anyone, anywhere who didn't like your husband?" asked Sigler, having offered to light yet another cigarette in the now beclouded suite.

"There is only one person who didn't like him," she exaggerated, her words mingled with exhaled smoke. "When he couldn't get him any other way, he had to kill him."

"You mean — "

"And I wish I could kill him!"

"You mean McKay?"

"That's right," she concurred, between puffs on the rapidly disappearing cigarette.

"What makes you think that McKay was that way?"

"Because Warren told me what he had told the grand jury," she declared.

The closeness of the room became more pronounced as Sigler cleared his throat and sought clarification of her last remark. "Because Warren had talked to the grand jury, is that it?"

"Of course," came the impatient reply, "Bill Green knew it, and don't you think that McKay knew it not two minutes after Bill Green knew it? I told Warren his life wasn't worth a penny from then on. I told him — "

"Yes," injected Sigler, not wishing to rehear her harping tale, "but he was too proud — "

"Yes," she finished for him, "he was too proud to ask you for any protection."

"Now, then, just what did he tell you about Bill Green?"

"He said," she halted long enough to replace her extinguished cigarette with a new one, "Bill Green was in the room and that you called Warren up and said, 'Warren, I've got Bill Green in here and I'm going to have you tell him to his face that he is the one who handed you this money.'" Blowing smoke into Sigler's scowl, she added smugly, "Evidently you couldn't crack Bill Green."

The smoky scowl grew darker as his face reddened. "Just go ahead and tell us what Warren said about it."

"Well, you asked Warren: 'Warren, Bill Green did give you this $300, is that right?'"

"It was $500," corrected Sigler.

"No, $300," came the equally self-assured reply.

"No, $500," bickered Sigler.

"Well," huffed the witness, "I never heard anything about $500. I still say $300. Anyway, Bill didn't say anything. That's when I told Warren his life wasn't worth a penny."

"What did he say to you after you told him that?"

"Nothing. He got deathly sick with one of his nervous spells. He had been having his warm milk and cookies, like he always did before he went to bed. After I made that remark, he just got up and threw up." Then, in such a detached manner that even Sigler was taken aback, she added: "So I fixed the furnace temperature and shut the house for the night. From then on Warren wasn't the same."

"And you had to be mean and nasty to – " Sigler cut short his impulse to insert some heartfelt sympathy for the long-suffering senator. Still piqued, he asked bluntly, "Mrs. Hooper, frankly what was the relationship between you and him so far as affectionate love and that sort of thing is concerned, say during the last few months?"

"Well, there wasn't – well, it wasn't any different than it ever was."

"Are you sure about that?"

"Yes," came the carefully worded, noncommittal response, "he was just as he was before. In fact, the Sunday before he was killed we were in the living room and I know he thanked me for all that I had ever done in helping him."

Choosing to ignore that self-serving reminiscence, Sigler stunned the witness with, "Did you sleep together?"

"Yes," she blushed faintly, "yes. Of course."[66]

Before the bloom had faded from her cheeks, she had grasped the intent of his queries and quizzed Sigler: "What has all this got to do with the murder? You don't think that I had anything to do with it, do you?"

"No," responded the lawyer, his eyes widening in feigned astonishment, "I haven't said that you had. What makes you think for a minute that I believe you had anything to do with it?"

"Well," she confided, while fumbling to extricate a handkerchief from her purse, "I don't know your work and I shouldn't question it, but why are you asking all these personal things?"

Slowly removing his pince-nez and letting them dangle at the end of their black ribbon – much the way the witness was now suspended from his rope of intimate questions – Sigler methodically rubbed his temple. Still gazing directly at her, he asked in a measured tone, hesitating between each word, "You wouldn't have had anything to do with it, of course?"

"My God, no!" she screamed. "I thought so much of him! I thought so much of him!"

"Did you really think so much of him?" Sigler inquired rhetorically. "Did you really love him?"

"Oh, yes, I did!" she pleaded, her eyes begging him to stop.

Unmindful of her unspoken prayer, he continued the torture. "Has there been any other man in your life since you and Warren were married?"

"No, no, not a soul." As the questioning swung from the dead to the living, her mood instantly transformed from melancholia to defiance. "You can't find any affair like that," she challenged.

"Well, it would be very embarrassing for us all if — "

"Well, I'm not afraid one bit! It isn't true!" Her voice was barely audible above the smashing sounds of her fists on the armrests.

Sigler commented casually, "Did Warren ever accuse you of having anybody?"

"Yes, he did at one time, but he never mentioned his name," she snapped, casting daggers in her stare.

"Did he ever say anything about Dr. Morehouse, or accuse you of anything as far as Dr. Morehouse was concerned?"

Turning a ghastly pallor, Mrs. Hooper pulled back in her chair as if she had been slapped. Unable to steady herself, she stammered, "Uh-uh-no."[67]

Smirking, Sigler turned his back, leaving her alone with her thoughts for a few moments.

Having achieved his aim of demonstrating what a devastating circumstantial case could be developed against her should she refuse to assist the special prosecutor in his crusade to link McKay to the murder, Sigler shunned further delving into her personal affairs and turned to the issue of her late husband's professional ethics. Eliciting from her the facts that she handled all the family finances, that Warren had earned $291.66 per month from the osteopathic association, that he had to repay a loan from her father at $25 monthly installments and cover all insurance premiums on each member of the family from his $3 per day legislative salary, and that she generously permitted him to keep what was left of his lawmaker's stipend as "pocket money," Sigler asked if her husband had ever taken money from individuals while serving in the legislature.[68]

"Yes, he did, but I didn't see any harm in it. I don't know where a lot of it came from. He did mention Bill Green though." Then, as an addendum, she recalled: "He did say that McKay stopped him in a hall somewhere — I don't know where it was — it was something about the bank bill — and he asked Warren how he felt about it and Warren said he had already made up his mind. He told McKay what

60

it was and McKay said, 'It's OK with me. Don't change it. There will be a gift for you,' or something like that. That's all I remember."

"Did he mention the name of Charles Bohn of the Bohn Aluminum Company?" Sigler inquired in an offhand fashion.

"No. I've never heard that name before."[69]

After hearing a capsule summary of her earlier testimony on Floyd Fitzsimmons, Sigler asked if Warren always had come home and informed her when he received such remunerations. "Oh, yes," replied the woman who, shortly before, had sworn that her husband never took the time to chat with, let alone confide in, her. "I didn't see any harm in it. They weren't bribes. We needed money to pay off bills, but we always turned down bribes."[70]

Another "we," noted Sigler, doubting if Hooper really had a private life and, at the same time, while possibly chortling to himself at her convenient distinction between "gifts" and "bribes." Nodding at Mrs. Hooper, he proposed a brief recess during which, despite the subfreezing temperature, the windows were thrown open to allow the wispy layers of smoke to escape.[71]

Fifteen minutes later, the session resumed. "Mrs. Hooper," began Sigler, "do you think there is any danger to you now?"

"I don't know. I just figure that if McKay thought that Warren had talked with me — whether they could prove it or not — if I would say anything about it — that they would just shut me up. You know McKay lied — " her voice trembled, "he lied about a lot of things. He knew me. He said he didn't in the newspapers, but he met me once. We had breakfast together at the Morton Hotel one morning."[72]

"Well, I'll assign a man to be at your house in the evenings, but not during the daytime, if that is agreeable with you. I'd like not to have to tie up too many men on that detail," he said with unemotional honesty.

"That will be fine. It may not be necessary. I should think you can be the best judge of that," she agreed. "You know, I will feel better after the trial of Fitzsimmons next week."[73]

Before adjourning, Mulbar sought Mrs. Hooper's opinion on the state police theory on how her husband was slain. "Well," she eagerly volunteered, opening a new package of cigarettes and graciously receiving a light from Olander, "another man must have gotten in the car and driven. Warren certainly never was driving the car that day. He never left it in neutral, which is how you say it was found. It was always in second. And the bag was always on the floor, never on the front seat where you found it."

"You mean," growled the chief of detectives, "that he let this other man drive the car?"

"No," she shook her head in disgust, "that is not what I mean at all. Warren didn't let him. Warren didn't like to have anyone, even me, drive the car. Warren never let anyone drive the car unless he was sick or sleeping."

"Well, who would drive for him?"

"I just know sometime somebody got in that car. He didn't leave Lansing alone. Warren always put the bag on my side of the car, where I would be sitting, on the floor. So evidently somebody opened the door and said move over, with a gun, and moved that bag. But what I can't understand," she asserted, "is if they wanted to kill him, why didn't they do it right away? Why did they wait until he was eighteen miles from home? That is the thing that is driving me crazy. He never drove fast, but the car skidded and there was no snow on the pavement that night."[74]

Cutting the discussion off abruptly with a curt "Do you have any other questions, Captain?" Sigler thanked Mrs. Hooper for making the trek to Lansing and repeated his pledge to furnish protection at her home.[75] After escorting her to a waiting State Police car, Sigler retired to his room to mull over the preceding three hours' events.

V Early that evening, Sigler dictated a press release for the following morning in which he would reveal that the two snowplow operators who had ordered a parked maroon sedan to move from Bradford Road on the day of Hooper's assassination had identified the first part of the license plate as HC8, which was an Ingham County designation. "We are making a canvass of every car storage plant in that county to determine if license plates had been stolen without the owner's knowledge," the statement read. "This could easily happen where cars have been put away for the winter. If it was an Ingham County car, we have an extremely important lead."[76] As a postscript, he announced that having worked night and day for sixteen days, he would take "a few hours rest" over the weekend with his family at Battle Creek.[77] That should keep the fifth estate content until he returned, he must have thought, as he summoned his driver to escort him to a late dinner.

CHAPTER FIVE

UNRAVELING THE WEB

I February opened at a hectic pace for Sigler on another front as well. Amid the continuing sensational rumors surrounding the Hooper murder, the special prosecutor was busy with the trial of Benton Harbor sports promoter Floyd Fitzsimmons. In 1941 he had allegedly offered $500 to State Representative Gail Handy to influence his vote on a bill to regulate horse racing and increase state revenue from the Detroit Fair Grounds through the installation of totalizers to assure honest tabulation of bets. This case never could have come to court on its merits alone, because it was based not on evidence but merely on the testimony of one man — Handy — against another — Fitzsimmons. However, Sigler chose to use it as an opportunity to assert once again his contention that former Republican National Committeeman Frank D. McKay, a close friend of Fitzsimmons, was somehow linked to the brutal assassination of the Albion senator. On the surface, this seemed tenuous at best; but, unbeknownst to defense counsel, Sigler had ascertained from interviews with Mrs. Hooper and Agnes Wickens both the depth of Hooper's involvement with, and his fear of, Fitzsimmons.[1]

Ironically, the 59-year-old, stooped and emaciated Fitzsimmons had been responsible for Sigler's involvement with the grand jury probe. When Bill Green, a 60-year-old, eight-term rural Republican legislator, was indicted by the Ingham County grand jury in August 1943, he had no counsel. While relating his plight to his crony Fitzsimmons, the latter suggested that Green retain Kim Sigler, a noted criminal lawyer from the small town of Hastings. Fitzsimmons, because of his boxing promotions, was friendly with Sigler, himself an ex-pugilist, and the two had spent many hours making small talk about "the manly art of self-defense" and the days when "Fitz" was chief promoter for Jack Dempsey. As a favor to his friend, Sigler agreed to handle Green's case for less than his normal fee and promised his new client an easy acquittal. Within weeks, however, Sigler betrayed his client by resigning as defense counsel and joining the grand jury prosecutional staff. Green was furious, as he had confided much information to his attorney concerning grafting legislators. In turn, the Hastings barrister violated the rule of confidentiality and used the knowledge to impress Circuit Judge Leland W. Carr, the grand juror, with his deep insight into legislative corruption and to convince the jurist that he would be an indispensable addition to his staff. Fitzsimmons likewise fumed that his old "sparring partner" had set both Green and himself up to "take a dive," but it was to no avail. Inadvertently, through Green, Fitzsimmons had made Sigler the grand jury's "white knight" as well as setting the stage for his own conviction.[2]

Fitzsimmons' lawyer, Fred R. Walker of Detroit, had spent much of January trying to postpone his client's trial on grounds that newspaper coverage of the Hooper trial had prejudged the case against him. Defense allegations rested heavily on Sigler's repeated statements to the press that Hooper was to have been the state's star witness in another upcoming case charging that McKay, Green, and Fitzsimmons had conspired to defeat a 1941 horse racing bill. Despite the similarity in the indictment, that case was entirely separate from the one for which Fitzsimmons alone was now standing trial. Appearing before Judge Carr on January 17, Walker dramatically pointed to a stack of newspapers and berated the magistrate in an attempt to convince him "that a fair trial is impossible at this time in view of the many newspaper stories linking Fitzsimmons' name in the Hooper murder." He argued that because "Senator Hooper was killed by someone with a motive, the public is bound to assume that Fitzsimmons is a person who would have an interest in what happened to Senator Hooper" and that "no court could remove that cloud of suspicion from any juror."[3]

Sigler opposed the motion, claiming that the learned Detroit counsel was implying that Ingham County residents would not fulfill their oaths as jurors and listen impartially to the evidence. Judge Carr, as usual, concurred with his new protege and denied the request.[4]

The trial opened on January 29 in the Mason Court House, with Circuit Judge John Simpson presiding. Walker again moved for a postponement, this time making an emotional presentation in which he pleaded with Simpson to examine his position carefully. "When you read or hear that Judge Leland W. Carr said that Fitzsimmons stands to gain by Hooper's death and that the writer or commentator fails to add that Hooper did not figure in this particular case," he intoned, "I say it creates a cloud of suspicion that makes it impossible for my client to have a fair trial." Like Carr, Simpson was unmoved by the "cloud of suspicion" speech and tersely denied the motion, noting that he did not think people took seriously what they read in the newspapers.[5] He added that in an earlier graft case in which twenty of twenty-two defendants were convicted, "we managed to get a jury and conduct a fair trial, and I seen no reason why we can't repeat [that] now."[6] Sensing a tone of predestination in the judge's remark, Walker retreated to the defense table. A jury of five farmers and nine housewives was then selected within two hours and the trial began.[7]

The next day, Walker again moved for a continuance, claiming that "because it has not been made clear that Senator Hooper had no part in this case, the prejudice created in the mind of the public cannot be removed by any court." Sigler countered by chiding his opponent for basing a protest on "inference and supposition," and gently reminded him that under the American system of justice "no juror can sit who has a fixed opinion on the guilt or innocence of the defendant." Simpson again rejected Walker's plea, this time adding sarcastically, "Under your theory, Fitzsimmons could not be brought to trial if the murderers of Senator Hooper are not caught."[8]

On February 1, the special prosecutor embarked upon a relentless onslaught to associate the defendant with both Hooper and McKay, neither of whom had any connection whatsoever with the case. The small courtroom was crowded as the state's most colorful trial lawyer began his inquisition.

"During the past ten years, by what means have you made your money?"

"In the last seven years I didn't make any money in politics," Fitzsimmons replied. "I lived off the money I had."

"All right, who did you make the money from in politics?"

"Well, I handled Governor Fitzgerald's campaign in the fourth congressional district."

"Who paid you?" demanded Sigler.

"Mr. Fitzgerald paid me."

"Did Frank McKay pay you anything?"

"He never gave me a nickel," said the defendant.

"How much money did you make on that campaign?" asked Sigler.

"I don't know."

"That political campaign in which Frank McKay was involved?"

"I don't know," said the witness, leaving unchallenged Sigler's remark about McKay's involvement.

"Tell the jury how much!" Sigler shouted.

"I don't know. I don't remember," pleaded Fitzsimmons.

"Can't you give us any idea?"

"No," whispered Fitzsimmons, "I can't give you any idea."

"Couldn't you tell us whether it was $1 or $100 or $5,000?" sneered the prosecutor in mock disbelief. "Can't you give us any help?"

His nerves fraying, Fitzsimmons yelled back, "No! No! I didn't — I don't go out looking for money — chiseling. I worked for three months for your campaign for state senator..."

Hurriedly, Sigler tried to stop the witness, but Fitzsimmons continued, "...and didn't get anything." Judge Simpson loudly banged his gavel and sternly warned the trembling witness to pay attention to the questions and answer only the questions put forth. Fitzsimmons then asked the judge to "let him ask me the questions properly." Simpson snapped, "Are you in a contemptuous mood toward me? I want you to pay attention to the questions and the answers and answer the questions. Don't talk back like that to me or you'll find yourself in contempt of court."

Smiling, Sigler then repeated his query: "How much money did you make in politics?" to which the defendant meekly replied, "I didn't make any."

"Then what have you done — work, business, or anything to make money — to make a living during the past six years?" demanded Sigler.

"Nothing," said the witness.

Sensing that he had worn his old friend down, Sigler then moved to his main area of interest. "All right, Floyd," he said, "how many times were you over to see Frank McKay after you were before the grand jury on the 31st of October, 1944?"

"I often went over to Grand Rapids," said Fitzsimmons, "because I have relatives there and I dropped into McKay's office because he was a friend of mine to find out what was going on politically. I do not run errands for McKay. I carted his lawyer down to Detroit once. Gene Garey, a friend of mine from New York City. I got acquainted with him because he was connected with Madison Square Gardens. I believe McKay asked me to drive him."

"Do you know Bill McKeighan, the former mayor over at Flint?" asked Sigler.

"I do. I don't know how often I've seen Bill McKeighan. I did see him the night I took Gene Garey in. I was in Detroit and went up to his room in the Book-Cadillac."

"Why did you go see Bill McKeighan?" pressed Sigler.

Flustered, Fitzsimmons blurted, "I wanted to ask him if he knew where I could get some nylon hose for my wife for her wedding anniversary."

"You drove all that way about some nylon hose," replied Sigler smugly.

"And other purposes as well," said the promoter, "maybe to see someone."

"Whenever Frank McKay or Bill McKeighan want you to?" shouted Sigler, brandishing a clenched fist toward the witness.

"No! No!" screamed Fitzsimmons. "That isn't true!"

Then, in a complete change of tone, Sigler calmly asked, "Who signed your bond in this case, Floyd?"

"Frank McKay."

Having established the McKay link, Sigler wheeled to the Hooper connection. "How many times did you see Warren Hooper and where?"

"Twice," replied Fitzsimmons hesitatingly, as he sensed that the final nails were being driven skillfully into his coffin. "Once in Albion and at the House of Representatives."

"When did you see him in Albion?"

"I was going to the World Series in Detroit and was low on gas coupons so I stopped and asked Warren if he could help me out with a couple of tickets."

"So you knew Warren Hooper well enough so you could ask him to give you some of his gas tickets?" wondered Sigler aloud, while deciding that he could save the rest of his revelations on Fitzsimmons' visits to Hooper for a later trial — that of Frank McKay for conspiracy to murder.

Suddenly realizing the impact of his incriminating statement, Fitzsimmons blurted,"No." The damage had been done, however, and Fitzsimmons now was firmly ensconced in the jurors' minds as an intimate of McKay, McKay's chief henchman Bill McKeighan, and the late, lamented Warren Hooper. His fate was sealed.[9]

While the jury was deliberating, Sigler, in a jovial mood, had grabbed Fitzsimmons by the arm and joked, "Well, Fitz, we went the full fifteen rounds, eh?" Pulling away, Fitzsimmons merely glowered at his adversary.[10] Still smiling, Sigler then went into a hallway to banter with newsmen. Incredibly, he brazenly told reporters who had not witnessed the courtroom scene moments earlier that, in response to his comment, Fitzsimmons had said warmly, "It was a fair trial, Kim. I haven't any kick coming. I'm still your friend. If there's ever a time you need help, come see me."[11]

It took the panel only ninety minutes to return a guilty verdict. Visibly shaken, with head bowed, Fitzsimmons listened impassively as Judge Simpson sentenced him to serve three years at Southern Michigan Prison in Jackson.[12] Once again Sigler had "got his man," but it would mean nothing unless it led him another step closer to McKay.

II To Sigler's dismay, the next seven weeks added virtually nothing to further his goal. Despite the best efforts of state and local law enforcement agencies, it appeared that Warren Hooper was the victim of a perfect crime. By the middle of the month, the murder investigation was relegated to the inside pages of newspapers. By March, it had totally disappeared. Sigler could only pray that the coming of spring would brighten not only the cold, foreboding Michigan skies, but also shed light on his elusive quarry.

III April began much as March had ended, with the daily temperatures growing warmer and the trail of the assassin becoming colder. In a desperate effort to keep his name, if not the case, in the headlines, Sigler continued to hold "no new news" press conferences. On April 3, the special prosecutor, resplendent in one of his dark chocolate brown three-piece suits, which he favored because he thought they accentuated his shock of silver hair, met with reporters at the Lansing Court House. The increasingly skeptical members of the fourth estate were once again assured that "a lot of progress" had been made and that he was "convinced that the case was going to be solved." The flamboyant orator could issue only a terse "no comment," however, when asked if the solution was imminent or if reports of underworld involvement in the murder were accurate. After repeating his oft-told belief that the occupants of the maroon automobile seen near the murder site played a role in the crime and that the senator's troubled personal and marital home life had no connection with his death, Sigler confided that he did possess vital new evidence, but that to reveal it at the present moment might hamper progress in the manhunt.[13] Having heard that well-worn evasion from the special prosecutor in the past, veteran crime reporters concluded that he was at a dead end and agreed that the story was no longer newsworthy.

For the next eight days the only mention of Sigler in any major state publication was a single sentence in the *Michigan State Digest* questioning whether he was earning his $100 per day salary.[14] This was unsettling to Sigler, partly because he truly did have important secret witnesses whom he believed eventually would break the case wide open, and partly because his ego demanded that his name be constantly before the public. Newspaper clippings detailing his exploits as special prosecutor were preserved carefully by Sigler in leather-bound scrapbooks purchased with grand jury funds, and he was determined to maintain his high profile even if it meant manufacturing news and resorting to cheap sensationalism.[15]

On April 11, disregarding state police claims that the killer took the murder weapon − a .38 calibre long-barreled Colt revolver − with him as he made his escape, Sigler announced he was ordering an intensive one-day search for the missing gun. Aiding state police detectives would be members of the Springport High School Future Farmers of America and Boy Scouts from Eaton Rapids, whom the special prosecutor had requested be excused from classes to participate in the important work. He admitted that there was no reason to suspect that the gun had been left near the scene, but insisted that the search was necessary and had been postponed only because snow depths had been too great. Nothing was found, but Sigler had rekindled public interest in the investigation.[16]

Meanwhile, state police detectives, having sifted through hundreds of clues and leads offered by anonymous tipsters and citizens eager to receive the $25,000 reward put up by the state, finally made a breakthrough. On March 22, Sam Abramowitz, a 36-year-old ex-convict from Flint who had ties with Detroit's notorious Purple Gang, was brought in for questioning. Under interrogation, he claimed − and a polygraph test corroborated − that he and another ex-convict, 28-year-old Henry "Heinie" Luks of Lansing, had been hired by Harry Fleisher, head of the Purples, to kill Warren Hooper.[17] On April 4, Luks was brought to the Jackson State Police Post and a polygraph test indicated deception when he denied any knowledge of, or participation in, the Hooper murder. Five days later another test was performed with similar results, and Luks was ordered to return on April 17. On that date, Luks was confronted by Abramowitz. After listening to Abramowitz retell his allegations, Luks shouted that his accuser was a liar who did not know what he was talking about. Visibly shaken, Luks asked to speak with his parole officer. Having done that, he admitted the truth of Abramowitz's story.[18]

Based on information furnished by Luks and Abramowitz, warrants were issued for the simultaneous arrests of five persons early on the morning of April 20. Purple Gang leader Harry Fleisher (or Harry Fleish as he was sometimes called), 42, was aroused from bed in his Detroit home shortly after 8:00 a.m. After a search of the premises for concealed weapons, he was escorted to the Jackson

State Police Post where he was fingerprinted, photographed, and sent to jail. Fleisher's younger brother Sam, 33, was seized at his Detroit residence. Notwithstanding his protestations of ignorance of the Hooper murder, he, too, was taken to Jackson. Gunman Mike Selik, 32, and his wife Naomi, 28, were apprehended in their Detroit apartment. Both were taken to the Jackson Post, but after questioning, Mrs. Selik was allowed to return to Detroit. The final arrest was that of 43-year-old Peter Apostolopoulos, better known in Detroit gambling circles as Pete Mahoney, who, while not a gangster himself, enjoyed being in their company.[19]

Afternoon daily newspapers were quick to headline the arrests, but two chief state police officials and Sigler were cautious in their remarks. Commissioner Oscar G. Olander refused to comment and Captain Donald S. Leonard said only that the prisoners had been brought in for questioning. Sigler added that no formal charges had been made against those arrested and emphatically stated that "the Hooper case has not been solved." He also criticized state police for making what he termed "a premature announcement" which he feared might "seriously handicap the prosecution of the murderers." Looking grim, with his head bowed, the special prosecutor related in solemn tones that "the police and I had a definite understanding that no statement would be made until we knew that we had the killers and that we could apply for warrants. A police officer has violated that understanding."[20] Pressed by persistent questioners, he again attempted to downplay the significance of the arrests, saying that they were "only a part of the routine investigation" and that "there has been a tremendous amount of money spent in this case and there are many people who are implicated." Before leaving the room, Sigler urged patience and promised that "there will be no more news until we really have something."[21]

Many high-ranking members of the state police, however, were infuriated at Sigler's interference in their investigation and were more than willing to undermine Sigler's plans by talking to media representatives. Captain Harold Mulbar, the hulking chief of state police detectives, eagerly told reporters that there were indications that Hooper's murder was a "paid killing in which large sums of money passed hands." To him, the arrests made the ultimate solution of the crime look "pretty promising." Mulbar not only detailed the procedure by which questioning, which lasted until nearly midnight, was done, but also how all of the prisoners were placed in separate cells in different jails in order to preclude communication. He even told of a secret "show up" in which the witness who saw the two men in the maroon car at the murder site was shown the four gangsters who were in custody. Somehow the chief managed to refrain from disclosing the results.[22] Captain William Hansen, when asked if the investigation was getting somewhere, replied: "You bet your life. We have made great progress." Like Mulbar, Hansen refused to comment on the results of the "show up," but he did reveal that the witness's identity had to be kept closely guarded because he was a "well known public figure." This revelation led to speculation that perhaps some lawmakers had stumbled upon the murder scene and now had to be protected lest they, too, fall victim to an assassin's bullets. Almost as an invitation to the curious reporters, Hansen nonchalantly added that another secret "show up" was scheduled for that evening.[23]

Angry at this police effrontery, Sigler met with Olander and extracted from him a pledge of department support. Sigler then returned to Lansing, where he was prosecuting a naturopathic conspiracy case for the Ingham County grand jury. While in the Capitol City, Sigler hoped to persuade Judge Carr to speak with Attorney General John R. Dethmers regarding the possibility of the special prosecutor being named an assistant attorney general for any trials which might result from the recent arrests. Dethmers, who like Sigler was thinking of running for the Republican gubernatorial nomination in 1946, was loath to bestow more prestige upon his potential rival and had summarily rejected a similar earlier request. Because of this rebuff, Sigler now sought Carr's intercession on his behalf.[24]

Throughout the legal turmoil at Jackson, the prisoners seemed to be enjoying themselves. They joked, laughed, and bantered with reporters, and when photographers approached, they quickly covered their faces with hats and coats as though they were starring in an Edward G. Robinson gangster film. This lightheartedness may have been merely a show of public bravado, however, as on April 23 the state trooper in charge of transporting Harry Fleisher from the county jail to the Jackson Police Post related to his superiors that the captive was uneasy and had asked: "Are all those reporters out there again? I hope they're not. They don't care what kind of publicity they give a man. They'll do anything for a story." It was the trooper's opinion that "if it were not for the publicity, Fleisher would like to get something off his mind."[25]

Curiously, the only stories written on Fleisher during the first two days of his incarceration, which were obviously the ones which upset him, appeared in the *Detroit Times*, a Hearst newspaper specializing in sensationalism. The Detroit hoodlum was depicted as a blond, debonair man of the underworld, whose criminal record included thirty arrests. The articles also recounted his alleged participation in the Lindbergh baby kidnapping, his eight years in Alcatraz for violating prohibition laws, and his ascension to the leadership of the Purple Gang after Ray Bernstein and Harry Keywell received life sentences for their parts in the bloody 1931 gangland slayings known as the "Collingwood Manor Massacre."[26] Yet this was common information and its publication should not have affected Fleisher.

The question then became: what prompted Fleisher's concern? One possibility was that he resented references to the prison records of his brothers, Sam and Louis. The former had served six years at Alcatraz and Leavenworth for prohibition violations and forgery, while the latter, along with his wife, was serving a thirty-year sentence in federal prison for possession of unregistered firearms. The *Times* had made it seem that the three sons of a poor immigrant Albion junk dealer had made crime a family affair.

A more intriguing possibility was that Fleisher, who had been a frequent visitor of Bernstein and Keywell at Jackson Prison, was fearful of what might befall him when his former comrades learned of his arrest. For years, underworld gossip labeled Fleisher as merely a high-priced errand boy, and insinuated that the real power of the Purple Gang still rested with its imprisoned former leaders. If this allegation was true, and if Fleisher had been involved in the murder of Senator Hooper, two scenarios — neither of which offered solace to Fleisher — could be drawn. First, Fleisher and his accomplices decided to act on their own in the Hooper job but had bungled the work by being apprehended. Testimony given at their trial would certainly threaten the operation of the gang, hence whether found innocent or guilty, Fleisher and the others faced the wrath of Bernstein and Keywell. Second, Fleisher had acted upon the orders of Bernstein and Keywell. Again, his capture and subsequent trial represented a threat to the continuation of the gang and would bring certain punishment. In either instance, Fleisher would have good cause to seek anonymity from the press. The impression that Fleisher feared for his safety grew stronger when his attorney, Edward H. Kennedy, Jr. of Detroit, obtained a writ of habeas corpus for his client, who promptly rejected freedom saying that he was content in jail and would "get out when I'm good and ready." Chagrined, Kennedy told reporters that he had no further intention to seek his client's release.[27] Shortly thereafter, Fleisher was brought before Judge Carr, who informed him that cooperation with the grand jury would help his cause should he be formally charged with a crime. The gangster steadfastly refused to answer questions put to him by Sigler and was subsequently sentenced to serve thirty days in the Ingham County jail for contempt.[28] Once again, Fleisher had opted for the security of a cell.

IV On May 3, Municipal Judge William H. Bibbings of Battle Creek, who had no legal training before being elected to the court, signed warrants charging Harry and Sam Fleisher, Mike Selik, and Pete Mahoney with conspiracy to murder Warren G. Hooper. Because the charge was conspiracy rather than the actual deed, the warrants were issued in Calhoun County where the alleged conspiracy occurred. Arraignment was set for 2:00 p.m. on Saturday, May 5 in the judge's city hall office. At that time the examination date would be set.

Wearing a tailored, light summer suit and white shoes, Sigler met reporters in Judge Bibbings' courtroom. In a brief statement, he reminded his audience that Hooper had been slain before his testimony could be taken. Therefore, he had urged the judge to schedule the examination "as quickly as possible so that the testimony of the witnesses can be recorded," and pledged that "there will be no more murders in this case." Theatrically glancing at his gold wristwatch, Sigler brushed aside questions, saying only: "This is not a solution to the murder case by any means. It is merely a step, incident to the solution. The officers will continue their investigation of the murder itself."[29]

With eager reporters at his heels, the special prosecutor then strode to the nearby courtroom of Circuit Judge John Simpson, where a decision on whether to grant a writ of habeas corpus to Pete Mahoney was to be rendered. Simpson, known as the "Honest Judge" in his home district of Jackson, had denied the previous week a request for such a writ by Mahoney's attorney, Theodore Rodgers, on the grounds that counsel had failed to meet statutory requirements by not furnishing a copy of the petition to Sigler. The judge, who prided himself in courtroom decorum, vividly remembered the events of that day and hoped that they would not recur.

At the initial hearing, Rodgers, a large man with a booming voice and caustic manner, had argued that his client's constitutional rights had been violated: that Mahoney not only had been held for two weeks without being charged with a crime, but also had been secretly moved from one jail to another, which precluded him from being able to meet with his attorney. Sneering contemptuously, Rodgers pointed his finger at Sigler and bellowed: "This Beau Brummel, in all his Broadway magnificence, is arrogant. My client has rights. He's being held in jails. This horsing around must stop." Simpson, rapidly pounding his gavel, peered down over his shell-rimmed glasses and warned Rodgers "not to use such language in this court." When Sigler arose to address the judge, Rodgers repeatedly interrupted. Finally, in a condescending fatherly tone, Sigler suggested that his brother attorney from Detroit "sit down, be a gentleman, and try to get along better."[30]

Unfortunately for Judge Simpson, the second encounter was painfully reminiscent of the first. The request for a writ of habeas corpus was again denied, this time because Mahoney had that morning been charged with a specific crime. Rodgers again raised the issue of his client's constitutional rights, saying that Mahoney had been "badly mistreated, mentally or otherwise, although I don't think physically."

"Mahoney has been treated kindly in every way," retorted Sigler.

"Does this warrant mean," Rodgers asked Sigler, "that Mahoney now goes to Calhoun County and gets out of your clutches?"

"He has never been in my clutches," Sigler nobly replied. "He has been in the jurisdiction of the law."

Shaking his head, Judge Simpson restored order and remanded Mahoney to the custody of State Police Captain William Hansen. With a sigh of relief, the judge left the bench, pleased that he would no longer have to preside over the verbal jousts of those silver-maned legal gladiators.[31]

Sigler's dislike for Rodgers was real and not merely part of his courtroom theatrics. In later years, the special prosecutor revealed a trick he had played on his antagonist. Knowing how angry Rodgers was about Mahoney being moved from jail to jail, one rainy night Sigler telephoned Rodgers in Detroit and, using a disguised voice, whispered, "Pete Mahoney is in jail at St. Johns," and then hung up. Rodgers borrowed a car and made the three-hour drive to St. Johns, only to find a bewildered police chief who had never even seen Mahoney, let alone house him in his jail. The bedraggled Rodgers stomped back to his car and returned home while Sigler, who had watched the entire scene from a nearby parked car, roared with laughter.[32]

On the afternoon of May 5, Judge Bibbings arraigned the four defendants, each of whom appeared in court relaxed and smiling as he entered a plea of "not guilty." Bond was set at $25,000 despite defense counsel contentions that the standard amount for the charge of conspiracy was $10,000. Among the crowd of spectators was Mike Selik's beautiful wife, Naomi, who took advantage of her new celebrity status by posing for photographers. Only after being forcefully directed by Rodgers did she refuse to give interviews.[33]

That afternoon the *Detroit Times* ran James Melton's exclusive account of the Hooper murder. Melton, a hard-drinking, heavyset Southerner in his late thirties, had been the *Times* crime reporter for several years and enjoyed the friendship and confidence of many of the city's leading underworld figures as well as that of members of law enforcement agencies.[34] According to Melton's "authoritative source," who was probably his friend Donald S. Leonard of the state police, the identity of Hooper's killer had been revealed to the police by gangsters who sought to ease pressure on themselves. The alleged suspect, whose name was not revealed by Melton, was William "Candy" Davidson, a noted Detroit triggerman who was sought for murder in three states. Davidson, who at 5'6" had feet small enough to match the imprints found at the murder scene, reputedly boasted to his gangland pals that he had been hired to kill Hooper. Supposedly, he left Detroit on the day of the slaying and had not been seen since.[35]

While this story sounded authentic, it was discounted by police officials the next day when pictures of Davidson were shown to the witness who claimed to have seen the two men in the maroon car. "Well, it could be him," the witness said; but after viewing recent pictures of the four defendants at the conspiracy trial, he became much more certain and swore that Sam Fleisher was the driver and that Pete Mahoney was "the killer at the car."[36] When this classified information was leaked to Melton, he dropped his Davidson theory. Later it was discovered that on the day of Hooper's slaying, Davidson was in a Los Angeles, California jail.[37] Yet unsubstantiated stories of the assassination, such as that of Melton's, continued to make headlines for the next several years.

V Early on the morning of May 11, hundreds of curious spectators began to arrive at the courtroom of Judge Bibbings, where at 10:30 examination of the four Detroit gangsters was scheduled to begin. To accommodate the unexpected throng, the proceedings were moved to a more spacious circuit court facility. Excited onlookers nudged people in the seats next to them to point out Senator Hooper's widow who was attending with her two young sons. At the prosecutor's table sat a distinguished quintet of legal talent: Kim Sigler, Wayne County Prosecutor Gerald O'Brien, Jackson County Prosecutor Murl K. Aten, Calhoun County Prosecutor James Dunn, and Ingham County Prosecutor Victor C. Anderson. Present for the defense were Theodore I. Rodgers representing Mahoney and Robert G. Leitch for Sam Fleisher. Max Klayman, counsel for Harry Fleisher and Mike Selik, had not arrived from Detroit.

Immediately after court convened, Rodgers requested a delay to allow Fleisher and Selik to obtain legal assistance in lieu of the absent Klayman. Sigler objected, sneering that seeking postponement because of a missing attorney was "a trick as old as the hills."

"I can't go without no lawyer," shrieked the elder Fleisher, leaping to his feet. "You know you didn't let no one see us. You kept us locked up like in a dungeon. I don't want no kangaroo court. I want a fair trial!"

"That's not true," snapped Sigler. "You'll get a fair trial. And let me tell you, brother, we are not going to be horsed around in this manner!"[38]

Having calmed the bellowing barristers, the judge granted a two-hour delay. When the examination resumed at 1:30 p.m., the courtroom was an armed camp, with police officers everywhere. The initial prosecution witness was Sergeant Leo Van Conant, who methodically recited the dates of grand jury appearances by Hooper, Floyd Fitzsimmons, William Green, and Frank McKay before embarking on a tedious description of each of the twelve rooms on the tenth story of the Olds Hotel, which comprised both the grand jury headquarters and Sigler's living area.[39]

"On the evening of the twenty-ninth or thirtieth day of November, 1944," shot Sigler, with a suddenness which instantly transformed the tranquil scene into one of electricity, "did you see the late Senator Warren G. Hooper in the grand jury conference room, which is located immediately to the rear of the room occupied by myself?"

"Yes, he was with Prosecutor Victor C. Anderson of Ingham County," came the crisp reply.

"Then what occurred?"

"Well," began the blue-uniformed officer in a tone of confident authority, "you walked through my room, which is connected by a common door to your parlor, and beckoned me to follow you and Mr. William Green. You went through your room and into the conference room. I was immediately behind you and you walked up to the opposite side of the table to which Mr. Anderson and ex-Senator Hooper were seated. Mr. Green was on your right and I stood immediately to the right of Mr. Green. Mr. Anderson was talking with Senator Hooper at the time. When they finished, you said, 'I presume you gentlemen know each other.' After they exchanged greetings, you asked Senator Hooper, 'Did this man ever pay you any money?' Senator Hooper looked directly at William Green and said, 'Yes, sir.' Mr. Green dropped his head down and didn't look at anyone the rest of the time he was in the room. You then asked Senator Hooper, 'How much?' and he said, '$500 on the 1941 horse racing bill.'"[40]

Slowing rising for what would prove to be a familiar refrain, Rodgers registered an objection. "I will ask that all this testimony be stricken," he said, pacing with bowed head before Justice Bibbings. "These men here are defendants and any conversation between the late lamented Mr. Hooper and anyone else is not admissible in this courtroom. These people who were not present on the twenty-ninth day of November in the Olds Hotel Tower have no way of refuting anything that might have been said. It is strictly hearsay. I submit, if the Court please, that any conversation between Mr. Green and Mr. Hooper is not relevant on the issue at hand."[41]

Oblivious to the finer points of the law and reliant on Sigler's advice on legalistic interpretation, Bibbings summarily denied the objection and instructed the witness to continue. "You asked Senator Hooper," Van Conant went on with unrestrained self-assurance, "'Did this money come from Frank McKay?' and he said, 'Yes, sir.' Then you turned to Mr. Green and said, 'You see what we have got on you!'"[42]

Defense counsel, having no cross-examination of the state trooper, listened anxiously as the next witness, Victor C. Anderson, corroborated each detail of Van Conant's account. Despite a reiteration of the previous objection, the testimony of the bespectacled, steely-eyed prosecutor was allowed to be admitted into the court record.[43]

While the defense fumed over the dubious legality of the evidence and assured their clients that it would never be permitted in a formal trial before a trained jurist, they did not yet comprehend how absolutely crucial the testimony was to Sigler's recreation of the events leading to the Albion senator's assassination. The special prosecutor was convinced that after the confrontation in the Olds Hotel the Grand Rapids boss, in order to prevent the testimony from being repeated in open court, put up $25,000 to have his accuser slain. Sigler, without any substantive proof, had concluded from gossip and rumor that the deal to remove Hooper had been made at McKay's winter retreat in Miami, Florida, with Leo Wendell, a Detroit private investigator who had been on the Ingham County grand jury payroll and had access to confidential material affecting McKay. Wendell, according to Sigler, then hired Charles Leiter, McKay's bodyguard and former Purple Gang gunman, to act as go-between with the Fleisher brothers. Monty Wendell, Leo's son, and "Nightshirt Charlie" Spare, a former leader of Detroit's Ku Klux Klan and Black Legion who had also been employed by the Ingham County grand jury as an investigator, were assigned to hang out at O'Larry's Bar in Detroit, a gangster abode, to keep tabs on the Fleishers and report whatever progress was being made on carrying the plot to fruition.

This entire scenario was pure speculation on Sigler's part, but he had become so obsessed by the dream of gaining public adoration and fame through the downfall of McKay that he was willing to gamble that his flamboyant style and oratory could overcome a jury's doubts concerning the lack of facts.[44]

With the arrival of the third witness, murmured excitement pulsed through the gallery. Alfred Kurner, a Detroiter serving a 7- to 25-year sentence in Jackson's Southern Michigan Prison for armed robbery, took the stand, and spectators leaned forward to catch every word the gangster would utter against his fellow criminals. Meanwhile, the four defendants smirked and giggled.[45]

The 23-year-old, pencil-thin Kurner, sporting a crewcut and close-clipped moustache, looked more like a college student than a thief as he began his tale. Under questioning by Sigler, Kurner admitted that, while in the Wayne County jail awaiting sentencing on his robbery conviction, he had penned a letter to Judge Carr saying he had important information concerning the Hooper murder, hoping that this act might result in a reduced prison term. Occasionally stammering from fear when he glanced toward the defense table, Kurner elaborated upon the contents of the letter which first directed police attention to the alleged conspirators.[46]

"We were all sitting in O'Larry's Bar, Mike Selik's place on Dexter and Boston Boulevard in Detroit, on Christmas night, 1944," Kurner recalled. "There was Sam Abramowitz, Mr. and Mrs. Dave Mazroff, Henry Luks, and a couple of ladies. Harry Fleisher and Mike Selik was sitting to the left of us, about five or six feet, I guess."

"Pardon me for interrupting," smiled Sigler, "but did Sammy Abramowitz go over to the table where Harry Fleisher and Mike Selik were?"

"Yes, sir," answered the witness over an objection by Leitch that the question was leading.

"I suggest that Mr. Leitch read the criminal code," urged Sigler, and then suggested curtly that his adversary sit down and remain silent.[47]

"Sam got up from our table several times and went to where Harry and Mike were sitting," Kurner continued. "He was gone about five or six minutes on each occasion. He called me into the men's room and asked if I was interested in making $3,000. I told him I was always interested in making big money. He told me he had a big job on the line in two or three days, but he didn't say what it was at that time. He told me..."

"What's the matter?" asked Sigler, surprised by Kurner's pause. "Do you want a drink? Are you afraid of anybody here?"

"Just a moment!" gasped Rodgers, fumbling to get to his feet. "I rise in proper indignation. After all, if he is afraid, I don't blame him. If he has a conscience, he should be afraid."

"If you keep on making speeches — "

"I am going to keep making speeches from now until doomsday!"

"I don't doubt it, brother," sighed Sigler noisily. "You can't keep your mouth shut!"

"Don't call me 'brother,'" smirked Rodgers. "After all, I am rather particular as to the kind of people — "[48]

Ignoring the now addled Rodgers, Sigler urged Kurner to resume his story. "Well," continued the witness in a confidential tone, "about three days later I went to Sammy Abramowitz's apartment on Linwood in Detroit. Sammy asked me if I was still game to make $3,000. I said, 'Yes, I am.' He asked me if I'd seen anything in the papers lately and I said, 'No, I haven't.' He said, 'I don't mean in Detroit. I mean in Lansing.' I told him I just seen a lot of riffraff going on up there — a lot of politicians having quite an affair with Judge Carr. He says, 'Well, that's it.' I says, 'What do you mean?' He says, 'There's a party we're going to try to talk to.' He told me that it would take us about two hours to get to where this party lived from Detroit. He stayed up there about two hours himself and nearly froze."

"Did he tell you that he had cased the job, or words to that effect?"

"Yes, he did."[49]

Again lumbering to his feet, Rodgers took issue with Sigler's tactics. "Mr. Sigler has been posing leading questions throughout this examination, Your Honor. Would you instruct him to just state direct questions and get direct answers, if possible? I don't think he has to coach the man. He seems pretty apt."

His face flushed, Sigler strode toward Justice Bibbings. "I've stood just about all this smart-aleck talk that I'm going to. There is — "

"So have I!" raved Rodgers, arms raised heavenward as if in supplication.

" — no occasion for this brilliant individual to come into this court and charge me with coaching anyone. I don't need to coach anybody."

"Well, you openly put words in this man's mouth."

"You must try to be courteous," chided Sigler, while the courtroom spectators laughed and Justice Bibbings stared in bewilderment.

"I'm sorry," mocked Rodgers, "but I'm not susceptible to lessons from you, sir, on deportment."

"No," came the cutting reply, "you couldn't learn them from any-body. It isn't in you." Shaking his head in resignation, Sigler walked past the still silent judge and softly said, "Go ahead, Al, and tell us what he said on that occasion."[50]

"He said we were supposed to bump off some politician mixed up with the grand jury in Lansing, but that there was another party in on the deal. That night I met Sammy in O'Larry's Bar. He must have left the bar three or four times to go talk with Harry Fleisher and Mike Selik at their table. Anyways, Sammy Abramowitz told me that the thing was called off because they was trying to reach the guy by money — to try to get him to keep his mouth shut. If not, we was supposed to go up there to quiet him, or shoot him."[51]

Shifting uneasily as Harry Fleisher glowered at him and Mike Selik made faces while playing absent-mindedly with his bright hand-painted necktie, the youth related how he had taken a friend, David Butler, with him to O'Larry's that evening, but that the latter had remained in the car which was parked at the curb near the tavern's entrance. Kurner said he asked Abramowitz for a gun and that Sam went to the back of the bar, which was reputed to be the Purple Gang's arsenal, and returned with a .38 calibre revolver. Kurner and Butler later used the pistol to rob a downtown Detroit saloon, in a heist which Kurner ruefully remarked netted only $18. Following the stick-up, Kurner borrowed money and fled to Los Angeles, where he was subsequently apprehended and returned to Michigan to stand trial.[52]

Taking several gulps of water, Kurner nervously darted glances toward the defendants as he awaited cross-examination. In a pro forma maneuver, Leitch asked that Kurner's testimony be stricken as far as Sam Fleisher was concerned because the younger Fleisher had not been implicated in the testimony. This was merely a tactic to get the objection in the court record and, as Leitch anticipated, it was overruled by Bibbings. Rodgers then embarked upon a series of inquiries which accomplished little more than nettling Sigler. In response, Kurner detailed his early life of petty crime, the names of the girls seated with him at O'Larry's Bar on Christmas night and in Abramowitz's apartment three days later, and the eating, drinking, and social behavior of Harry Fleisher and Mike Selik at O'Larry's. Finally, when he appeared to have completed his questioning, Rodgers casually remarked, "Say, how much do you weigh, Al?"

"About 166," was the cautious reply.

"What size shoe do you wear?"

"About 9½," said Kurner even more warily.

"Do you want to know the size of his collar, too?" sneered Sigler, in an attempt to discover if his adversary intended to pursue the matter of the imprints left at the murder scene.

"No, just his feet," Rodgers smiled, and with a wave of his hand dismissed all further interest in the witness.[53]

After a brief appearance by David Butler, who verified Kurner's story, Sigler produced a surprise witness, Mrs. Evelyn Iris "Bessie" Brown, the 37-year-old waitress and manager of the Top Hat Tavern in Albion. Clad in flaming scarlet, Mrs. Brown primly entered the witness box and adjusted her skirt as she awaited the opportunity to reveal her evidence.[54] Her testimony was that on Thursday, January 11, 1945, two men — one tall and large, the other smaller and nervous — entered her establishment and sat in the third of five red upholstered booths along the right-hand wall. The smaller man, whom she identified as the defendant Pete Mahoney, ordered Stroh's beer by the bottle. During their one-hour stay, which saw them consume parts of four or five bottles of beer apiece, the smaller man continuously glanced at his vest pocket watch and the wall clock behind the bar. He further attracted her attention by going to the restroom several times. She could not accurately describe the larger man because he sat with his back to the bar and kept his hat pulled low to conceal his features, which she regarded as highly suspicious.[55]

"Can you tell us in more detail the actions of Pete Mahoney," prodded Sigler, "as to whether or not he was nervous?"

"Your Honor," began Rodgers with grim resignation, "I still insist that Mr. Sigler be instructed by this Court — and I would deem it a great favor — not to put words in the witness's mouth. If she thought he was nervous, she would tell us. She doesn't need any help. She seems to have had plenty of it."

"That's another of your smart aleck remarks. If you'll just — "

"Yes," smirked Rodgers, "I'm getting to be an awful smart aleck."

"Tell us a little more about the man's conduct," commanded Sigler, still barely able to control his contempt.

"My impression," said the witness, who was seemingly oblivious to the courtroom antics, "is that he was waiting for someone or had someplace to go."

"Just a moment," countered Rodgers, not bothering to rise. "If it please the Court, her impression — that calls for an operation of the witness's mind and I ask that the remark be stricken."

Bibbings stared plaintively at Sigler, in hopes of receiving a sign of what would be the proper response. To extricate the jurist from his predicament, Sigler said, without gallantry, "All right. After the speech we consent to it being stricken. Counsel was right in his objection. It's the first time he has been right today. Now, tell us what he did that caused you to form an opinion regarding his conduct."

"Well, when they only drank about two-thirds of each bottle of beer. I thought that was rather strange. And he was watching the clock," she stated while pointing to Mahoney, "as if he had an appointment somewhere or was waiting for a friend. Then by watching his watch several times. And I thought it was strange that he should go to the toilet so many times."

"All right. You may examine, Mr. Rodgers."[56]

"Thank you," grinned the Detroit lawyer, "I haven't examined so good looking a lady in a long while. How old are you, Mrs. Brown?"

"Why don't you speak up?" grumbled Sigler. "If you're going to speak privately to her, wait until after court."

Knowing that he was goading the special prosecutor into another display of temper, Rodgers maintained his smile and asked softly, "By the way, Mrs. Brown, are your eyes weak?"

"No, sir."

"Would you mind taking off your glasses for a moment?"

Almost as if on cue, Sigler exploded. "Why don't you open up your coat and let him see that nice red thing on your blouse. And be sure to give him your telephone number."

Laughing, Rodgers gave a low bow. "My friend," he said sarcastically, "when it comes to describing the effects of sartorial adornment, I can't do that as well as you." Turning, he leaned on the witness box rail to face the befuddled woman. "I would like to see the red flower, as long as Mr. Sigler has suggested you show it to me."

"Well, maybe I have something to say about that," she huffed, while willingly revealing the pin on her blouse.

Through this performance Sigler fumed, Rodgers smirked, spectators guffawed, and Justice Bibbings sat as impassive as a stone monument. The hearing was rapidly becoming the best show in Battle Creek.[57]

Rodgers then launched a barrage of questions intended to find out why, of the more than dozen patrons she had served during that hour, she would remember only the man she claimed was Mahoney and his companion. Her explanation was that they were strangers, acted nervous, and the smaller man pronounced "Stroh's" with a foreign accent. This pleased Sigler, since Mahoney was a Greek immigrant who spoke broken English.[58] The witness also revealed that Detective Bion Hoeg had come to the tavern to speak with her about another matter. When she told him of the January 11 events, he showed her a packet of 25-30 mug shots to see if any were the visitors. She chose one "who resembled Pete Mahoney" but was not actually the Detroit gambler.[59]

"When did Mr. Hoeg come to your tavern?" asked Rodgers.

"I don't remember the date."

"How many times have you been in Lansing to identify photographs at the state police barracks?"

"Just once."

"Remember the date?"

"No, but it was a week ago last Monday," she snorted belligerently.

"How many weeks before that had you picked out the photograph of the man who resembled Mahoney?"

"I don't know," she said, giving forth a sigh of boredom. "It could have been two or six. It was a few weeks before I went to Lansing."

"Yet you did remember so easily," thundered Rodgers in mock amazement, "the exact day Mr. Mahoney came in sometime in January and ordered a bottle of beer!"

"That's objected to as argumentative," shot back Sigler, casting visual daggers toward Bibbings, who quickly sustained the prosecutor.[60]

"Isn't it a fact, Mrs. Brown," spit Rodgers, not permitting her to compose her thoughts, "that you were told by the police to identify Mahoney?"

"No, sir. I wasn't told — "

"And isn't it a fact that somebody told you that Mr. Mahoney spoke with an accent?"

"No," she insisted, grasping the box rail.

"You're going to blow up in a minute," snapped Sigler, trying in vain to sidetrack Rodgers' onslaught.

"That's right," puffed the reddened counsel, "I will blow up. Have you ever been arrested and convicted, Mrs. Brown?"

"Wait a second," urged Sigler to the meandering lawyer. "Why don't you light somewhere? Are you nervous?"

Ignoring the jibe, Rodgers relentlessly persisted. "Have you, Mrs. Brown?"

"No, sir. Never. Until today I'd only been in a courtroom once and that was right here for my divorce."[61]

In a deft change, Rodgers caught the witness and Sigler unawares. "Was Mr. Hooper a customer in your bar?"

"No, sir. I never saw him in there in my life. I didn't know him personally, but I used to know of him when he ran a filling station in North Albion on the corner of Albion Street and Austin Avenue around 1934."

"You never went out with Mr. Hooper?" he asked, casting a sideways glimpse toward Sigler.

"Maybe I'm particular who I go with," she said noncommittally.

"I don't blame you," Rodgers reassured. "You just didn't want to go out with Mr. Hooper."

"If I wanted to, I would," she asserted, with a toss of her head. "Or with anybody else. But I think that's a little bit personal and I refuse to answer."

Coming to rescue what remained of her virtue, Sigler warned: "You don't need to pay any attention to him. He's just that way. He can't help it."

"I don't make $100 a day and expenses, like you. It's just that I always thought Mr. Hooper was a very lovely person and I wanted to know if she ever went out with him."

"Oh," blurted the soft, firm voice from the stand, "it don't make no difference to me what you make. Maybe I'm just the type that looks like I go out. But Mr. Hooper, he never asked me for a date and I was never out with him."

"Ever have any difference with Mr. Hooper's wife?"

"No, sir. I never saw her until today to know who she was."

"What size shoe do you wear, Mrs. Brown?"

"I wear a four."

"May I see your foot?"

As she extended her leg toward Rodgers, Sigler said approvingly, "A very small foot," which brought a beaming "Thank you" from the witness.

The mood was broken, however, when Rodgers interrupted, and slyly remarked, "I think there was something in the newspapers about small feet, and since Mrs. Brown was questioned in the death of her former employer in Detroit, I — "

"I object to this tomfoolery," reacted Sigler, realizing the last vestige of the witness's credibility was about to be shattered. "I also object to his running around the courtroom. First thing we know, he'll be climbing up the side of the wall here."

"That's okay," mocked Rodgers, "I might be taking after you."[62]

Bibbings again sustained Sigler, and Rodgers continued. "Isn't it true, Mrs. Brown, that Detective Hoeg came to see you not on any other case, but because he suspected that you had been out with Mr. Hooper before the killing?"

Ignoring Sigler's shout of "Don't answer that!" the witness stated flatly, "No, sir."

"How do you like that?" sneered the prosecutor.

"That's okay," answered Rodgers. "I don't like anything she says, because I don't believe the lady. This is all a frame-up on her part."

"Frame-up!" blared Sigler, his voice echoing throughout the room. "We'll show you whether it's a frame-up or not!"[63]

Staring into Brown's eyes, Rodgers renewed his probing. "You served Mahoney, brought him beer, and were very close to him?"

"Yes, sir."

"The lights were on and you had a good occasion to see his face, did you?"

"Yes, sir."

"Did you notice anything peculiar about Mr. Mahoney's face?"

"No, sir."

"Step over here, would you, Mr. Mahoney?"

The well-dressed, clean-shaven defendant strode to his attorney's side. His face was grotesquely seared and scarred, with a long, deep gash on his left cheek. "Take a good look at me," he ordered. "Are you sure it was me?"

Mrs. Brown took a long look, as photographers' flashbulbs burst like machine gun fire, and whispered, "Yes."

"The only thing you noticed about me was being nervous and walking up and down and watching the watch?" pleaded Mahoney. "My liberty is at stake."

"What right have you to talk to me?" she asked indignantly.

"Wait a minute," chimed Sigler, "I am going to ask that he be ordered to sit down."

"Mr. Sigler," implored the defendant with sincerity, "I only want her to take a good look at me. I want the lady to hear me speak. I want her to be positive I'm the man who was in her place at Albion. That's all."

"She is positive, Mr. Mahoney," snarled Sigler. "In fact, I think she is almost as positive of it as you are."

"May I ask something, Mr. Sigler?" pleaded Mahoney.

"You go back and sit down," came the terse reply. "I won't argue with you."[64]

Following the exchange, Bibbings adjourned court until 9:30 a.m., at which time Mrs. Brown was to retake the stand. However, her police escort failed to have her back at the appointed hour and, rather than waste time waiting, both prosecution and defense counsel agreed to hear the next scheduled witness, Henry Luks. A hush settled over the gallery as the 29-year-old, tall, dark-haired former safecracker admitted that he was a "three-time loser," having been sent to prison in 1934, 1937, and 1940. While serving as a trusty at Southern Michigan Prison he met Mike Selik, who was working as

Warden Harry Jackson's houseboy, and they became "very good friends." He recounted how he had vehemently denied any knowledge of the Hooper slaying when the state police brought him in for questioning in April and how it was only after his parole officer explained to him that, under Michigan law, a fourth criminal conviction carried a mandatory life sentence that he agreed to testify, in return for immunity for his part in the conspiracy.[65]

Ill at ease and rarely looking at the defendants, Luks began his shocking tale of premeditated murder. "On December 23, 1944, at around eleven-thirty at night," he said in a soft, barely audible, tone, "I was sitting in O'Larry's Bar having a drink when Mike Selik came up and said, 'Harry and I want to talk to you in the office as soon as you get through drinking.' So I went down the back corridor behind the piano to Harry Fleisher's office. In there, Harry said, 'Well, if you want to get in on a deal, you can make yourself about five grand.' I says, 'What is it — a safe?' and he says, 'No, it is getting dynamite and wiring a car.' I says, 'It sounds plausible and I would like to.' I told them I knew how to do it."

"What do you mean by 'wiring' a car, Henry?" interrupted Sigler.

"You wire dynamite to the sparkplug or starter, and once the starter is stepped on the fuses are set off and the dynamite explodes, killing someone," explained Luks with matter-of-fact simplicity. "Anyway, I told them I'd try to get the dynamite, and they told me to come back on Christmas Day."[66]

He coughed, sipped water, and then continued, his fingers steadily drumming against the arm of his chair. "Around midnight Christmas Day, I met with them again in the back of the bar. They asked if I got the dynamite, and I says it wasn't available. So they says, 'Would you be interested in taking care of this fellow in some other way?' They never mentioned the fellow's name, but they got to talking about him and said they knew where he lived and his habits and that he was supposed to testify against somebody. I asked where the money was coming from and Harry says that there was $15,000 in escrow someplace and my share would be $5,000. Then, after about five or ten minutes, I was asked if I cared if Sammy Abramowitz stepped into it. I says I didn't care. They says, 'Of course, the $5,000 that you're supposed to get will be cut in half and it'll be $2,500.'"[67]

"What happened then, Henry?" prompted Sigler, leaning on the rail of the witness box to make it seem that Luks was speaking only to him.

Draining his water glass, Luks moistened his lips and coughed under his breath. "Sammy joined us later that evening, or morning — it was after twelve. Harry and Mike then gave us a little more detail about how they knew all the fellow's habits and they asked us if we wanted to take a ride over to Albion and look things over and see how we liked it. If we didn't like it, we didn't have to take it."

"Where did you stay all that night, do you remember, Henry?"

"I went to a party on the west side of Detroit given by the bartender at O'Larry's Bar and we stayed there until about four or five o'clock in the morning and then took a cab over to the Wolverine Hotel so Sammy could drop off his girl. Then we took a cab to the Cream of Michigan Restaurant on Twelfth Street, where we were supposed to meet Harry Fleisher," Luks went on, his voice no longer quivering. "Harry was standing outside the restaurant and his black Cadillac was parked along the curb. We went in and had a cup of coffee."

"While you were there," asked Sigler, "did Mike Selik, the defendant with the hand-painted tie who keeps sticking his finger in his mouth, show up?"

"No, we drove to his apartment on Boston Boulevard, a couple of blocks from O'Larry's."

"He overslept a little that morning, did he?" the prosecutor added sarcastically.

"No," came the somber reply, "we planned to pick him up. Then after we got Mike we drove to O'Larry's because Sammy mentioned that he had a gun on him and Harry didn't want that. So Mike took it and put it away in the bar and then came out and got back into the front passenger's seat."

"Did you ever see where they kept the guns in O'Larry's Bar?" shot Sigler.

"I never did."

"Did you ever happen to look above the telephone booth that is near the kitchen?"

"I never did."[68]

"Just a minute," urged Rodgers, "there is no testimony here to show that any guns were kept in O'Larry's Bar. The prosecutor has gone far enough in asking leading questions. The judge might sustain me on this one."

"But he won't," smiled Bibbings, eliciting soft laughter from the audience.

"I thought not," fumed defense counsel. Turning to Sigler, Rodgers arms outstretched, angrily implored, "Let the witness, if he knows anything, go ahead and show it without any help, Mr. Sigler. Don't put guns into their mouths."

"No, these men didn't put guns into their mouths," snapped Sigler, removing his pince-nez and pointing them at Rodgers, "they held them in their hands." Spinning on his heel, Sigler asked, "Henry, then what did the man with the hand-painted tie do?"

"We know your brand of humor, Mr. Sigler," snarled Rodgers, while Bibbings maintained his stoic silence, "and we know when you mean Mr. Selik, who has a hand-painted tie. What we're interested in is guns."

"Oh, I'm glad you're interested in guns, too," grinned the prosecutor, "because then you won't object to the rest of my examination. Now, Henry, what happened after Mike came back to the car after he put Sammy's gun away?"[69]

"We started out for Albion. On the way there we didn't talk about the case at all. Mostly we talked about girls and other fellows. When we got to Albion around eight o'clock, we drove up to a white frame house with a Mercury or Ford parked in front of it. Either Harry or Mike said, 'This is where he lives. That is his car. We know it by the license number.' They also said they knew approximately what time he left his house for his office. We parked about a block away from the house and waited for him to leave for about half-an-hour."

"As you sat there, Henry," Sigler said in a hushed tone, "what did you discuss with these distinguished defendants?"

"They said he was some sort of a doctor," Luks responded, casting a wary glance toward the no-longer-gleeful mobsters, "and that he had a business place not far from there. That it was off the main street and that he was a neuropractor, or something, and that he had a business in Lansing also. They never said what his business in Lansing was, but they did mention that he had some testimony to give there. But they never said to who."[70]

"What else happened, Henry?" asked Sigler, positioning himself between the witness and the accused, so that their eyes could not meet.

"Well, I asked several questions and was told not to ask too many. Like I asked if Frank McKay had anything to do with it. Mike Selik told me never to mind about that. He says, 'The money is up for this case and that's all you have to worry about.' After that I mentioned, 'Does this fellow have something to do with the grand jury?' Mike told me the same as before to never mind and not to worry. In other words, he told me not to ask so many questions."[71]

Rodgers was stunned at the manner by which Luks had skillfully injected McKay's name into the testimony, but realized that it would be futile, given the temperament of Justice Bibbings, to question the propriety of the response, and decided to wait until his cross-examination to find out why the Grand Rapids financier was the only person the gangster thought would be masterminding the crime. Raising his hand to reassure his clients, Rodgers let Luks tell his tale without interruption.[72]

"Then we left and drove by his office twice, and then we started back for Detroit. I didn't know it then, but I now know that it was Senator Hooper's office. While we were driving around the office, all four of us discussed how to dispose of this fellow. It was suggested that Sammy Abramowitz, who had a bad arm at that time, go into his office and show the doctor his arm. While he was looking at it, I was supposed to come from behind and hit him over the head with a blackjack or blunt instrument. Sammy also suggested just walking in and shooting him. We also discussed strangling him, using his necktie or belt or rope."

"Who was to do this, Henry?"

"Sam and I."

"Where were Harry Fleisher and Mike Selik supposed to be while you and Sammy were doing the dirty work?"

"I don't know. They never mentioned they would be with us. It was agreed that they would have no part in the actual killing."

"Just a moment," burst Rodgers, unable to contain his wrath any longer, "there is not any evidence of 'dirty work' as yet."

"Oh, no," answered Sigler, with feigned horror, "we don't want to say, Mr. Rodgers, that killing is dirty work. We don't — "

"But there was no killing," asserted Rodgers.

"Then there are a lot of murders without killing, aren't there?" was Sigler's mocking retort.

"But there was no murder at that time. That's why I got up and objected — "

With a rap of his gavel, Bibbings cut him off. "We are overruling your objection," the judge proclaimed, nodding toward the prosecutor, who bowed in agreement. Noting the inadvertent, but accurate, use of the plural pronoun in Bibbings' statement, Rodgers flashed a contemptuous smile and resumed his seat.[73]

As Sigler adjusted his ruby cuff links with perfect aplomb, cheers and applause rang through the courtroom in appreciation of the performance. Only bows from players and unnecessary calls for an encore were missing from this summer stock legal revue.[74]

Not everyone, however, found the occasion entertaining. In the rear of the courtroom, trying unsuccessfully to avoid the prying eyes of the hundreds of persons who had crowded in to view the festivities, sat Callienetta Hooper. Looking prim in a dark blue dress trimmed with white lace, she listened intently as Luks unraveled the web of intrigue which led to her husband's death. Only when the callous discussion of how to commit the crime was described did tears roll down her cheeks. She then sent her sons to play in the city hall corridors under the watchful care of a police guard so that they would not hear how their father had been stalked like a wild animal by his would-be assailants.[75]

Concluding his story, Luks told of leaving Albion for Jackson around eleven o'clock. En route it was agreed that Abramowitz and Luks would meet an unnamed man with a truck the following morning. Mike Selik then ordered Luks to come to O'Larry's that evening to receive further details of the plan. Luks was let out at the Jackson bus depot and arrived in Lansing in mid-afternoon of the twenty-sixth. "I went to a barber shop," he recalled, "and got a shave and a massage and went to several bars. I drank. I had supper in a restaurant and went to a few more bars and finally ended up at the Rustic Village on Michigan Avenue. I drank there for a while and then I talked with this girl friend there that I was going around with. I asked her if she would make a long distance phone call to Detroit for me. She said she wouldn't because she thought I was calling up some other girl. I asked the waitress and she said she would. I gave her the number of O'Larry's Bar."

"Just a moment," sighed Rodgers, "I want to ask who the girl was that refused to make the telephone call."

"I might suggest, Your Honor," instructed Sigler acidly, "that my distinguished brother wait until he cross-examines the witness and then he can find out the girl friends and all their telephone numbers."

"That's correct," parroted Bibbings, shaking his head vigorously. "You may continue, witness."

"I gave her the number of O'Larry's Bar," Luks reiterated, "and I told her to ask for Mike Selik and she did. She asked me what to say and I told her to tell Mike that I wouldn't be there that night or the next morning, that I wasn't available, and that I'd been having trouble with my parole officer and couldn't very well leave Lansing for a while."

After Rodgers' objection that the testimony was hearsay was predictably overruled, Sigler inquired, "Was it true, Henry, that you were having trouble with your parole officer?"

"No, I was not," admitted Luks. "I didn't like the situation. I didn't like the thing. Anyway the girl came back and she says, 'Mike said okay. Tell him to forget about it.' That was the end of the case as far as I was concerned."

"You thought it was a little too hot, did you?" prompted Sigler shamelessly.

"Yes, it was too hot," agreed the amenable witness.

"I object," began Rodgers, "to the prosecutor — "

"Overrule your objection," chimed Justice Bibbings, not even affording the red-faced attorney the courtesy of completing the sentence.

"Again?" he sighed.

"That's right," smirked the black-robed magistrate, obviously relishing his momentary power over the high-priced, big-city criminal lawyer.[76]

Rodgers' cross-examination was an amalgam of subtle attempts at discrediting the witness and bitter invective aimed at the prosecutor and judge. At one point, after ascertaining that Luks, following his April 24 arrest, had been detained by the state police at several county jails, Rodgers sought, in vain, to discover the witness's current address. Sigler claimed the issue was immaterial and suggested that Bibbings not only sustain the objection, but also instruct Rodgers to keep quiet and refrain from being argumentative. The judge did both, which led Rodgers to implore rhetorically, "What chance has a poor lawyer got here?"[77]

Finally, to the delight of the spectators, a verbal brawl erupted when Rodgers insinuated that Justice Bibbings was shielding the witness from questioning through the use of legally unsubstantiated "judicial taboo." Rushing to the aid of his shocked ally once again, Sigler slowly began what would devolve into a tirade. "I must ask the Court to caution counsel against making such scurrilous remarks. Judicial taboo. I'm amazed that a lawyer would come into court and have the temerity to stand up openly and flaunt before the court the judicial rulings. Courts are to be respected and not treated in this manner, regardless of how distinguished the lawyer may be for the defense."

"I must, for a change, fight for my clients," shouted Rodgers, shaking with rage and indignation. "The pity of the whole thing is that I address the Court and I have objections, one after the other, brought into this court which have not been sustained. And, by everything that is holy, they should have been sustained at times. To me, on these rulings, these men are just not being given an even break."

"These men are being given an even break," countered Sigler. "Sit down and keep still!"

"I'm not going to sit down!"

"You haven't got a defense," ranted Sigler, "and you're making a fool of yourself."

"Gentlemen," begged the beleaguered judge, "kindly control your bantering in court."

"Will Your Honor kindly instruct this lawyer to be at least gentlemanly enough," demanded Sigler, "to shut his mouth when someone else has a right to talk and is trying to answer his foolish argument?"

"Carry on, Mr. Sigler," was the dutiful ruling from the bench.

"This Court has ruled properly. I will not object to any proper question that I earnestly and honestly believe tests the witness's credibility, but I am not going to stand here and let him or anybody else flaunt the rulings of this Court."

"I take it you're the defender of the helpless," jibed Rodgers in an unveiled reference to the untrained magistrate.

"I'm the defender of dignity in court, my friend," came the pompous reply. "You can come here and you can proceed with all your foolish tactics that you want to, but I'll be right here. And you're not going to ask silly questions that I am not going to object to."

"I don't care! What do I care? You're just railroading these men."

His integrity once more called into question, Sigler surprised everyone by slamming his fist on the prosecution table. "I'm going to ask that that remark of counsel's be stricken from the record, and I'm going to further ask that the Court instruct this lawyer to refrain from such tactics in the future. He and his clients have indulged in the old tactic of talking about railroading and kangaroo courts and all of that sort of thing and it's becoming nonsense. These men are going to get a fair hearing, but there isn't going to be any of this camouflage that my brother has so artfully attempted to throw over this proceeding."

His hands folded across his chest, Rodgers leered at his adversary. "You bring up a very interesting point, Mr. Sigler. When does the fair trial commence? I'm rather interested."

Flustered, Sigler sputtered, "I'm going to ask that counsel be instructed to refrain from making such remarks. I know he's doing it for no other purpose than to try to becloud the issue."

"At this time, you'll refrain from these remarks, Mr. Rodgers," mimicked Bibbings, "and I will instruct the reporter to strike that last statement from the record." With that the combatants took their chairs, the audience exploded with an appreciative ovation, and eventually everyone remembered that Henry Luks was sitting bemused in the witness box, patiently waiting to complete his ordeal.[78]

As Luks listed his repeated parole violations, Sam Fleisher and Pete Mahoney sat immobile, the gravity of the potential results of the hearing weighing more and more heavily on them, but Harry Fleisher resumed his hushed banter with Selik, who giggled noisily. Before Sigler could recite an oration of courtroom etiquette, Rodgers quieted his clients. He then asked the witness what had transpired immediately following his arrest by the state police.[79]

"On the second of April," Luks began, choosing his words with obvious care, "I was arrested as a violator of parole and put in the Lansing City Jail for two days. On the third day they took me out to take me to East Lansing and give me a lie detector test. After I took it, they said that the test hadn't come out just right and that they wanted me to take another test."

"Do you remember the questions?" said Rodgers, pacing before the witness.

"Well, I remember some of them. They asked if I was ever propositioned to kill a politician. I said no. They asked if Henry Luks was my name. I said yes. They asked if I had breakfast that day. I said yes. They asked me if I knew who killed Senator Hooper, and I said no. They asked me if I'd ever heard any conversation or heard anybody propositioned to kill a politician. I answered that no. If there was any other questions, I don't remember them. Anyways, after I took the test, they said, 'You're a little nervous for this test. We want you to be a little more composed the next time you come down here. You don't have to worry about nothing. Just answer the questions truthfully.' So they told me to come back the following Monday — the ninth. Then I had two or three more tests that Monday."

"Did they all come out okay?"

"No. They said that I had responded to certain questions unfavorably. They mentioned the question about being propositioned. They said that I responded to that question and the one about denying all knowledge of hearing about a proposition unfavorably. They questioned me more and then let me go that night. Shall I go on?"

"Yes," urged Rodgers.

"They told me to come back for another test the following Tuesday. Instead of giving me another test they cross-examined me. Well, questioned me."

"Did Mr. Sigler question you?" interrupted Rodgers.

"No, it was just Lieutenant Morse, a parole inspector, and several Detroit detectives. Anyways, they came out with the fact they knew about this trip and all, and that they wanted me to come clean about the case. I told them I didn't know nothing," Luks recounted, his voice reflecting nervous anxiety as he relived the encounter. "They told me the only thing they could do was try me on the case because they had evidence on me. Then they started to talk. They said, 'Now, you tell us the truth about this and it might go better for you. The truth may clear you up. We know that you are definitely in the case.' I still refused to say nothing. Then they says, 'There's a fellow wants to talk to you.' I says, 'Who is it?' They mentioned Sammy Abramowitz and I says, 'I'll talk to him.'"

Pausing only long enough to grasp his water glass with both trembling hands and raise it to his parched lips, Luks continued racing through his tale. "When I was confronted with him, he says, 'Well, I waited long enough for them guys,'" at which point Luks pointed to the defendants, "'I've told the police everything. I've told them about going to Albion. The only way you can straighten yourself out, Heinie, is to tell your side of the story. I told them about how you was propositioned and all that. And about you bringing me in and making the trip to Albion and all the facts in the case. At least you're not involved as far as I am. I know a little more about it than you do, so you'd better tell your story.' Well, I denied that I knew anything about the case. But after the police questioned me for a while, I saw there wasn't any use, so I told them that I would tell my side of the story. I only confessed because Sam Abramowitz had implicated me in the case and told his side of the story, and I was involved."[80]

"While in custody, you were told, were you not," accused Rodgers, still pacing, "by someone in the state police, that it would go easier if you made a clean breast of things?"

"No," Luks said earnestly, shaking his head violently, "they didn't tell me it would go easier. They said it would be better if I did."

"Were you told," hammered defense counsel, "that in the event you didn't play ball, there would be supplemental proceedings put against you so you would go into prison for life?"

"There was not, but I surmised that much."

"You thought it best to do business in order to save your hide by selling others down the river!" yelled Rodgers, finally stopping long enough to face Luks.

"I – "

"That's objected to as improper, incompetent, immaterial, and irrelevant," pleaded Sigler, who was, as always, sustained by Justice Bibbings.[81]

"Oh, yes," smirked Rodgers, casting a sly look toward the prosecution table, "do you remember the names of the girls you asked to telephone Mike Selik from Lansing?"

"Sure I do. The girl who made the telephone call was Florence. I don't know her last name. The girl who refused to make the call was Virginia Darling. They both lived together on East Michigan Street. I went around with them."[82]

After completion of Luks' testimony, court recessed until 1:25, at which time Evelyn Iris Brown retook the stand to undergo cross-examination by Rodgers. Concentrating on the uncertainty of her identification of the photograph of a man who resembled his client, Rodgers set out to discredit her testimony. "I think you mentioned there were eighteen photographs in the large envelope shown you by Detective Hoeg?"

"I said twenty-five or thirty," came the indignant reply.

"Yes," grinned the attorney, "so you did. May I ask you this then? When you identified that photograph that looked like Mahoney, were you told by any officer whose photograph it really was?"

"Yes, Mr. Hoeg told me. But I don't remember."

"Of course not," nodded Rodgers, who received a knowing smile from Sigler. "Well, yesterday you told us, I believe, that these two individuals left your place at exactly 1:30 Albion time?"

"I didn't give no correct time on when they left. I just said they was there an hour or more."

"Did Mr. Mahoney have any conversation with you — kid with you — tell you how he liked the town?"

"No. Just ordered his beer," she said curtly, fidgeting with the blue-tinted sunglasses she held in her lap.

"You say Mr. Mahoney went to the men's room on several occasions," inquired Rodgers, once again spritely walking the width of the courtroom.

"That's right."

"And he looked at the clock on the wall?"

"That's right."

"At that time there were several other customers there, who were well known to you?"

"That's right."

"But you don't remember who they were?"

"No, I don't."

"But you do remember Mahoney, who only came in once to your place of business many months ago?"

"I can't hear you when you're prancing around the courtroom," shot Sigler, requesting that the question be read by the reporter.

"That's right," answered Mrs. Brown after the prosecutor was satisfied with the propriety of the question. "The regular customers you don't pay so much attention to as a stranger when they come in."[83]

"Tell me, Mrs. Brown," quizzed Rodgers, making no effort to disguise his contempt for her, "when you were questioned by Mr. Hoeg, he let you know that there was a reward out of some $30,000, didn't he?"

"He did not," she huffed, straightening her back. "There was never anything mentioned of money matters."

"Well, I was just going to remind you that the reward was posted, as I understand it, for the murderer of Mr. Hooper, not the conspirators, so you would be out of luck on that."

As the witness gasped, either in dismay or indignation, Sigler issued a warranted objection.

Flashing a broad smile, Rodgers assured the court that he was merely trying to be helpful in gathering facts. Pleased with his thrust, he then queried, "Are you absolutely sure that Mr. Mahoney was in your place on January 11, the day Senator Hooper was murdered?"

"I'm absolutely sure."

"Why?"

"That's been answered at least a dozen times," blurted Sigler in disgust. "Here, I'll help you a little bit. He drank only a portion of his bottles of beer. He looked at his watch. He looked at the clock. In addition to that, he went to the toilet a number of times."

"Yes," posed Rodgers, "but don't lots of your customers go to the powder room, look at their watches, or glance at the wall clock?"

"Not that often, I bet," responded Sigler, to which Mrs. Brown eagerly added, "That's right."[84]

"You have children, don't you, Mrs. Brown?" asked Rodgers so sincerely that the witness relaxed for the first time.

"Yes," she boasted. "I have a boy. He works in a factory."

"Fine. I will ask just one more question of you." Without warning, he raised his voice and demanded, "Mrs. Brown, you wouldn't like someone who wasn't certain of a positive identification to identify your son if he was sitting in Mahoney's shoes, would you? This man is a mother's son, too!"

"Oh, if the Court please," muttered Sigler, "that's objected to. You ought to go to Hollywood and pull that one, Mr. Rodgers."

Despite Bibbings' ruling in favor of Sigler, Rodgers persisted. "You're not certain! You are not absolutely certain, are you, Mrs. Brown?"

"I am!" she bristled.

"You don't say you could make a mistake?"

"Absolutely not."

"On the eleventh day of January, Mahoney might not have been in your place, but he might have resembled someone else — resembled the man that you saw in that photograph that was showed to you by Hoeg. You don't concede that you might have made a mistake?"

"No!" she reiterated, clenching her fists tightly. "No!"

"But you did make a mistake on the photograph, didn't you?" Rodgers asked calmly. "Didn't you say that the officer said, 'Now take a good look at this photograph and see if it doesn't resemble a man by the name of Mahoney?' He did say that, didn't he?"

"Wait a minute!" shouted Sigler, drowning out Mrs. Brown's reply of "no, he didn't." Staring at his legal foe, Sigler thrust a finger toward the United States' flag near the bench. "We don't handle things like that out here in that way, Mr. Rodgers."

"My goodness. Wave the flag, Mr. Sigler."

"I've got to do something to meet your dramatics, you know, Mr. Rodgers."

"They're not dramatics. I just asked the lady a question. Didn't you say you received a fifty cent tip from Mr. Mahoney, Mrs. Brown?"

"I object to that. She has said yes to that over a dozen times."

"I'm just trying to get — " he paused, and then finished with sarcastic insinuation," — the two pieces of silver. Evidently it only took one piece of silver to get this man sent down the gangway. That's all. Call your next witness, Mr. Sigler."[85]

V I Bowing courteously in acknowledgment, Sigler summoned to the stand his principal witness, Sam Abramowitz. The 5'6½", 135-pound, bushy-haired thug, whom the police had characterized as possessing a "dull normal intelligence with an IQ of 90," volunteered that his criminal record was "bad, very bad." Elaborating, he stated, "I've been in prison twice, on probation once, and have probably been arrested a hundred times." During the preceding fifteen years, he added, all but three had been spent in jail.[86]

Like Luks, Abramowitz had met Mike Selik in prison where they became friends. After his parole on April 16, 1943, Abramowitz went to his hometown of Flint, where he attempted to practice his trade of barbering. Bitterly, he recalled having a good job in the prominent barbershop housed in the city's biggest office building, only to lose it when a well-known local attorney threatened to lead a boycott against the firm unless the ex-convict was fired.[87] After shouting at a photographer who exploded a flash in his face, Abramowitz boasted that his record while on parole was spotless, except for one arrest when he engaged in a saloon brawl when someone called him a "damned Jew." He did admit, however, to making the 75-mile trip to Detroit numerous times to visit Mike Selik at O'Larry's Bar.[88]

Abramowitz echoed Luks' account of the events leading to, and including, their trip to Albion, with the lone exception that he remembered that the means by which the murder could be accomplished were discussed at O'Larry's Bar, not during the ride to Albion.[89] He methodically detailed his later attempts on the senator's life. "On December 28 or 29, I think it was, I can't be sure of the date, Sam Fleisher picked me up at the Blaine Restaurant on Twelfth Street around 7:00 a.m. He drove a black Pontiac, I think. I never did take any notice of it. It might have been a Chevrolet. Anyways, when we got near Albion, Sam reached under the seat and pulled out a short-nosed .38 revolver with a nick in the handle. He put it on the seat between us, underneath some gloves. When we got to Albion, I put it in my topcoat."

"Had you ever seen that gun before, Sammy?"

"Oh, yes. At O'Larry's Bar. They kept guns there. Sam kept some hidden on top of the telephone booth."

"Well, go on," said Sigler, turning to watch the defendants. "What time did you reach Albion?"

"Right around ten o'clock. We did the same thing we did before. Just drove around by his house and office twelve or fifteen times. Just killing time because we never did see him. I didn't want to park. Sam wanted to, but I made him move on right away. We were there for about an hour and a half."

"Did you know at that time who you were gunning for?"

"Oh, yes. I asked Sam who he was, what kind of a doctor, and everything. Sam told me his name was Hooper and that he had to be silenced real quick before he could talk to the grand jury."

"Did Sam tell you," prodded Sigler, "that Hooper's talking would involve him or Harry or Mike, or that the job was being pulled for someone else?"

"No, he never mentioned anything like that. But I gathered from them telling me there was a $15,000 slush fund available for expenses that it was someone else that wanted it done."

"Then what happened, Sammy?"

"Well, Sam took the gun from me and we went back to Detroit to O'Larry's and told Harry we never saw Hooper. Harry just said, 'Jesus, he's a tough guy to get. We'll have to try again.' Harry and Mike later told me to meet Sam at the same place and time on January 2. So, on January 2, Sam and I went back to Albion again getting there about ten o'clock. We drove to the Hooper house, but didn't see anyone there so we drove to his office."

"Did you see the individual you were looking for?"

"Just before we left I saw this man sitting there, but I didn't see his face, only the top of his shoulders and the back of his head. He was very bald. He was sitting in a chair at a desk with his back to the window. He was almost laying on the window. It looked just like he had his head on it. He was talking to some woman. I don't know who she was. I noticed two little children over in the other part of the building playing in the window, looking out. The woman was sitting across the desk from him."[90]

An anxious hush fell over the courtroom as Sigler asked softly, "What happened then, Sammy?"

"Well, I said to Sam, 'We'll have to drop this, too. Too many people around.' Sam said, 'It does look bad. Let's just drive around a little while. Maybe whoever it is will leave.' After three or four times driving by, I said, 'We better get out of here,' and we finally left. Sam said he wanted to fix an alibi for himself so we stopped at a couple of junk places and Sam went in and talked for a minute or two. I figured maybe he had to prove to his wife he was there on business. Then Sam saw a farm advertising fresh eggs and we pulled in to get some. I got stuck in the driveway and the farmer's wife got us some ashes to put under the tires. Around three in the afternoon we got back to O'Larry's. We told Harry that we had seen Hooper but didn't shoot him because his wife and two kids were in the room. We said that we couldn't shoot him with kids around. Harry agreed that we had done the right thing. Then he said that he and Mike would probably have to do the job themselves."[91] On that note, court adjourned for the weekend.

On Sunday, Sigler received an anonymous tip that the underworld had passed a death sentence on Abramowitz. To protect his new "little package of dynamite," the special prosecutor promised to pack the courtroom with police. Nonchalantly, he added that word had reached him that he, too, had been marked for death, but that he had no fears for his safety.[92]

When court reconvened at 9:30 Monday morning, Sigler reviewed his witness's account of the last visit to Albion. Fully aware that Abramowitz's past criminal record showed no evidence of sympathy or concern for his victims, Sigler smiled at the jurors and asked, "Was that the real reason, Sammy, that you didn't shoot Senator Hooper?"

"No. Sam told me he was carrying a .32 automatic pistol on him and that he'd had it on the first trip, too, but didn't tell me. I said, 'That's pretty funny.' He said he had it in case there was any trouble. Well, I knew that if I did that killing, why Sam would have dumped me on the road somewhere using the gun he had. Even though Harry had given me a hundred bucks or so as an advance on the job, I decided I'd save my life and jump off the gravy train after that last trip."

"Just one more thing, Sammy," Sigler told the sallow-complexioned, impassive gangster. "Did you see Harry, Sam, or Mike after the murder?"

"Yes. I believe it was on January 12 that I went to Detroit. I went to O'Larry's Bar that evening and I was sitting at the bar and a little later Harry happened to go by and noticed me there. He came over grinning to me and I said to him, 'Well, it was done, huh?' He said, 'Yes.' And I said, 'Jesus, the description in the paper fits you and Mike. The only thing is the small shoes don't fit any one of you.' I had read something about the small feet, and I know Harry, rather I know Mike wears at least a nine shoe and he's got bigger feet than I've got. Harry said, 'No, it wasn't him because Mike is in St. Louis with his wife visiting her sick uncle.' Someone else just before this mentioned Mike was gone also."[93]

Robert G. Leitch, Sam Fleisher's attorney, launched the cross-examination with a determined, but futile, effort to confuse Abramowitz into changing his story.[94] Without warning, he snapped, "What size shoe do you wear, Mr. Abramowitz?"

The witness calmly replied, "an eight, and if you want to know, I believe it fits the imprint they've got."

"Have you ever been accused of the actual murder by the police?" inquired Leitch, his eyes wide with expectation.

"Yes, I was accused of it, but about a week ago Judge Carr granted me immunity if I would tell my story in court."

"The story you had been telling the police all along?"

"No, the truth. I had been lying for twenty-five days, but I finally decided to tell the truth."

"Was it the promise of immunity that convinced you to change your story?"

"No, I changed it before that. I — "

Sigler interrupted to point out that the granting of immunity was allowed by law and that Abramowitz had neither received, nor was promised, any remuneration by the grand jury.[95] Having established this, he waved to the witness to proceed with his tale.

Pointing to the defendants, Abramowitz sneered, "I'll tell you why I talked. It was because my friends over there didn't send me an attorney or try to help me at any time. You guys — "

"You're not any friend of mine!" yelled Selik.

"I know you're not my friend, Mike," Abramowitz went on, staring at his former comrades. "I lied for twenty-five days, but you guys let me lay in jail the whole time. I waited too long for help. I know by talking now I'm a rat, but I'm no stool pigeon. Stool pigeons get paid for it."[96]

Grinning, Abramowitz sighed, "You know, I've been wanting someone to ask me that."[97] Then, lapsing into sullen reflection, he seemingly made an apology to his old friends, muttering, "I know now it was a mistake for me to talk to Kurner. Otherwise we wouldn't be sitting here today." Turning to the judge, he added, "As far as I know, Your Honor, Pete Mahoney was not involved in any part of the conspiracy to kill Senator Hooper."[97]

Before Abramowitz was cross-examined by Rodgers, the attorney requested permission to recall Evelyn Iris Brown. As the brightly clad woman adjusted herself in the witness chair, Rodgers jibed, "You see, Mr. Sigler, I've always said that Mrs. Brown looked lovely in red. You know, I'm thinking of the good old days when Mr. Dillinger's sweetheart wore red."[99] As Justice Bibbings stiffened, Rodgers became serious. "Mrs. Brown, isn't it true that you were approached by Officer Hoeg and told that unless you identified Mahoney you would be linked to the murder of your former employer in Detroit?"

"Absolutely not!"

"But you were questioned in Albion by the homocide squad in reference to that murder, weren't you?"

"No, I — "

"Don't answer anything until I tell you," cautioned Sigler, "because this cute boy is going to try to get you in a hole, but I won't let him."

"Mr. Sigler," said Rodgers benignly, "I would never take advantage of this lovely little lady in red."

"From what I've heard, she'd be the first one, then," smirked Sigler, enjoying the laughter from the gallery.[100]

"Well, Mrs. Brown," continued defense counsel, "wasn't the picture you identified for Mr. Hoeg really that of Sam Abramowitz?"

"Objection!" said Sigler sharply. "She answered that last week."

"No, she didn't," insisted Rodgers, who was scolded by Bibbings for spending too much time talking to his clients and not enough listening to testimony.[101]

"All right," fumed counsel, pacing furiously, "let me ask you just one more question: Was the man in the picture you identified as resembling the man in your restaurant on the day of the death of Mr. Hooper really Pete Mahoney?"

"No, it wasn't," came the soft reply. "It wasn't Mahoney."[102]

Abramowitz then returned to the stand, and Rodgers subjected him to nearly two hours of sarcasm and ridicule in an effort to unhinge his story.[103] Failing in this, Rodgers turned to kindness and begged the witness to be truthful. "Didn't anyone tell you that if you did talk, Sammy — you know I'm not trying to ride you, but I want to find out what is doing in this case. That's my job. Didn't anyone tell you that your parole violation would be forgotten, because you know you have ten years to go in case you dump it on this thing?"

"They didn't have to make any bargains. I'd already made up my mind."

"You mean you gave freely from your heart of steel?"

"Absolutely," said Abramowitz, breaking into a wide grin.

"Are you now living in the Olds Hotel?" asked Rodgers in obvious reference to the preferential treatment afforded Charlie Hemans.

"That's a good one. Yeah, I'm a prisoner at the Olds Hotel! I'm not in any hotel! I'm in jail and have been all the time."

"Rumors are that you've been wined and dined by Mr. Sigler."

"Well, you must have been fooled," snapped the witness, flashing his temper for the first time.

"That's all," shrugged Rodgers. "It didn't hurt, Sammy, did it?"

"You couldn't touch him," crowed Sigler.

"I wouldn't want to," Rodgers rejoined, wiping his hands on his coat.[104]

The remainder of the hearing consisted of testimony on the armed robbery in which Abramowitz injured his arm, and accounts of police officers verifying Abramowitz's identification of Hooper's house and office in Albion.[105] Before final arguments began, Bibbings summoned all the lawyers to the bench and instructed them not to disrupt any closing statements under penalty of removal from the courtroom.

Rodgers initiated his summation with a plea of dismissal of charges against Mahoney on the grounds that only Brown had implicated him. Moreover, he asserted, even if she was correct and Mahoney had been unfortunate enough to be in Albion on January 11, that alone would not constitute participation in a conspiracy. Turning to his legal foe, Rodgers said solemnly: "In all conscience and in all truth and in all sincereness, with all bickering aside, I know Mr. Sigler is not interested in sending anybody to the bastille for something he has not done. Mr. Sigler is a conscientious, very clever lawyer, an admirable exponent, a veritable Daniel, who comes to sit in judgment on cases. But I don't think Mr. Sigler can dig up any law which will contend to keep Mahoney and bind him over to another court, because that would be a cruelty and an injustice. The only thing Mahoney can be held for is the unproven fact that he went to Albion, and that is not a crime."[106]

As to the other defendants, Rodgers based his defense primarily on the character of their accusers. "Is this Court," he pleaded, "going to take the word of these rodents — Kurner, Luks, and Abramowitz — these smelly insects of the underworld that crawl on their bellies and only appear at night? Is the Court going to take the word of these men who have been kept and transported from jail to jail, in preference to the word of the defendants? The word of this Abramowitz, who has been arrested a hundred times? Who tells you very glibly how he's going to do a killing? Abramowitz, who says he was going to kill a poor, helpless father of a couple of youngsters? A cold-blooded killing for thirty talents? This Abramowitz, this slimy thing, who would hang four persons just to save his little neck? Abramowitz, who tells you that at the scene of the killing, on the roadside where the late Senator Hooper was killed, that — "[107]

Hesitating, all of Rodgers' frustrations and anger erupted suddenly. "You notice, Your Honor, how nicely that was built up," he fumed, "because naturally Mr. Sigler, the maestro of this little farce that has gone on here, told the man: 'Well, Rodgers and the other gentlemen are going to ask what size shoe you wear, so be prepared for it.' So, this morning, Abramowitz said, 'I wear a size eight and my feet fit the prints that were discovered.' Then in the same breath, he tells Your Honor, 'I have been granted immunity. I am protected from murder and conspiracy to murder.'"[108]

Eyes blazing, defense counsel strode to the prosecution table and thrust a finger in Sigler's face. "Are you really looking for the murderer, Mr. Sigler?" he roared. "You don't have to do that. Just take this man Abramowitz out by his boots! Take the man that puts a number eight shoe in that moulage! I say there is the murderer! But evidently only I am interested in seeing law and justice done here. The special prosecutor is interested only in granting him immunity! I ask, Your Honor, that these unwarranted indictments against my clients be dismissed."[109]

Sigler forced a wan smile, stung by the knowledge that Rodgers had, however inadvertently, correctly assessed his motives in the case, and then began his argument. "Do try to stay within reason, brother," he said softly to Rodgers. "Your Honor," he began solemnly, "I'm always pleased when attorneys for the defense try hard to favor their clients because it happens we live in a country where every man is entitled to a fair trial regardless of what he has done. Where every man is entitled to his day in court, and he has the right to be defended by capable and competent lawyers. I am, however, a little surprised at some of the arguments that my distinguished brothers have advanced, because they are arguments which I know, and they know, are ridiculous. My brother Rodgers can stand up here and argue until he's blue in the face about his dear beloved Pete Mahoney, but the question is not whether Pete Mahoney is guilty beyond a reasonable doubt. At a hearing, it is not necessary for the People to prove that. The only question which is before this Court is whether or not there is sufficient evidence to believe he should be tried. Remember that all these men are accused not of murder, but of conspiracy to murder. The People claim that these four men entered into a vicious and wicked conspiracy forged in that den of iniquity known as O'Larry's Bar, and they sent their stooges off to Albion to spy upon this individual who had testified before the grand jury. He was about to take the witness stand. He was about to give testimony of the most striking nature, that would have shocked Michigan."[110]

"I hate to interrupt you, Mr. Sigler," sighed Rodgers, "but there is nothing to show that Mr. Hooper was about to make any disclosures, startling or otherwise."

"If you were a gentleman," replied Sigler, "you would let me proceed, because you know it is true."

"You've waved the flag at me so long," yelled Rodgers, "that I begin to think I'm a bum."

"You are, in some respects," agreed Sigler. "You know Senator Hooper was about to disclose facts that would have sent some very important people to jail, where they belong."

"But, Your Honor," insisted Rodgers, "what Hooper was going to do, he didn't do, unfortunately, but it has nothing to do with this conspiracy case at hand."

"Am I going to be heckled the rest of the afternoon, Your Honor, by my distinguished — "

"You may," shot back Rodgers.

"Look, brother," Sigler explained, "the point remains that Warren G. Hooper appeared before the Carr grand jury and confessed to certain offenses and those offenses included important people. Following his confession, an indictment was issued on the second day of December against certain important people. It is a startling, significant fact that when that case was set for examination on the fifteenth day of January this year — that just four days before Hooper was to walk into a court of justice and raise his right hand to his God and tell the world the facts — he was murdered."

"If it please the Court, let me raise my humble voice," injected Rodgers again. "There is no connection with this case and the murder of Mr. Hooper. Mr. Sigler has concocted an imaginative something or other because he can't find the killer. So he decides to shoot for — "

"I'm going to ask Your Honor to definitely instruct this lawyer to sit down and keep his mouth shut," ordered Sigler.

"I won't. There is no murder charge here."

"Your Honor," Sigler shrugged in exasperation, "this is the kind of thing that smart lawyers like Mr. Rodgers have been doing to obstruct the work of the grand jury. If Mr. Rodgers was in the legislature, he would have been in jail a long time ago for this kind of crookedness."

Turning to his adversary, Sigler continued: "Oh, you can call it waving the flag or whatever you want to, but when it comes to the point that men who have the nerve and backbone to tell the truth about crimes that are committed against the people are murdered through a conspiracy hatched at the end of some bar — well, waving the flag or not, I'm going to bring them to the bar of justice if it be within my humble power to do it."

"I agree, Mr. Sigler," nodded Rodgers, "because I don't condone crime either, but there is no connection between my clients and any possible murder of Senator Hooper."

"If this man doesn't shut up, Your Honor," commanded Sigler, glaring at Bibbings, "I will ask the Court to have one of the officers come in here and take him out of the room."

"And that's exactly what will happen," promised the judge, "if you don't keep still and let Mr. Sigler finish."

"And just let him sell my clients down the river?"

"The very reason, Mr. Rodgers," fired Sigler, "that your clients conspired to commit murder is because a certain senator testified to the truth about men with enough money to pay Harry Fleisher $15,000 to silence him."

"That is reprehensible, and I will not be ordered to keep still just because you are a special prosecutor. I am paid, Your Honor, to protect the rights of my clients, not to sell them out and not to be scared off because someone is in power. This isn't the Gestapo. This is still the United States, and I am going to fight for my people. In Hitler's day — "

"If you are fighting, it will be in the corridor," snapped Bibbings, who signaled to a state trooper who, in turn, seized Rodgers by the arm and escorted him toward the door.

"You're denying my clients a fair trial! You're denying them their rights!" insisted Rodgers as he struggled to free himself. Meanwhile, Naomi Selik, who had been sitting in the first row behind the defendants, rose and gave a stiff-armed Nazi salute to Sigler before she turned and followed Rodgers from the room. Scattered applause rewarded her defiance.[111]

When order was restored, Sigler picked up on his earlier theme, outlining how "those fiendish individuals" plotted "one of the most terrible offenses in American history" and promising to bring them to justice. Anticipating a call for a change of venue, he argued that while the assassination had been committed in Jackson County and much of the planning had taken place in Detroit, the law allowed that conspiracy could be charged in any county in which an overt act took place. He contended that the several trips made to Albion to try to slay Hooper brought the case within range of Calhoun County courts. He concluded by urging that the defendants should be bound over "so this case may be tried and a jury pass on it so we can tell whether or not in Michigan the time has come when any honest man who has the guts and the backbone to stand up and tell the truth is not going to fall victim to someone lying in wait to murder him along a state highway."[112]

At the conclusion of Sigler's oration, Bibbings permitted Rodgers to re-enter the courtroom, and immediately the Detroit attorney began to reiterate his earlier views. Sigler objected, with the terse note that "we've heard his statement before for four days here, and I'm sick of it," which drew from Rodgers an equally curt, "Well, I'm not getting a particular thrill in looking at your kisser either, you know."[113] Justice Bibbings concurred with the prosecutor; then, without taking time to review the evidence presented, he announced that the Fleishers and Selik would be bound over to circuit court "to await a prompt trial on charges of conspiracy to murder the late Senator Warren G. Hooper." A decision on Mahoney, he said, would be rendered the following afternoon. Bail for the defendants was set at $25,000.[114]

Rodgers submitted that the bail was excessive and asked the Court for a reduction, adding, "I think Mr. Sigler might be agreeable to that, for a change." When Sigler refused, defense counsel responded disgustedly, "I figured you wouldn't agree, but I was trying to get a little milk of human kindness out of you."

"I haven't any human kindness for individuals who conspire to murder people!"

"You haven't proved it yet, sweetheart!" challenged Rodgers.[115]

The next day, Bibbings proclaimed that Mahoney also would be bound over for trial. "The reason for adjourning the examination of Mahoney was to determine for myself just what disposition to make of the case," the jurist explained. "I have carefully considered the evidence and find that on one occasion he was in O'Larry's Bar, where he talked with Sam Abramowitz; that Mahoney was a close associate of these defendants; further, that O'Larry's Bar was a meeting place for planning crime and keeping weapons, and that the evidence shows he was seen in Albion on the day Senator Hooper was killed.

In view of these facts, I believe he should be held on trial and his bond will continue at $25,000."[116]

Rodgers evinced total disgust over the entire examination. "The travesty of the hearing which was conducted here is sufficient evidence to prove that these men could not expect a fair trial in Calhoun County," he told newsmen huddled around him in the city hall corridor. "The testimony under oath by the state's own witnesses shows that the conspiracy, if any, was in Wayne County. Therefore, a trial, if any, should be in Wayne. Sigler has maneuvered these proceedings into his home county of Calhoun, where he has friends and influence. Having a heavy police guard gave the impression of grave danger, which was deliberately prejudicial to the indictees." As to the ruling on Mahoney, the attorney expressed incredulously, "Even the state's own witnesses said that Mahoney had no part in any conspiracy — even Sam Abramowitz said that."[117]

When asked to comment on Rodgers' statements, Sigler said merely that he wished "to commend the Court and all the officers for the excellent manner in which this examination has been conducted."

"Well, that is a self-serving comment," retorted Rodgers sarcastically, "but if the Court had ruled with me one hundred percent, I probably would commend it, too!"[118]

Two days later, at 10:00 a.m., the defendants were arraigned before Circuit Judge Blaine W. Hatch. All pleaded innocent except Sam Fleisher, who stood mute and had a plea of not guilty entered for him. The four were then remanded to the Calhoun County sheriff until Monday, May 21, when Judge Hatch said he would hear motions for a reduction of their $25,000 bonds. He also set July 9 for the start of their trial in Battle Creek.[119]

Sigler agreed to a defense request that attorneys have an opportunity to speak with their clients privately and collectively at any reasonable time. However, he stipulated that the state had no intention of lodging the defendants in a single jail because "these jails have been built for many years and it's not fair to the sheriff to impose this burden on him in addition to his other duties." He intimated that Harry Fleisher and Mike Selik might continue to be housed in the Ingham County jail, with Sam Fleisher and Pete Mahoney held in the Jackson County facility.[120]

In a twist of ironic symbolism, Harry Fleisher's 19 year old son Henry was present to see his father arraigned. Unlike his lawless parent, the younger Fleisher, a Marine Corps private, was a war hero. While Harry had spent much of the war years plotting armed robberies and murders, his son had earned a Purple Heart, a battle star, and service ribbons while fighting to preserve the American system of government.[121]

The following week, Judge Hatch reduced bail to $15,000. Sigler vigorously opposed the decision, imploring the judge to keep in mind that "we are not dealing with some youngsters who have committed a crime for the first time. We're concerned with a gang of Detroit hoodlums who sat in a bar and planned to murder a man who did not keep his mouth shut."[122] Despite Rodgers' joyous claim that his clients would be on the streets within hours, most courtroom observers sensed that their freedom would be short-lived and that the heavy doors of Jackson Prison soon would swing open to await their arrival.

Senator Warren G. Hooper
(Courtesy of Michigan Dept. of State Archives)

Kim Sigler
(Courtesy of the Michigan Dept. of State Archives
© John Henderson)

Leland W. Carr
(Courtesy of the Michigan Dept. of State Archives)

Frank D. McKay
(Courtesy of the Michigan Dept. of State Archives)

Callienetta Hooper
(Permission granted by The Detroit News, Inc., a
Gannett Newspaper, © 1945)

Harry Fleisher (Permission granted by The Detroit News, Inc., a Gannett Newspaper, © 1932)

The Purple Gang: Irving Milberg, Raymond Bernstein and Harry Keywell (Permission granted by The Detroit News, Inc., a Gannett Newspaper, ©1931)

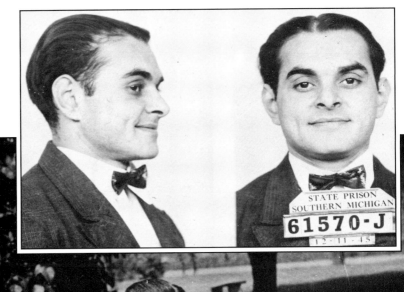

Myron (Mike) Selik (Courtesy of the Michigan State Police)

Jackson Prison inmates at the wedding of Deputy Warden D.C. Pettit's son.
Henry Luks (#2), Harold Johnson (#5) (Courtesy of Michigan Dept. of State Archives)

O'Larry's Bar (Courtesy of Michigan State Police)

Kim Sigler and Donald S. Leonard with State Police (Courtesy of the Michigan State Police)

Kim Sigler and his gubernatorial portrait (Courtesy of Michigan Dept. of State Archives)

Portrait of three State Police Detectives, Joseph Sheridan (center) (Courtesy of Michigan Dept. of State Archives)

Senator Hooper's automobile (Courtesy of the Michigan State Police)

Senator Hooper's grave site, Albion, Michigan (Hooper actually was born in 1904) (Courtesy of J.L. Loehr)

CHAPTER SIX

TOWARD THE
MAGNIFICENT OBSESSION

I During the six weeks between the arraignment of the alleged conspirators and the onset of their trial, Sigler maintained his high public profile by continuing efforts to bring legislative grafters to justice. After a four-day trial in early June, two chiseling lawmakers were ordered to jail for lining their pockets on horse-racing legislation.[1] Then, on June 16, Michigan's crusading white knight captured coveted national press coverage when he announced that Judge Carr had that morning signed a warrant charging Frank D. McKay and seven others — among them McKay's bodyguards Charles Leiter and Isadore Schwartz, former members of the Purple Gang — with conspiracy to violate the state's liquor laws in 1939 and 1940.[2] The grand jury's first indictment against McKay had collapsed with Hooper's death, but this time, Sigler had so sullied McKay's name with repeated innuendos implicating the Grand Rapids boss in the senator's murder that the prosecutor was convinced his foe would not escape.

II In a surprise move, on June 10, Sigler obtained warrants against Harry Fleisher, Myron Selik, Pete Mahoney, William "Candy" Davidson, and Samuel Chivas accusing them of the December 1, 1944 armed robbery of the Aristocrat Club in Pontiac. The robbery of owner James "the Greek" Dadas' illegal Oakland County dice joint had never been reported to the police, but during the murder conspiracy examination Abramowitz had mentioned that his arm had been bandaged during his trips to Albion. "I'll tell you how I hurt my arm," he had volunteered. "We stuck up a handbook in Pontiac early in December and I used my fist to smash in a glass door." Under prompting by Sigler, the witness had related that Harry Fleisher, Mike Selik, and Pete Mahoney had furnished guns to Luks, Davidson, and himself (Abramowitz) and had driven them to Pontiac to pull the heist. The purpose had been to harass Dadas because he had refused to give Fleisher "a piece of the joint."[3]

Sigler's move, while a shock to the general populace, had been carefully planned and followed several secret conferences with Oakland County's circuit judges and prosecutor, Donald C. Noggle. The entire grand jury staff had been brought to Pontiac to assist in the investigation, and two state police detectives had been assigned to work with local authorities gathering evidence. A special Oakland County grand jury subsequently was created specifically to examine the case. Sigler did all this over a relatively insignificant crime because the robbery represented a potential method by which to end the self-imposed silence of the Fleishers, Selik, and Mahoney as to who paid them to have Hooper slain. As Sigler was quick to note, the maximum penalty for conspiracy to murder was five years, but conviction for armed robbery could result in a life sentence. "That's what we can ask for in this crime," he explained, "and it may serve if we are unable to break further developments in the Hooper slaying."[4]

By late afternoon, June 11, all the defendants except Davidson had surrendered to authorities. Three days later, the noose around the defendants' necks grew tighter when Sigler announced that a Detroit waitress, Jeanette Welker, whom he described as "Harry Fleisher's sweetheart" (doubtless to encourage the gangster's wife to come forward in a jealous rage to testify against her unfaithful spouse), had been apprehended and was being held in protective custody by the state police. "She has important information on the whereabouts of Harry Fleisher on January 11," Sigler revealed, "and since Fleisher and Selik refuse to give us that information themselves, for her own safety she could not be released on bail. Also, since she is a person with no ties, if threatened she might try to flee."[5]

This new attempt to impel one or more of the alleged conspirators to talk aroused anxiety among the friends and admirers of McKay. Among such persons was Edwin Goodwin, editor of the *Michigan State Digest*, a weekly Lansing political newspaper, who was an ardent enemy of the Ingham County grand jury. A stylistic writer with a rapier wit, Goodwin had engaged in a steady stream of ridicule against "Sir Kim, the prosecutional generalissimo who considers himself an island of legalistic dynamism entirely surrounded by suspects."[6] In his June 20 editorial, Goodwin responded to a remark in the *Detroit Times* that "the bribery case against Frank D. McKay collapsed when the state's witness Warren Hooper was murdered." His comments reflected the direction McKay's defense would take should it become necessary to deflect accusations from the Detroit hoodlums:

Warren Hooper never said that McKay offered him or anyone bribe money, nor did Hooper say that anyone else had said that McKay had done so. Adroitly, Hooper cautiously said that money 'came *from* McKay,' not that McKay tendered it. Thus, subtly, Hooper's allegation carried with it its own loophole of escape from responsibility on Hooper's part. He could edge from under by insisting that he had never said that McKay offered anyone a bribe; but merely that he, Hooper, had understood that the money 'came from McKay.' Therefore, it's scarcely surprising that, as the *Times* says, the allegation is 'collapsed.' This statement of Hooper's would never convict. McKay must have known that if Hooper were to live and were to testify as above, namely, that it was the understanding of the witness that money 'came from McKay,' such testimony would do McKay no harm other than to redden his face should his name be mentioned at all in connection with so ignoble a subject. Therefore, incidentally, McKay could not in anywise benefit from Hooper's death.[7]

Having offered the reason why McKay would not have been involved in Hooper's death, Goodwin put forth an explanation as to why the senator would have tried to implicate McKay in an illegal act.

Warren Hooper, more than any other man then living, stood to profit and to escape prison, by promising the authorities thus to involve some notable person. It publically had been explained that there was 'no other way' to induce such as Hooper to 'talk' except under promise of immunity from prosecution and prison. Hooper, admittedly, was a bribe craftsman.... But, having become cornered, he also was quick to see that his one way out was to involve some 'big name' man, known through connection with public political affairs. Hooper positively knew that Governor Harry F. Kelly bore antipathy towards just such an outstanding Michigan political figure in his own political party, and that Kelly had publically announced his irrevocable purpose to affect that political figure's overthrow. Hooper knew that the Governor would not lack facility towards his avowed end. Hooper knew that every Governor has political favors to bestow.... In winning for himself immunity from prison, Hooper need not claim to have personal knowl-

111

edge that so and so or anyone in person offered a bribe. He would need only to insinuate and infer sufficient knowledge to appear to justify official inquiry. Therefore, not being dumb, Hooper knew precisely whom to seek to involve.[8]

By opting to defend McKay through defaming an assassinated martyr and one of the state's most popular governors, Goodwin must have brought a smug smile to Sigler's lips. The special prosecutor's foes were running scared.

III On July 3, Judge Hatch, who had been assigned to hear the murder conspiracy case, agreed to postpone its beginning until July 16. The one-week delay had been requested by Sigler on the grounds that the Lansing examination of McKay's liquor conspiracy charge was scheduled to start on July 5 and was expected to last as long as ten days. Overlapping trials, he argued, would work a hardship on the prosecution staff. Defense counsel concurred, primarily because they had previously claimed that the July 9 date did not afford them sufficient time to prepare their presentation.[9]

Harmonious relations were short-lived, as the hearing preliminaries grew stormy when Rodgers and Leitch moved to have the charges against Pete Mahoney quashed because of insufficient evidence introduced in justice court. Sigler contended that a conspiracy could be established through circumstantial evidence and that that had been done when witnesses testified that Mahoney had been in Albion the day Hooper was slain, had been present in O'Larry's Bar when the conspiracy was planned, and had been an intimate associate of the other respondents. "Evidence will disclose that Pete was one of the closest friends Harry Fleisher had," he promised. "Harry even took Pete along when he took his girl out. Most important, Your Honor, he was in Albion in January 11 for the specific purpose of acting as an outpost for this job." After vigorous objection from Rodgers, that final remark was stricken.[10]

In his rebuttal, Rodgers reminded the Court that only two of the state's ten pretrial witnesses even mentioned Mahoney. Abramowitz had assured Justice Bibbings that, to the best of his knowledge, Mahoney had not been involved in any conspiracy, while Evelyn Iris Brown had all but admitted that Mahoney had not been the man she saw in her tavern. "But even if that were not the case," implored counsel, "what difference would it make if Mahoney sat on Hooper's back fence on the day Hooper was killed? That doesn't prove a conspiracy." Calling for order, Judge Hatch said he would present a written decision. Then, before adjourning, he admonished attorneys on both sides to restrain themselves and "leave personal matters out of this case."[11]

The motion concerning Mahoney was rejected and, on July 13, three days before the case was to be heard, Leitch filed a motion for a separate trial for Sam Fleisher, saying that his client had "a good and meritorious defense which would be prejudiced if he was compelled to go on trial with the other defendants." He argued that since the arraignment of the four defendants, all but his client had been arrested on a robbery charge in Pontiac which had no connection with the murder conspiracy case and in which his client had been neither accused nor implicated. Turning his fury on Sigler, the normally mild-mannered lawyer bristled: "The spectacular tactics of the prosecutor, and the prominence of the persons accused, have resulted in the formation of a group of newspaper reporters and photographers who follow Mr. Sigler from place to place, and who write sensational articles concerning the trials that are highly prejudicial to Sam Fleisher. Many of these articles have contained false and detrimental statements concerning Sam Fleisher, describing him as being held for the Pontiac offense, as a hoodlum, a member of a gang, and these articles have mentioned underworld retribution, depict the arrest of a girlfriend witness, describe separation of the defendants in cells, and charge the defendants generally with being involved in many crimes and moral lapses, none of which apply to Sam Fleisher. The questionnaires answered by many of the 101 prospective jurors in this case indicate that they are regular readers of newspapers which have carried sensational and false stories to the detriment of Sam Fleisher."[12]

Rodgers then submitted a motion seeking a continuance until the September term of circuit court. Twelve reasons were cited, including claims that the charge of conspiracy gave the prosecution such wide latitude that the defense had not had time to prepare its case, and that the location of the trial was far removed from the residence and place of business of the defendants. Hatch took the motions under advisement, saying he would rule on them Monday morning.[13]

In its Sunday, July 15 edition, the *Battle Creek Enquirer* was guilty of exactly what had inspired Leitch's complaint. A front-page story sought to stir local passions, and perhaps prejudice prospective jurors, by predicting dramatics at the upcoming "sensational criminal trial." Sigler's pet theory that "prominent men, including Frank D. McKay of Grand Rapids, wanted Hooper dead" was set forth as fact. Sigler was glorified as the "dramatic and colorful" hometown hero who would unfold the "bizarre story" of the "coldly planned murder." Spectators were alerted that the special prosecutor would have to battle a new adversary, Edward H. Kennedy, Jr., a "wily courtroom practitioner" from Detroit, who had joined with Rodgers and Leitch in an unholy attempt to thwart justice. However, it confidently predicted a prosecution triumph because "Sigler would not be Sigler if he had not saved sensations."[14]

At 10 a.m. Monday, July 16, Hatch met with the attorneys. Press crews representing the United Press, Associated Press, *Detroit Times, Detroit News, Detroit Free Press, Battle Creek Enquirer,* and *Jackson Citizen Patriot* crowded together, note pads and pencils ready. A special room had been equipped on the fourth floor of the city hall with telephones and teletypes, the latter linked directly to the *Detroit News* and *Detroit Times.* Eagerly the reporters listened as Rodgers ambled forward to restate his motion for a continuance. Sigler responded by reminding the judge that the McKay and Aristocrat Club trials were scheduled for early September and October, respectively. "This is yet another attempt by the defendants and attorneys in this case," Sigler asserted, his light blue eyes flashing in anger, "working with the defendants and attorneys in the liquor graft conspiracy case against Frank D. McKay and others to stall the McKay trial. Your Honor, I would move to dismiss this conspiracy case rather than delay those other trials."[15]

"Does the prosecutor consider this case a sort of prologue to the McKay case?" fired back Kennedy. "After all, most of the state's witnesses in every case, including this one, are in the penitentiary — or should be there. We deny, individually and collectively, Mr. Sigler's contention that we are involved in any conspiracy to aid and abet the defendants or counsel in other trials." Hatch admitted that Sigler's accusation seemed unfounded, but still denied the motion for delay.[16]

Responding to Leitch's request, the judge noted that Sam Fleisher had been erroneously described as a participant in the Aristocrat Club robbery in several press accounts. "However," he ruled, "I believe such publicity would be as harmful for the defendant at a separate trial as it would be if he were tried with the others. The Court will attempt to see that this man is not prejudiced before the jury. We will not be trying these men for anything that happened in Pontiac." With that, he announced that the selection of a jury would commence at 1:30 p.m. that afternoon.[17]

Sigler whipped the process off to a fast start when, for twenty-two minutes, he dazzled the first tentative jury with a memory display. With machine gun-rapidity, he ran through the original jury selections, calling each by name, mentioning their residences and backgrounds, and discussing details of their lives. After this feat had been accomplished, and Sigler had implanted the seed with jurors that his memory was so exceptional it should never be questioned on matters of fact, the preliminaries settled down to the tedious choosing of veniremen.[18]

As the selection droned on, the Fleishers, Selik, and Mahoney sat stolidly with their attorneys and whispered exchanges among themselves. During intermissions, they playfully dodged news photographers in the city hall corridors, chuckling at every successful escape. At the urging of Kennedy, they eventually posed for one group picture.[19]

Finally, after a two-day, 8½-hour search, at 3:20 p.m. Tuesday, a predominantly rural jury of eight men and six women, averaging sixty years of age, was impaneled. Before final agreement, Sigler asked the entire group if any of them knew, or had political connections with, Frank D. McKay, William H. McKeighan, or Edward N. Barnard, but he offered no reason why such an association would disqualify them in the present case. He also inquired if anything they may have read or heard about him as grand jury prosecutor prejudiced them. Both queries were met with negative responses, and the taking of evidence began.[20]

Judge Hatch called upon Sigler to make his opening remarks, and, in an hour-long oration, the special prosecutor outlined the state's case. Beginning with a review of the lower court examination in mid-May, Sigler moved to a discussion of the nature of the charges against the defendants. "The state will prove that these men entered into a vicious conspiracy to kill Senator Hooper because he had testified before the state graft grand jury," he declared, moving along the jury box railing so that each member could see the grim determination in his eyes. "Hooper testified against certain men before the grand jury. He was an important witness in several cases. The purpose of their conspiracy was to silence his testimony. Remember always that it is not essential in a conspiracy that all parties meet together or that all should even be aware of the full plan. It makes no difference in the case whether or not the state proves that the defendants actually carried out their vicious, cruel plot. It is sufficient to prove that there was a general plan. It is the claim of the people that a conspiracy can be proved in this case in part by circumstantial evidence."[21] Momentarily removing his black-ribboned gilt nose-glasses, Sigler launched into a slow, forceful, meticulously detailed account linking each defendant to the crime. Despite his air of supreme confidence, Sigler harbored a secret dread. As he spoke, he reanalyzed each juror and pondered what he must do — not to win, but rather to retain, their confidence in his righteousness and that of his cause. Six housewives, six farmers, a retiree, and an automobile dealer: all old-fashioned, middle-class citizens with a deep-rooted belief in the traditional values of hard work and honesty — people who had done their best to live their lives by the Ten Commandments. Could they, despite their sworn oaths that it was immaterial if a witness was a convict, not let it subconsciously color their opinions? Could they be convinced that would-be assassins and armed robbers were capable of telling the truth? Could they cross that invisible barrier which separated their concepts of right from wrong and align themselves with admitted evil-doers to achieve social and legal justice by avenging the death of a local martyr? If this was to be his finest hour, Sigler knew it could be attained only through his finest effort.

"The state will prove," he continued, "that Harry Fleisher and Mike Selik, reputed by police to be members of the Purple Gang, received $15,000 to arrange Senator Hooper's death. They met at O'Larry's Bar, owned and managed by Mike Selik's brother Charles, on December 23, 1944, to plot the crime. They were joined in the saloon by Henry Luks, a habitual convict. Fleisher and Selik knew Luks by reputation. He had recently been paroled from prison for the third time. They tried to hire him, and did hire him, to go to Albion and murder Hooper. Mike Selik and Henry Luks had been buddies for some time. They met in a saloon at Boston and Dexter, which was their habit. Harry Fleisher and Mike Selik knew Luks' reputation as a sort of expert on explosives. They wanted him to get dynamite to attach to Hooper's car. Their scheme was to blow Hooper up when he stepped on his starter. The people will show that Fleisher promised Luks $5,000 to go to Albion and rub out this man. We will prove that Luks came back to O'Larry's Bar after a few days and told Fleisher and Selik he had failed to get dynamite and so the deal fell through. We will produce not only Henry Luks to tell his story, but also Sam Abramowitz and Alfred Kurner, both ex-convicts, who will testify how they entered into the conspiracy to murder Hooper."[22]

Extending his left arm toward the defendants, who had sat expressionless during the discourse, Sigler singled out with his index finger the suave, blond, younger Fleisher. "The state will prove," he solemnly asserted, "that this man, Sam Fleisher, not once, but twice, drove the gunman hired by his brother Harry and Myron Selik on missions of murder. Both times he had to return to Detroit in failure."[23]

When Sigler had embarked upon his remarks, 90 degree temperatures and high humidity had made the courtroom uncomfortable. By the time he neared his conclusion, it had been transformed into a Turkish bath. Women jurors refreshed themselves with palm leaf fans furnished by the court, while male panelists swabbed their faces with brightly colored bandanas. While not perspiring noticeably, Sigler did not wish to appear superior in any way to his audience, so he, too, withdrew a white handkerchief and dabbed his forehead before turning his attention to the fourth defendant, Pete Mahoney.[24]

Addressing the jurors, he piqued their curiosity by intimating that the close ties between Harry Fleisher and Mahoney might have brought them together as partners in the actual murder of Hooper. "The state will produce evidence," he promised, "that Mahoney was Harry Fleisher's best friend. The evidence will show that Harry Fleisher never went anyplace without Mahoney. Last Christmas, Mahoney was the only outsider to have Christmas dinner at Harry's home. Pete Mahoney sat in the Top Hat Tavern in Albion on the day that Hooper was murdered and a man built like Harry Fleisher sat across from him, with his hat pulled down over his eyes, and nervously watched the clock as he consumed beer."[25]

Sigler ended by pledging to prove that Harry Fleisher, after several unsuccessful attempts had been made on Hooper's life, told accomplices that he and Mike Selik would do the job themselves. Court then adjourned until 9:00 a.m. the next day, when Henry Luks would be the first of the state's twenty-three scheduled witnesses.[26]

Despite a forecast for continued blistering, record-breaking heat, Sigler arrived in court on Wednesday in all his fabled sartorial splendor. Garbed in a light tropical gray suit, red and white striped tie, a red point-pressed handkerchief showing swankily from his breast pocket, and white shoes with spats, he seemed to be defying the elements. No matter what the conditions, he always maintained his carefully cultivated courtroom image of imperturbability.[27]

Wearing a new tan sport coat, black tie, and dark brown slacks, Luks placed his hand on the Bible to swear to tell the truth. Reporters snidely remarked among themselves that state-supplied meals obviously agreed with the witness, as he had put on weight while in custody since his earlier testimony.[28]

Sigler guided Luks through a reiteration of his statement at the hearing, and then turned him over to defense counsel for cross-examination. Kennedy, along with Maurice Walsh of Chicago, had assumed the defense of all the defendants except Sam Fleisher when

Rodgers resigned to protest Judge Hatch's refusal to grant a continuance. He now began to grill Luks in an effort to undermine the witness's credibility. "When were you arrested, Henry," he asked, "and where have you been held since your arrest?"[29]

"I was first arrested and tried for this particular case," Luks stated in a firm voice, "when I was working at the REO plant in Lansing. I came back from Detroit the day after Easter, which was on April 1, and the following night I was called into the office at work and the police took me down to the Olds Hotel and questioned me until about two o'clock in the morning. I was lodged for two days in the Lansing City jail, and then I was taken to the Michigan State Police headquarters in East Lansing and had a lie detector test. They told me I was lying and to come back in a week. I told them I wasn't lying. They gave me a few more tests, but I was never in custody after them two days until Sam Abramowitz confessed. Right now I'm in the custody of the Michigan State Police at the Battle Creek Post. Before that I spent five or six days at the Ingham County jail and at a jail in Charlotte, near Lansing. I was never held in the Olds Hotel. I talked there, but I never slept there."[30]

"You did tell the state police a different story later than you first told them, didn't you, Henry?"

"That's right. When I first went before the grand jury I refused to testify on the ground I might be incriminating myself. I refused to come in and tell what I now claim is true until the State of Michigan granted me full immunity from all prosecution."

"Isn't it correct," badgered Kennedy, "that you didn't tell what you now claim to be true until Mr. Sigler said to you, in effect: 'You come in here and tell this jury what you claim to be facts and, even though you admit it to be a fact, we won't prosecute you?'"

"I ask that remark be stricken, Your Honor, and ask that the Court read Section 17.220 *Compiled Laws of 1929* so that the jury may understand the rules regulating the issuance of immunity." Hatch sustained the objection and, overruling defense complaints, read the statute to the panel.[31]

"Mr. Luks," asked Kennedy, "is it your understanding right now that even if it should develop eventually that you had something to do with the actual killing of Senator Hooper, that nothing you say here could be used against you?"

"To tell the truth to you, I'm not worried about that. My parole officer told me to tell the truth," Luks smirked, "and I always thought that if I was implicated in murder they could use what I said."[32]

118

"When you get to drinking pretty heavy, Henry, like you were the night before your trip to Albion, are you likely to do things that you don't know anything about?"

"Well," smiled the witness shyly, "sometimes when I drink pretty heavy I don't remember where I've been or what I did."

"That's a pretty good defense, too, isn't it?" sneered Kennedy, as Sigler arose to protest "another typical smart crack" by his opponent.

"But I do remember everything that happened on December 25 and 26, Mr. Kennedy," insisted Luks gravely, "because it takes at least twenty to thirty three-quarter-ounce shot glasses of liquor to get me that drunk, and I only had fifteen and a couple of bottles of beer Christmas night and the next morning."

"Thank you, Henry," said Kennedy with obvious sincerity, as he noticed the look of shock and disbelief on the jurors' faces. "I have no further questions."[33]

The special prosecutor then summoned Al Kurner to the stand and requested that the slim, well-groomed youngster recount his dealings with Sam Abramowitz. "I had a talk with Sam Abramowitz on December 18, 1944, in his apartment. There was a young lady on the floor of the bedroom sleeping. Sam was trying to get rid of her for an hour and a half," he recalled with a grin. "After she finally left, he asked me if I was still game to make that $3,000 he had told me about earlier at O'Larry's. I told him I sure was. He told me we had to bump off some guy. He didn't say where, just that it was about two hours from Detroit. He said they first were going to try to get to him with money, but if he didn't meet the terms, we'd kill him. He said some fellow would drive us there, and we would shoot him in his office."

"Did he tell you the politician who testified lived in Albion?" prodded Sigler.

"I object to counsel leading the witness with suggestive questions," protested Kennedy.

"All I've been doing," replied Sigler innocently, "is trying to get the facts. My brothers sit there, talk with each other, and suddenly come to life here part of the time. However, rather than listen to a speech from Mr. Kennedy, I'll strike the question."[34]

Court adjourned until 9:00 a.m. the following day, at which time Kurner was cross-examined with the intent of raising doubts as to his veracity. Next to testify was Detective Inspector George Branton, twenty-four-year veteran of the Detroit Police Department, who verified that he had accompanied Abramowitz to Albion and that the mobster had pointed out Hooper's house and office. Sigler then moved to call the Senator's widow as a witness. Surprised, because her name had not been among those endorsed before the trial, Judge Hatch ordered all counsel into his chambers.[35]

Kennedy strongly opposed the request, saying that Mrs. Hooper's presence in the courtroom with her two small children was damaging enough to his clients, without adding what would certainly be a "highly prejudicial" appearance on the stand. The defendants, he argued, were strangers in the community and had been prejudged in the press. Producing the widow, he feared, could be the "last straw" in the minds of the jurors.[36]

Sigler pledged that his only intent was to ask Mrs. Hooper to identify the pictures of her house and her husband's office. Hatch consented to her endorsement, but cautioned the special prosecutor that he would not tolerate anything beyond those limited inquiries.[37]

IV During the interlude, Mrs. Hooper's children became restless, and when four-year-old John stood on his chair seat, the bailiff asked him to behave. Shortly afterward, she and the children went into the corridor. Surrounded by reporters shouting at her, Mrs. Hooper, looking tired but cool in a white, two-piece, cotton pique suit and small white hat, held a press conference. "After I testify," she anticipated, "I'll take the boys home. Naturally, I want to attend the trial, but the boys are too small. They're awfully good, but they are just not big enough to sit through all that. Ever since this happened, we've been poison in Albion. I can't get anyone to stay with them." Hearing this, the elevator operator offered to let the boys ride up and down with him for the rest of the day and then to find a nearby nursery for the future.

"Do the kids know what happened to their father?" insensitively pried a scribe from the Associated Press.

"Oh, yes, the children know all about what happened. We had to tell them. Bobby is in school and naturally the children talked about it. Of course, John is too little to understand. He knows his Daddy is dead, but he also knows he went away and didn't come back. Now whenever I leave him, he's afraid I won't come back either."

"What are you doing now that the senator's dead?"

"I'm taking care of two children and a fourteen-room house. I don't have a job yet. So far I have been trying to keep the little tea company together that my husband started as a sideline, but it doesn't mean any income."

When a reporter pressed the financial issue, Mrs Hooper evinced her first real emotion of the interview. "People think we got money from the state, but we haven't — not even funeral expenses. People should know there was no state pension, even though it was promised by the state. All I got was $45 due my husband for the first eleven days of his work this year."

Asked how her suit against the senator's insurance company — which refused to honor the double indemnity clause on the technicality that Hooper's death was not accidental — was progressing, she replied, turning to reenter the courtroom, "Whether or not we get it, I guess, depends a lot on this case."[38]

V Mrs. Hooper was on the stand for less than five minutes, but her impact was substantial. Jurors were moved when she identified photograph's of "Daddy's office" and said softly that her husband's desk chair was situated so that the back of his head could be seen from the roadway. As she stepped down, she barely glanced at the state's next witness, Sam Abramowitz.[39]

Abramowitz began by recounting how he had met the defendants. He and the Fleishers had grown up in the same Detroit neighborhood, but he knew Sammy better because they were closer in age. Harry Fleisher had introduced him to Pete Mahoney at O'Larry's Bar in 1944, and he had become "good friends" with Mike Selik while they both were serving time at the Ionia (Michigan) State Reformatory.[40]

Sigler then ordered the slight, would-be assassin to tell the jurors how he participated in the conspiracy contrived by the defendants. "Well," he said nervously, "on the twenty-sixth of December, 1944, I arrived at O'Larry's Bar around midnight with Al Kurner and five other people. We sat at a corner table in the back room. I saw Harry Fleisher, Mike Selik, and Henry Luks sitting at a table in the front of the same room. After about forty-five minutes, Pete Mahoney sat down with us, but when Mike Selik came back Pete walked away. Mike asked me if I wanted to go on a job with Henry Luks. I said sure, and Mike went back to talk with Henry. Mike then hollered for me to come join them at their table, which I did. Either Harry or Mike asked if I knew anything about dynamiting a car. I said I didn't. Harry and Mike then started to talk about how to do the job. Henry didn't have anything to say. Since the guy was supposed to be a doctor of nature, or something like that, and I had my arm in a sling, Mike suggested we go to Albion and I could walk into his office and have him examine my arm, and Henry could sneak in behind him and hit him on the head. Then we could kill him in any way we saw fit. We also talked about catching him on a secluded spot on the highway and killing him there. We discussed shooting him. Strangling him with his belt or necktie was mentioned, but Henry Luks and myself didn't want to do it that way. Mike said there was $15,000 in escrow, and that Henry and I would split $5,000. Mike Selik said the guy was mixed up with the grand jury in Lansing, but didn't mention his name."[41]

Head bowed, Abramowitz repeated the stories first told in justice court about his initial trek to Albion with Harry Fleisher, Mike Selik, and Henry Luks to case the area, and about his later two unsuccessful murder missions with Sam Fleisher. In the midst of his account of Sam Fleisher warning him that there was a deadline of Thursday, January 11, for the killing, court adjourned until nine o'clock the next morning.[42]

When he resumed his tale, Abramowitz admitted being on Harry Fleisher's payroll. "I started getting money about the first of December, 1944, and received amounts varying from $10 to $50 throughout that month and January, 1945. He gave me the money either at O'Larry's or his place on Twelfth Street whenever I asked for it. I would say the total amount of money Harry Fleisher gave me was around $300-$400."[43]

Having demonstrated to the jury that Abramowitz was a trusted henchman of Harry Fleisher and Mike Selik, Sigler skillfully extricated his star witness from further complicity in the crime by having Abramowitz explain his fear of being slain by Sam Fleisher. "The last time I spoke to either Harry Fleisher or Mike Selik about this matter of the murder of this man was Tuesday, January 2. I am certain that January 2 was the last time I had anything to do with it," he added for emphasis, his hands tightening around the arms of his chair. "I asked Harry Fleisher if there were any more chances to get down there. He said, 'No, I think Mike Selik and myself will do it ourselves.'"[44]

Cross-examination by defense counsel tried to establish doubts in the jury's mind as to both Abramowitz's character and truthfulness. Leitch managed to gain an admission from the witness that he had "misspoken" at the hearing about on which trip Sam Fleisher stopped to purchase eggs. "I testified at the examination that it was on the second trip I went with Sam, but it was the first time," he explained, in an earnest tone. "It was the second time I had gone to Albion, but not the second time I had gone there with Sam Fleisher."[45]

Walsh elicited that Abramowitz was a frequent, heavy drinker, harbored no remorse about the thought of taking a man's life, had a reputation for felonious criminal activities, had willfully lied to authorities for nearly a month concerning his role in a murder conspiracy, and could have been mistaken when he said he met the defendants in Detroit on December 26, as it might have been the following day. Under Walsh's unrelenting thrusts, Abramowitz admitted that he had been wrong earlier in the trial about the deadline date for Hooper's slaying, confessing that it was not January 11, but rather January 2, a Tuesday. Even his shoe size was reduced from the 8 which fit the imprint at the murder site to a $7^1/2$.[46] By the end of his appearance, Abramowitz's credibility seemed all but destroyed.

After Abramowitz left the box, the remainder of Friday afternoon and early Monday morning saw Sigler desperately try to restore the jurors' confidence in his chief witness. The special prosecutor produced Clarence Chapman and Peter Blyveis, the junk dealers with whom Sam Fleisher had visited while in Albion; Mr. and Mrs. Earl Nice, the farm couple from whom Sam Fleisher had bought the eggs; and Maurice Cuyler, an Albion service station owner, who had been working on Hooper's car in early January when Sam Fleisher dropped by to talk for a few minutes. Each positively identified Sam Fleisher, and the Nices swore that Abramowitz had been Fleisher's companion on the day of the egg purchase.[47] It was not much, but it was the best Sigler could do to show that Abramowitz was capable of telling the truth.

Evelyn Iris Brown was sworn in and repeated her story of Pete Mahoney's visit to her Albion beer garden on the day of the senator's death. Upon receiving the witness for cross-examination, Leitch and Kennedy launched a ruthless assault on both her memory and character. It was shown that over the years she had falsified her birthdate on a marriage certificate, been mistaken as to the exact year of her divorce from her first husband, and was unsure of the year in which she was born. When Sigler protested Leitch's line of inquiry, the attorney replied, "Mr. Sigler has asked the jury to believe this woman, Your Honor. I'm simply trying to show she cannot be believed." Hatch concurred with the defense.[48]

Kennedy continued the onslaught, asking Brown about her positive identification of Mahoney. "It was that man," she swore, pointing at Mahoney. "I'm sure it was him in the tavern. When Officer Hoeg came in to question me the first time, it was about some ex-boxer who was alleged to have been in my place and who was a suspect in the Hooper murder. I didn't know the man. The next visit by Mr. Hoeg was a few weeks later. He brought 20-25 pictures in an envelope and asked me to see if I recognized any of them as being in the tavern on January 11. I said no, but there was one who resembled a man who was there. Both had deep lines in the side of their mouths. At the time, I didn't know whose picture I had seen. He didn't tell me. Now I know it was Sammy Abramowitz."[49]

As a gasp went through the room, Sigler rose to re-examine his beleaguered witness. "We understand that the picture was not of Pete Mahoney," he reassured, "but merely resembled the man in the Top Hat. However, have you ever made an identification of Pete Mahoney in person?"

"Oh, yes," she nodded. "When I was at the Jackson Michigan State Police Post, Captain Hansen, Detective [Edward] Johnston, and some other officers took me to a little room in the back, which had a window covered by venetian blinds. The blinds were drawn so I could see through the cracks. About ten feet away, Pete Mahoney was standing outside on the sidewalk with three other men and a state trooper. Captain Hansen asked me if there was anyone out there that I ever saw before and I pointed to Mahoney. I didn't know who the others were at that time. I had never seen them before. I later found out from the officers that they were Harry Fleisher, Sam Fleisher, and Mike Selik."

"I object," blustered Walsh, "to this lady telling us who the police officers said the other men were. That is hearsay evidence."

"Your Honor," implored Sigler, "these gentlemen have questioned this lady's identification of Pete Mahoney in a long, gruelling cross-examination. I have a right to show what actually took place when she pointed out the defendant Pete Mahoney."

"You have that right," agreed Hatch. "Let the answer stand."

"You may step down, Mrs. Brown," Sigler said sympathetically, all the while hoping that the jurors would retain only the latter part of her testimony.[50]

The prosecution's next witness was Harry Richards, Jr., owner of Albion Motor Sales, who had known Sam Fleisher since 1935. Like Cuyler, he stated that Sam Fleisher had been in Albion on January 9 or 10. He had talked with the witness for 30-45 minutes in the corridor between the showroom and parts department, never taking his eyes from Cuyler's service station across the street.

"Can you give us the gist of the conversation you had with Sam Fleisher on that occasion?"

"Well, he asked about my father and brother. Then he asked me what some of the boys were doing that he used to be connected with in the local junk business. I told him what I knew. Also, he told me his past experience for the last few years."

"Is that all you can remember?" urged Sigler expectantly.

"Well, he told me his experiences at Alcatraz."

"I move that be stricken," thundered Walsh, his face reddened, "and that the jury be instructed to disregard it. I also have a motion to make, but not in the presence of the jury."

"The objection is overruled, and I will meet counsel in my chambers. Court is recessed until 1:30," Hatch snapped, rapping his gavel.[51]

During the break, all three defense counsel moved for a mistrial. Kennedy sternly claimed that the remark about Alcatraz was so highly prejudicial that any opportunity for a fair trial was now precluded. "It is common knowledge, Your Honor," he lectured, "for anyone who is of age that Alcatraz is a federal penitentiary where the most incorrigible convicts are sent. Any reference that a man might have been in any prison is prejudicial, and when you say he was in Alcatraz that is the ultimate in stigma. Even if Your Honor were to go back and instruct the jurors to disregard the remark, it would be like rubbing salt on an open wound. It is one of those things you cannot remove. It is like driving a dagger in a man's back and pulling it out. The dagger is removed, but the fatal wound is still there."[52]

Walsh seconded his comrade's motion, claiming that the prosecution had "purposefully and intentionally dragged in something on direct examination which he could properly bring out only on cross-examination of Sam Fleisher."[53] Hatch continued to listen in silence, eyes closed and arms folded across his chest as he reclined in his high-backed chair.

"Your Honor," Leitch began, shaking his head, "I agree with what Mr. Walsh and Mr. Kennedy have said, and I, too, ask for a mistrial because it is now apparent these defendants cannot have a fair trial. The prosecution has known for a long time that the picture Mrs. Brown identified was of Sam Abramowitz, yet he did not furnish that evidence to the defense. Moreover, Officer Hoeg, who knew about the identification, has not even been endorsed to be a witness in this case." Glowering at Sigler, he continued scornfully: "It has never been the intention of the prosecutor to give these defendants a fair trial."[54]

Totally unmoved by these diatribes, Sigler adjusted his cuffs, flashed a cold smile at his adversaries, and began to slowly pace the floor near the judge. "Your Honor," he sighed, "the shoulders of the prosecutor are broad. It has been the sincere effort of the prosecution in this case to be absolutely fair. Counsel for the defense has cleverly attempted throughout the trial to claim that the prosecution was attempting to prejudice the rights of the defendants. That's an old procedure. It is axiomatic in trial work to attempt to try the prosecutor or try the prosecutor's witnesses. With regard to this matter, I was not trying to bring out this particular fact. I was attempting to show that Sam Fleisher went to the garage to lie in wait for Senator Hooper, and that thereafter he went into the showroom of Richards' garage where he could look across the street and observe the actions and conduct of the senator. My good faith inquiry was to establish that he went to the garage and showroom to do one or both of the following: one, to establish an alibi; or two, to be in a position where he could observe Senator Hooper. I promise this Court and counsel that I had no intention of bringing out anything about Alcatraz. When counsel for the defense have the temerity to stand up before this Court and claim that I have intentionally intended, and attempted, to prejudice these defendants, then I am convinced that either they are overly sensitive on this hot day, or they are simply attempting to make a mountain out of a molehill in an effort to try the prosecuting attorney."[55]

"But, Your Honor," injected Leitch, "the fact still remains that he surrendered Mrs. Brown to us without bringing out the fact that she had identified Abramowitz's picture."

"I don't agree," shot back Sigler. "You blew up before because you know you haven't a leg to stand on. But because I want to try this case fairly and impartially, I am willing to have Mr. Hoeg endorsed. In fact, Mr. Leitch, if you continue to yell constantly that I am unfair, I want the jury to hear the facts from Mr. Hoeg, so I can watch you run for cover."[56]

Hatch agreed, and at 1:30 Bion Hoeg was sworn in. After recounting his meetings with Mrs. Brown, he explained the procedures he used and the results. "I took thirty pictures of individuals taken by various police departments and prisons. Included was one of Mike Selik, but not of the other defendants. No one else was present in the Top Hat Tavern with us. I handed her the pictures and she sorted through them. She came to this one, marked Exhibit 48, the picture of Sam Abramowitz, and said that the fellow who was in the Top Hat Tavern the day Hooper was killed had this man's features, only he didn't have a moustache and the wrinkles on his face around his mouth were deeper. She didn't say he was the man who was in the tavern, only that the picture resembled the man. That was the extent of her identification, so far as the picture was concerned." Defense counsel had no questions and after Hoeg was dismissed, court was adjourned until 9:00 a.m. Tuesday.[57]

VI Despite a forecast for sunny skies and continued scorching temperatures, Sigler knew that Tuesday did not bode well for him. Days earlier he had been tipped by Kenneth McCormick, his *Detroit Free Press* confidante, that on July 24 Michigan Attorney General John R. Dethmers was planning to release to the press the first of four daily installments of his report on conditions at the Southern Michigan Prison at Jackson. For seven months the state police, Corrections Commission, and the attorney general's office had been busily gathering evidence, and the long anticipated findings were sure to grab the headlines from the Hooper trial. The timing of the release bothered Sigler, who felt that the attorney general was a potential rival for the Republican gubernatorial nomination in 1946. Since Sigler's carefully planned dream of power rested majestically, if precariously, on the outcome of the Battle Creek case, he nervously awaited Dethmers' pronouncements so that he could plot his counteroffensive.[58]

A wily politician, Dethmers knew that the initial report would receive the most public attention, so he made certain the Tuesday revelations would be the most shocking. After presenting a copy of the report to Governor Kelly, Dethmers somberly met media representatives at the state capitol and related some of the horrors he had uncovered when he "tore the lid from the world's largest walled prison." Prominent hoodlums such as Mike Selik, Ray Bernstein, Harry and Phil Keywell, Raymond Fox, Joseph Medley, and Henry Luks, had received favored job assignments. For a price, a more desirable cell block was assigned. At least ten bookies operated within the prison, handling large and small wagers on horse races and ball games. Several inmates established pawnshops and loan shark operations, while others, working in the kitchen, pilfered large amounts of nutmeg for the manufacture and sale of drugs known as "speedballs." For fifty dollars, the attorney general revealed, Deputy Warden D. C. Pettit would allow private conferences to be held in his office between incarcerated Purple Gang leaders and known criminals such as Harry Fleisher and Mike Selik. Pettit often hired "lifers" to serve as houseboys and entertained inmates in his own home. Several prisoners, including Henry Luks, were invited to the wedding of Pettit's son and posed for a group photograph in the deputy warden's new red roadster.[59]

In tones of righteous indignation, Dethmers accused Harry H. Jackson, warden of the prison for fifteen years, of allowing the institution to devolve into a brothel. For a one dollar bribe, a nurse would admit a prisoner to the infirmary under the guise of showing dangerous symptoms, especially a high fever. "Thereafter," he explained, "the inmate could have a female visitor in bed with him behind a screen or a sheet hung over the doorway." More prominent inmates were afforded the luxury of having liaisons in the warden's office. Mike Selik, while serving as the warden's houseboy, met his future wife, Naomi, when she was visiting her imprisoned current husband. In a less-than-storybook romance, Mike and Naomi became lovers and, after each visit to her husband, she had a tryst with Selik either in the warden's or the deputy warden's office.[60]

What should have been the most significant revelation was dimmed by the lurid, titillating sex scandal. As many reporters scurried to the telephones to try to scoop their rivals, Dethmers recounted that prison cars often had been used to "run liquor from O'Larry's Bar in Detroit to D. C. Pettit's home, where it was consumed by inmates and prison officials." On several occasions, Pettit himself went to Detroit with inmates and returned in a drunken stupor. On other times, favored prisoners were permitted to leave the prison, while still officially "on count" as being in their cells, to visit houses of prostitution in Detroit and Jackson, to go to Detroit Tiger baseball games, or to attend weekend parties at resort cottages owned by prison officials. In every instance, prison automobiles were utilized and civilian garb was furnished by prison officers.[61]

Dethmers concluded by charging that Jackson, Pettit, and others impeded the investigation by telling inmates not to testify. He alleged that Jackson promised an inmate that if he refrained from telling the truth about prison affairs, the warden would "do something for you when this blows over." The attorney general stated that Jackson and Pettit had even conspired to frame the escape of certain inmates and then blame it on a guard "who happened to be president of the CIO local" when the union pushed for an investigation in 1941 on charges of mismanagement in the prison.[62]

Later in the day, Jackson — a crude, lumbering, obese man who fit the Hollywood image of a warden — issued his expected perfunctory disclaimer of any wrongdoing. "It's the first time I ever heard of more than half the purported incidents which make up Attorney General Dethmers' report," he announced gruffly. "All of us know that when one has that purpose in mind, the meaning of comparatively innocent acts may be twisted to imply something far different. Those inmates at Pettit's son's wedding, for example, went not as guests, but to help with the arrangements. One was a musician. I will not discuss the charges until the report is complete. This prison administration, in due time, will make a full statement. Until then, there will be no piecemeal discussion."[63]

In Battle Creek the response to Dethmers' account was immediate. When court opened on Wednesday, defense attorneys Walsh and Kennedy filed a motion for a mistrial on the grounds that release to newpapers of stories about prison irregularities was highly prejudicial to Harry Fleisher and Selik. Walsh read into the record accounts of Dethmers' statements as reported in the *Detroit Free Press, Detroit News, Detroit Times,* and *Battle Creek Enquirer.* Defense counsel also had the attorney general subpoenaed as a witness in support of their motion. During Walsh's reading, court was recessed briefly to enable Judge Hatch to answer a telephone call from Dethmers, who wished to know if the subpoena was official. The judge assured him it was and instructed him to "come to Battle Creek right away."[64]

Shortly after 11:00 a.m. the attorney general, escorted by state police troopers, entered the courtroom and took the witness stand. Spectators in the packed courtroom eagerly leaned forward in anticipation of seeing the state's chief law enforcement officer being grilled by both defense and prosecution lawyers.

After Walsh elicited the information that the attorney general possessed no proof to substantiate his statement that Selik and Henry Luks had met at O'Larry's Bar to plot Hooper's murder or that the murder plan might have been hatched, and even carried out, by inmates of the prison, Kennedy probed into Dethmers' career in Republican politics and his experiences as a prosecuting attorney. During the questioning, Dethmers agreed that no criminal trial should ever be interferred with by the issuance of personal opinions; but he categorically denied that he had ever stated, even though he may have intimated, that his findings would solve the Hooper assassination.[65]

As defense counsel hammered at Dethmers' apparent improprieties, Sigler nonchalantly leaned back in his chair and maintained a stoic silence. Annoyed by the tone of certain queries, Dethmers plaintively sought protection from the court, saying to Judge Hatch, "I notice that the prosecution is getting back to the practice of making no objections to any questions."

"Do you think I should be making objections?" Sigler shot back sardonically.[66]

Judge Hatch interjected with the suggestion that the remainder of the prison report be withheld until completion of the conspiracy trial. This was emphatically spurned by Dethmers, who explained: "In view of the loose practices outlined in the report, I felt it was important that we impress upon the state's Corrections Commission the necessity for immediate action." He assured the judge that the third section, to be released the next day, would have "no bearing on this case whatsoever," but he reiterated that "things are so bad at the prison that it is imperative action be taken at once."[67]

Sigler then set upon his adversary with a fury nurtured by political ambition. The jury having been dismissed until the mistrial motion was decided, the special prosecutor approached the bench and angrily informed the judge: "This action by the attorney general is nothing new to us, Your Honor. Ever since Judge Carr and I started to bring politicians to justice, attempts have been made to frustrate our efforts. Men such as Frank D. McKay, John Dethmers, and others like them — politicians — are willing to give their bottom dollar to see something happen to cases coming out of the grand jury. And let there be no doubt, Your Honor, John R. Dethmers is a bedfellow of Frank D. McKay and is only interested in helping himself politically."

Wheeling, Sigler strode menacingly toward Dethmers, who involuntarily winced in expectation. "You have been both a criminal lawyer and a prosecutor in your career, haven't you?" Sigler fairly shouted.

"Yes, sir," came the curt response.

"You never liked to have the People's witnesses plastered all over the papers when you were prosecutor, did you?"

"What do you mean by plastered?"

This display of feigned innocence only stirred Sigler's wrath. "Oh, come on now. Answer my question. You know what I mean."

"No, I don't," smiled Dethmers.

"I mean besmirched," Sigler screamed, holding up a copy of the *Detroit Free Press* with a five-column picture of the inmates at young Pettit's wedding. "Where did they get that picture to print in the newspaper?"

"I gave that picture to the press," said the witness, who now began nervously tapping his fingers on the arm of his chair.

"Did you know that the man identified as number 2 in the picture was Henry Luks?"

"I didn't know," murmured Dethmers, still tapping his fingers.

"You didn't know?" gasped Sigler incredulously. "Oh, come on! Let's talk plainly about this!"

"Take it easy, Kim. Take it easy," urged Dethmers in a soft voice that held both a plea and a warning.

For the first time since the trial began, Sigler showed the effects of the stifling courtroom. Fury had accomplished what nature could not achieve. His collar wilted, the silver hair matted, and perspiration eavestroughed down his temples. Shaking his fist, Sigler raged on. "Oh, I'll take it easy, all right. When did you hand out this picture to the newspapers?"

"I believe it was last Monday."

"After this trial had been on for a week?"

"I didn't know just when the trial started," admitted the attorney general amid snickers of laughter from the spectators, who were bemused by the ever-increasing admissions of ignorance on the part of the witness.

"Didn't you release the prison scandal reports in installments in order to spread the publicity out over a longer period?"

"No," replied Dethmers, obviously pleased to be able to answer a question, "if I were going to spread it out, I could have released it weeks apart and got more publicity." Again, whispered laughter snaked through the gallery as onlookers asked each other if the attorney general regretted not following that course.

"Didn't it ever occur to you that the release of this story might hurt the lawsuit that is going on here? As an old prosecuting attorney, didn't it impress you that it might do irreparable harm?"

"No, it didn't and it doesn't now. I don't feel it would do any harm and I don't now. It was my utmost desire to avoid influencing this case," solemnly intoned Dethmers. For a third time, spectators turned to each other, asking how the attorney general could avoid influencing a case which he did not even know was taking place. Dethmers' performance was clearly galling his constituents.

"Didn't it occur to you," pressed Sigler ruthlessly, "that the statement in the press that the Hooper murder may have been committed by someone in that prison might take the heat off the four defendants?"

"No, and I don't think so now."

"Didn't it occur to you that by distributing that picture of Henry Luks, one of the state's top witnesses, in the company of murderers and rapists, you would be doing the people of Michigan irreparable harm?"

"No," asserted Dethmers flatly, perhaps never comprehending that by this time he had convinced everyone that absolutely nothing had ever occurred to him.

Sigler dropped his chin, gazed at the floor deep in thought, and shook his head while walking slowly to his seat. Turning to face Dethmers again he said softly, "And to think you're the attorney general of Michigan — the attorney general." With a wave of his hand, he then announced that he had no further questions.[68]

Judge Hatch promptly ordered a noon recess. Following the hour's adjournment, the judge asked for closing statements. Sigler, having changed clothes, approached the bench looking cool and composed. "Your Honor, I submit that when the attorney general uses the press for an opening campaign statement, it is pretty bad. I further submit that the defense has not been hurt. It has been the state's case which has been damaged. He named Henry Luks, who was the state's principal witness, as one involved in prison scandals and then has the temerity to say that he wouldn't believe a convict or ex-convict under oath unless it were corroborated. If anything happens to this case as far as the People are concerned, no one but Dethmers will be to blame. Dethmers was the leading light in the Republican party when Frank D. McKay was boss. Jackson Prison has been rotten for years, but it wasn't until Judge Carr and your humble servant got close to them that they did anything. Then this attorney general — this former bedfellow of Frank D. McKay — got busy. It is ridiculous for him to say that his report has to be issued at this time. Politicians like him want to see the grand jury fail, but it will not. In September we are going to do our best to put that crooked political boss McKay where he belongs."[69]

Kennedy was also critical of Dethmers' action in announcing the prison investigation while the Hooper case was in progress. "I have been fortunately, or unfortunately, mixed up in Republican politics," he said soberly, "but I got disgusted in 1936 and left. I want to say that I never thought I would see the day when the attorney general of the state would take the stand and say that when he issued a report like this that he didn't believe it would affect this case. And it wasn't a completed case. It was like writing a play in four acts with the grand finale to come on Thursday. If public officials would pay more attention to their jobs and less attention to getting their names in the headlines, maybe we would have better officials. A condition has been created here by the state's chief law enforcement officer where it is now impossible for these defendants to get a fair trial. I'm here to defend them on the charge made on the information. I didn't come in to answer an opening campaign statement by Mr. Dethmers."[70]

Walsh echoed the two previous speakers, saying that Dethmers' report was "of such general interest that it will be associated and discussed so widely that the jurors cannot help but being affected. Copies of newspapers with the story have already been found in quarters used by the jurors. I am sure that the court does not want this case to proceed beyond the probability of a fair trial. I find it difficult to believe that this was not done purposefully. And what does this prison story do? It induces the possibility that the defendant Myron Selik might have killed Hooper and even includes Dethmers' conjecture that perhaps a convict was let out of Jackson Prison to kill the senator and then come back to jail and establish an alibi by never having been reported as absent from his cell."[71]

In making his decision, Judge Hatch joined the others in chastising the attorney general. "I feel it may be my duty to deny the motion for a mistrial at this time. I don't feel that the published reports are prejudicial to this case. It is unfortunate that the attorney general handed out his report at this time, but that does not show that this jury will be prejudiced by it. I believe the Court can give the jury a charge and make allowances for every right of the defense and that a just verdict will be brought in." Court was then adjourned until 9:00 a.m. Thursday.[72]

Without doubt, Dethmers was both personally and politically damaged by this episode. Any chance he might have had for the governor's race was gone. The verdict on Sigler's performance, however, was less certain. His admirers boasted that their hero "Sir Kim" had slain another would-be dragon. More objective political analysts wondered about the wisdom of Sigler's intemperate tirade against one of his party's most influential members. Michael Gorman, prominent Republican editor of the *Flint Journal*, berated Sigler for an "unfair and ridiculous" blast upon a "forthright and courageous" public servant. He deplored the special prosecutor's mudslinging and praised Dethmers for not engaging in similar tactics. Even the friendly *Detroit Free Press* editorialized that the verbal battering of Dethmers had earned Sigler the wrath of powerful men in the Republican party. It also pointed out that few, if any, knowledgeable persons believed Sigler's charges linking Dethmers with McKay. The attorney general had been the leader of the anti-McKay forces since 1941 and it was his active anti-bossism that earned Dethmers the Republican state chairmanship in 1942. Facts notwithstanding, Sigler was very pleased with his performance. He had maintained his image of a crusader against evil and had once again invoked the specter of Frank McKay in the trial. The people still loved him and, as he smugly confided to his staff, it would be the public, not the party leaders, who would select the next governor.[73]

Sigler's good fortune continued when, with little public fanfare, Governor Kelly ordered Warden Jackson, Deputy Warden Pettit, and five others suspended and placed State Corrections Commission Director Garrett Heyns in control of the prison. An ardent admirer of Sigler, the new acting warden could offer invaluable assistance to the special prosecutor in his ongoing search for the actual killers of Hooper by giving him inside information on convict gossip about the murder.[74] Kim Sigler must have fancied himself at that moment the luckiest man alive.

VII As if the prison scandal report had not been enough to try Sigler's patience on Tuesday, he also had encountered unexpected courtroom problems earlier in the day with one of his own witnesses. Jeanette Welker, the strikingly attractive 26-year-old, red-haired paramour of Harry Fleisher, was the state's key witness linking Pete Mahoney to Harry Fleisher. All eyes were upon her as she moved to the stand, attired in an expensive black dress, pearl earrings, and a black hat worn at a jaunty angle. A black veil hid most of her face from the jury. Since May 18 she had been held in the Kalamazoo County jail as a material witness because she had been unable to post a $5,000 surety bond. Physically she showed no effects of that ordeal, but it obviously had embittered her, for when she faced Sigler her jaw was firm and her thin lips were set in a tight sneer.[75]

She answered numerous preliminary questions, relating her early years in Fort Wayne, Indiana, before moving with her mother to Detroit in 1936. For several years, she stated impassively, she had worked as a secretary. Then, in January 1943, she accepted a job as kitchen manager at O'Larry's Bar.

"Why did you leave a respectable position with an accounting firm to take over the kitchen in that bar?" asked Sigler.

"I thought it would be a good way to make money."

"Wasn't it really because you wanted to be near Harry Fleisher?" smiled Sigler as he deftly led her toward the important testimony.

"Yes, it was a case of six of one, half a dozen of the other."

"When did you start going out with Harry Fleisher?"

"Since July 1942, I have seen him occasionally."

"Did he assist you in paying the rent for your apartment?"

"No," whispered the witness, withdrawing a large white handkerchief from her handbag and wiping away tears.

Stunned, Sigler's eyes widened and he stood momentarily speechless. Smiles were exchanged at the defense table, while reporters, wondering at Sigler's shocked expression, asked each other, "What is it? What's wrong?"

"Your Honor," intoned Sigler, having regained his composure, "this is not the same testimony the witness gave to the grand jury on May 18. Consequently, I request that this witness be declared hostile."[76]

Judge Hatch recessed court briefly to meet counsel in his chambers. He declared that he would not consent to Sigler's request until a question which was material to the case was asked and the witness's response clearly was contradictory to her prior testimony. Upon returning to the courtroom, Sigler resumed his interrogation.[79]

"Did you go out with Harry Fleisher?"

"Occasionally."

"Did you see Mike Selik around the bar?"

"Yes."

"Did you see Harry Fleisher and Mike Selik together?"

"Well," she replied sarcastically, "if they owned the bar they would naturally be together."

Ignoring the impudence, Sigler asked, "When did you leave O'Larry's Bar as an employee?"

"August 1944, after I got into a fight with the bartender. I hooked on at Turk's Music Bar and then the Gold Dollar Bar on New Year's Eve."

"Did you go places with Harry Fleisher when Pete Mahoney was along with you?"

"A couple of times. We went out to eat."

"Isn't it a fact, Miss Welker," Sigler pressed, staring into her veiled, defiant eyes, "that every time you went out with Harry Fleisher, Pete Mahoney went along, too?"

"No, sir."

"What places did you go with Harry and Pete?"

"I can't remember any places," she snapped with contempt.

Judge Hatch immediately rapped his gavel and announced that the witness would henceforth be considered hostile and subject to cross-examination by the state.[78] Thanking the Court for its consideration, Sigler began to read from a transcript of her grand jury testimony and then inquired, "Do you remember being in your apartment the day after the Hooper murder with Harry Fleisher?"

"I believe so. But did I say that Harry was definitely there with me? I think maybe I just spoke with him on the phone."

"Didn't you read about the Hooper murder in the newspapers?"

"Oh, yes."

"And didn't you testify before the grand jury that you asked Harry if it was his brother Sammy who was involved in the case and that Harry said, 'I don't know. Could've been'?"

"Gee, I just don't remember, but I really don't think so," came another sneering retort.

Straightening herself, she lifted her veil and with wide-eyed innocence asked the judge, "May I please try to clear myself of any impeachment of myself, Your Honor?" Angered by her betrayal, Sigler stood before the prosecution table with folded arms, waiting to hear what tale would issue forth from her less-than-reliable lips.

"Well, Your Honor, when the newspaper writings first appeared," she explained, "I saw where Sammy was supposed to be in Albion. I asked Harry, 'Was that supposed to have been Sammy that had been there?' I said, 'Are they trying to get Sammy into it?' Then Harry said, 'What the hell would we want to have anything to do with a case like that?'" Turning from the judge, she glared at Sigler with unconcealed hatred. "Your grand jury stenographer must have gotten it mixed up. It was noisy there. You asked me to take off my hat because the judge couldn't see my face and to talk louder because the clerk could not hear me."

Adjusting his nose-glasses, Sigler thanked her for that information. Without warning, he then shot, "Did Harry Fleisher ever deny knowing about the Hooper case?"

Before she could respond, Kennedy leapt to his feet shouting, "This is a fair example of what happens in that grand jury! I object!"

"Are you casting aspersions on Judge Carr and the grand jury?" challenged Sigler.

"No, just on you and your tactics," yelled Kennedy, now nearly nose to nose with his adversary.

Judge Hatch rapidly and repeatedly gaveled for order and the bailiff escorted Kennedy back to his seat. All remarks were stricken from the record and each attorney was advised to respect proper decorum. He then asked Miss Welker whether if released from custody she would make herself available for further questioning. "I certainly will," she promised. "I don't like the bedbugs in that jail." She was led to an adjoining office where she began to sob loudly. "Must be for effect," Sigler wrote on a note passed to Victor Anderson. "What a performance. What a day."[79]

VIII When the Thursday session convened, the atmosphere in the courtroom was noticeably less electric than that of the two preceding days. Initially, Sigler suffered an apparent reversal when Judge Hatch sustained a defense motion that none of Jeanette Welker's testimony relating to Harry Fleisher's visits to her apartment or conversations with her was admissible and therefore was to be stricken from the record. The special prosecutor accepted the decision without comment because he knew, as do all lawyers, that despite the judge's admonition to jurors not to consider what they had heard in making their decision, it was impossible to blot that testimony, or the manner in which it was given, from their minds. He was certain Jeanette Welker would be remembered by the veniremen and that this would not help the cause of the defendants.[80]

The prosecution's first three witnesses that day were Albion residents who verified that Sam Fleisher had been in their city a day or two prior to the assassination of Hooper. Henry Richards, Sr., an automobile dealer, nervously stated that he had known Sam Fleisher since 1935, but quickly added that he had not seen him for nearly nine years before he dropped in at the dealership for a visit on January 10, 1945. He said Fleisher told him his car was at the Buick Garage being repaired. After two or three minutes, Fleisher left.

Louis Robinson, owner of the garage to which Fleisher brought his overheated 1941 Pontiac to have a new thermostat installed, recalled that the date was January 9 but added he could be mistaken. He noted that there were two other men with Fleisher. "One looked like a Jew, chunky like Sam but shorter. The other one was short and skinny. Maybe 5'6" or 5'4". He was dark and looked like an Italian." The third witness, Guy Vroman, a farmer, drawled that he was in the garage "on either January 9 or 10," when Fleisher drove in. They talked about Sam wanting to buy a truck — if he could find a good one — for use in his Eaton Rapids junk business. Vroman smiled when he recalled, "I told Sam he should have bought mine when I offered it to him a few years back." He corroborated Robinson's descriptions of Fleisher's two companions and then was excused. Sigler sensed that the jurors no longer harbored any doubts that Sam Fleisher, for some unknown reason, had been in Albion shortly before Hooper's death. A thin smile fleetingly crossed his lips as he knew the web of circumstantial evidence he had woven was forming Fleisher's shroud.[81]

Next on the stand was Sergeant Leo Van Conant of the state police detail assigned to the grand jury. Over defense objections, he swore that Judge Carr had issued a warrant, which he had served, for the appearance of State Senator Warren G. Hooper to offer testimony at the trial of Frank D. McKay and others on charges of corrupting the legislature on a horse racing bill.[82]

Sigler's final witness was Ingham County Prosecutor Victor C. Anderson, who confirmed that all charges against McKay and others in connection with the horse racing legislation had to be dropped as a result of Hooper's death. The small, bespectacled prosecutor accusingly added that Hooper would have been the principal witness against McKay in a pending case alleging corruption on state highway legislation, which also had to be dropped.

Once again, Sigler had deftly swung attention from the defendants to Frank D. McKay, the man he desperately sought to prove funded the slaying. Sometimes subtly and other times bluntly, the prosecutor's thrust throughout the trial had been to intimate that McKay not only was endangered by Hooper's potential revelations, but also possessed both the financial resources and gangland connections to have the senator's lips permanently sealed. Pleased with the morning's accomplishments, Sigler abruptly announced shortly before the noon recess that the state rested its case.

Defense counsel summoned only one witness, Clare Spears. The District Supervisor of Paroles in Detroit testified that in December 1944, he was residing in Flint and serving that area. Under probing by Kennedy, he claimed to have seen, and spoken with, Sam Abramowitz in front of the Flint Tavern in Flint at approximately 11:20 p.m. December 27, 1944. That was the same night that Abramowitz testified he was plotting with Harry Fleisher and Myron Selik in O'Larry's Bar in Detroit. "I also talked with Abramowitz in Flint about two or three days later," he added, which would have been during the time Abramowitz swore he was making a trip to Albion and he was living in Detroit hotels.

"How did the defense find out about this?" demanded Sigler.

"I don't know," insisted Spears, "unless it was learned from my written report on Abramowitz I filed with my department in March 1945."[84]

With this important blemish on Abramowitz's veracity fresh in the jurors' minds, Kennedy rested the defense. Judge Hatch proceeded to dismiss the jury until 1:30 the following afternoon so that he might hear a defense motion for a directed verdict of acquittal for Pete Mahoney.[85]

For nearly two hours, defense attorneys peppered the judge with arguments in support of their position. "There is not a word of evidence to show that Mahoney has done anything to further a conspiracy or to make one possible," Walsh told the Court. "The state is asking us here to guess a man guilty — to convict him on conjecture." Leitch methodically read nearly a dozen court decisions covering culpability in conspiracy cases, which the judge patiently received while leaning back in his high-backed chair, his arms folded, his eyes closed. Then Kennedy arose and flew into one of his usual flamboyant, emotional presentations. "I want to read what the state said in its opening argument that they were going to prove about Pete Mahoney," he stated, his voice resounding through the packed gallery. "They said he was Harry Fleisher's best and closest friend and confidante and that he was Harry Fleisher's guest at Christmas dinner; they said that he was seen in Albion on January 11 with a man closely resembling Harry Fleisher. None of these things have been proven in this court. Where is the evidence, Your Honor, to support what Sigler was going to prove? I submit that Mr. Sigler cannot have it both ways. If he insists that Henry Luks and Sam Abramowitz are telling the truth, then they must be believed when they say that Mahoney was not a part of this alleged conspiracy." Tossing the transcript aside, Kennedy threw a look of hate, tinged with disgust, at Sigler before sitting down to hear the prosecutor's response.

In reply to his "learned brothers in the law," Sigler put forth a lengthy recitation of precedent-setting cases involving proofs required to establish a conspiracy, with emphasis on the manner in which circumstantial evidence could be utilized. In contrast to his behavior during Leitch's reading, Judge Hatch now leaned forward attentively, as though hanging on Sigler's every word. This was not lost on Kennedy who, in anticipation of an appeal, jotted a note on the judge's behavior in his notebook. "Little significance might be attached to single acts of this defendant," Sigler concluded, "but when they are all strung together they comprise a set of circumstances which involve Mahoney."

Sigler had barely taken his seat before Judge Hatch rendered his decision to deny the motion. Again, Kennedy scribbled in his notebook. "I attach great significance," the judge proclaimed, "to the fact that at this trial, Mr. Abramowitz testified that on Christmas night at O'Larry's Bar, Mahoney sat down with Abramowitz, and that Mahoney, after calling Myron Selik to the table, walked away. In the lower court hearing, according to the record, Abramowitz claimed that he merely greeted Mahoney, but did not sit with him. I see no reason not to allow the jury to decide on his fate as well as that of the other defendants." With a bang of his gavel, he rose and retired to his chambers.

As the gallery emptied, Kennedy haphazardly stuffed papers into his briefcase, whispered something to Walsh and Leitch which elicited grim smiles, and stormed away, brusquely shunting aside reporters with a terse, "No comment." By contrast, Sigler, calm and self-assured, exchanged light-hearted banter with the press and promised that there was much fireworks yet to come. As he left the courtroom all smiles and waves, no one could doubt how he had captured the public fancy with his contagious enthusiasm. There never had been another like Kim Sigler.[86]

IX For nearly two long, hot weeks, an endless maze of testimony and arguments had assaulted the jurors. Now it was almost over. The panel prepared once again to be pleaded with, shouted at, and cajoled to use their great intellect to further the cause of justice. Subconsciously, they confronted the approaching climax with conflicting emotions. It was a time-consuming and tedious task, but never before in their lives had they felt so important.

Appearing somber in a dark blue suit and matching tie, Sigler paced in front of the jurors before launching his opening argument. In a soft voice which commanded attention, he reiterated his earlier explanation of the leeway allowed by law in conspiracy cases. "It is not necessary," he reminded them, "that each conspirator knows the others engaged or that they meet together or that one must have knowledge of what the others are doing or that each knows the plan as a whole. I submit to you that the state has established that a diabolical conspiracy of wicked men was born and bred in the wicked den of iniquity that is O'Larry's Bar in Detroit. There sat in that den of iniquity two of these defendants — Harry Fleisher and Mike Selik. These men undertook to hire killers for 15,000 lousy dollars that had been put up to rub out a man who had talked too much. They plotted the death of Senator Hooper as if he were a rabbit! They went at it as you would buy a bag of oats!"[87]

Point by point, he refreshed the jurors on the scheme which had been outlined during the nine days of testimony, graphically detailing the accounts of Luks and Abramowitz going to Albion with Sam Fleisher to case the job. "They went in Harry Fleisher's big Cadillac," Sigler said scornfully as he directed the gaze of the less-than-affluent panel toward the defendants. "The big shots in the front seat and the scurvy little hired killers in the back. They stalked the senator like a hunted animal because they had been told his lips had to be sealed. But unlike a hunted animal, he had no chance. Oh, to think that a man's life, my good brothers and sisters, should be taken because he went before a tribunal of the People to tell of graft and corruption in high places."[88]

Adroitly shifting direction, the special prosecutor reflected on the work being done by Leland W. Carr and himself in ferreting out improprieties in state government through the grand jury system. He briefed the jurors on the testimony Hooper had presented before the grand jury against Frank McKay — testimony which had been rendered worthless because of the senator's mysterious death four days before McKay's trial opened.

Playing on the admiration in which Carr was held by mid-Michigan residents, Sigler, in a tone generally reserved for a worshipful son toward his father, praised the grand juror as "a stalwart old circuit judge — a stalwart judge who is performing the sacred duty of investigating graft and corruption." He then set forth a lengthy and devastating arraignment of "political interference" in the judge's efforts, such as that of Dethmers a few days earlier, and concluded with a plea that the jurors never forget that "the grand jury is the People's tribunal, set up to protect democracy against corruption, wickedness, and sin."[89]

Having spoken for slightly more than an hour, Sigler closed by telling the jurors, who, like the spectators, were spellbound by his Bryan-like oratorical prowess, that "the people of Michigan owe a debt of thanks to Sam Abramowitz and Henry Luks for, despite their unsavory pasts and selfish motivations for testifying, such crimes as this would never be solved without their coming forward. Thank God we are permitted to grant immunity to men such as them." Dramatically raising his arms skyward, as if making an oath to God, he vowed: "Somewhere, sometime, the law will find the man who put up that dirty, lousy money, and someday, God grant, that man who passed that money to these men will be brought to the bar of justice."[90] Applause erupted and Judge Hatch permitted it to continue briefly before restoring order.

The prospect of following such a spectacular performance in no way awed Maurice Walsh. Smiling, he approached the jurors and stated frankly, "You have heard the state's case in the way Mr. Sigler wanted you to hear it. Now I'm going to show you how it was that Mr. Sigler heard about it."[91]

The affable but hot-tempered Irishman recounted Al Kurner's letter to Judge Carr advising the jurist to see him "before my trial" if he wanted to learn who killed Senator Hooper. "Who was Kurner talking about?" he asked rhetorically. "It wasn't these defendants here because he had no dealings with them. No, he was talking about Sammy Abramowitz. Then, after Kurner's story, Abramowitz was arrested either for Hooper's murder or for investigation of the murder and he was in the soup. Abramowitz says he sat in jail twenty-five days saying nothing. Isn't it fair for me to infer that Sammy may have been asked by Mr. Sigler if Frank McKay gave him the money, and kept asking him that same question? Finally, Abramowitz made up his mind that that was what Sigler wanted to hear — so he told him. It took him twenty-five days to think it out, but that's pretty good for him. Sammy wanted to get out, so he slipped them the McKay angle. When Luks then was confronted by Abramowitz, Sammy said: 'Come on, Luks, hear my story — repeat it — and you'll get immunity, too.'"[92]

Grinning sardonically at the scowling prosecutor, Walsh continued. "Sammy Abramowitz learned his story so well from Mr. Sigler that the prosecutor in his argument today made the same mistake that Sammy did. Sammy first testified that he and Sam Fleisher stopped to buy eggs on their second trip to Albion, but when Mr. and Mrs. Earl Nice failed to confirm this, he changed his story. But today, Mr. Sigler had him buying eggs on the second trip, just as Sammy Abramowitz had first related. Mr. and Mrs. Nice are reputable citizens like yourselves and they wouldn't change their story. But Abramowitz will change his story. He'll tell any story he thinks will fit this case."[93]

Walsh refused to let up in his ridicule. "More than fifty exhibits were introduced during this trial," he sighed, "and most of them were photographs of various places and buildings introduced by Mr. Sigler." Holding the entire collection in his hand, the attorney moved toward the jury. "Mr. Sigler introduced picture after picture in this trial. I sat there, just like you, waiting and wondering what big development is coming now? But nothing ever happened! Look at these again. The outside of O'Larry's Bar, the inside of O'Larry's Bar, another picture of the inside of the bar, and, look, here's another picture of the outside of the bar!" Hurling the packet of photographs onto the prosecution table, Walsh spat, "All your pictures are just plain bunk, Mr. Sigler. Just plain bunk!"[94]

Regarding the story of Henry Luks, Walsh implored the jurors to apply logic to the state's theory concerning the alleged initial attempts on Hooper's life. "Does it make sense to you intelligent people that, as he claims, Luks was brought from his home in Lansing to Detroit in order to be driven to Albion to stalk a state senator who was still in Lansing because the legislature was in session? That is nonsense, yet Mr. Sigler expects you to believe it. Also nonsense is Mr. Sigler's contention, based on the stories of Luks and Abramowitz, that Harry Fleisher and Mike Selik had cased the job thoroughly and knew all about Hooper. If that is true, why did Luks and Abramowitz never even see Hooper? The closest they came was to spot the back of a bald-headed man's head, who somebody said they thought might be Hooper. How does this tale of ineptitude demonstrate a diabolical, well-conceived plot? The answer is, of course, that it does not, simply because the state's witnesses lied."[95]

"What Sigler has done here with his poor evidence he has done beautifully," Walsh smirked, "but after all, his story depends upon just two witnesses, Luks and Abramowitz. You pull them out and the house of cards falls down. I further compliment Mr. Sigler on the way he shocked you at the start of this trial. They were going to blow Hooper up with dynamite. However, when we asked Luks to trace all his movements, he had made no effort whatever to get any dynamite. Mr. Sigler must have forgotten to tell Henry something."[96]

In reference to Sigler's descriptions of Judge Carr, the grand jury, and Frank McKay's alleged improper activities, Walsh somberly lectured the jury: "Kim Sigler wants you to join his anti-McKay crusade. I don't object to you joining if it's outside this court. The information charges these four defendants with conspiracy to murder in conjunction with an added person unknown. Mr. Sigler tried to tell you who the unknown person is. He wants you to infer that Frank McKay put up $15,000 to have Hooper killed. I don't think Mr.

Sigler believes that himself, because if he does believe it he should have Frank McKay down here with the opportunity to have counsel and to defend himself. If you bring in a guilty verdict here, it will be a help in the Lansing case against McKay. But you jurors are not a prologue to the McKay trial. If you find these men guilty on the theory of the state, you will be finding McKay guilty in his absence. Why didn't Sigler continue his investigation and get the murderer? I'll tell you why — he needed a conspiracy trial to precede the McKay case! You're being asked to take part in a political football game and these defendants are the footballs."[97]

Having laced the jury with these rapid blows to the body of Sigler's case, Walsh withdrew in favor of Leitch who picked up the onslaught. He urged the jury to consider not only the witnesses who took the stand, but also the potential witnesses the state failed to produce. "Luks claimed that he had a waitress telephone for him to notify Selik that he was dropping out of the job," Leitch recalled. "With all of the facilities of the state police, why wasn't that girl here to confirm that story? At O'Larry's Bar it was claimed that the place was open for business and many other persons were present while this conspiracy was going on. Several were supposed to be at the same table, such as Dave Mazroff and a girl named Avo. We can assume that these people were interviewed and that their stories might not have been wanted. But wouldn't you jurors have liked to have heard some testimony from someone who has not been granted immunity?"[98]

After detailed factual review of the evidence from the defense standpoint, Leitch closed with an opinion on the so-called "McKay angle." "Is it sensible," he posed, "to believe that a man in McKay's position would hire a killer simply because a confessed bribe-taker like Hooper had accused him of something? I don't really think so, do you?"[99] With that, Judge Hatch recessed court until Monday, July 30, at 1:30 p.m.

X The weekend afforded Sigler the opportunity to reflect upon what damage, if any, had been inflicted by Walsh and Leitch. Sitting alone in his office Saturday morning, his mind was probably comforted by the thought that contrary to defense contentions, his case did not rest flimsily on the testimony of two ex-convicts. Rather, it was solidly based on an intangible quality which was immune to all assault — the character of the jurors. He had always been pleased with the panel because, while he did not know them individually, he was familiar with their collective mentality. He could feel that they were haunted by the specter of having to face their friends and families if they turned their backs on the chance to free the state from having these four known felons walk its streets, and by the prospect of having to live with the knowledge that any crimes committed by the defendants in the future would have occurred because they refused to put these men behind bars. Their consciences simply would not allow any verdict but "guilty", and, Sigler reasoned, they would not listen to defense arguments even when, as they had on Friday, they contained a goodly amount of truth. Still, his pride was at stake and public ridicule had to be rebuffed. It would be rough-and-tumble improvisation on Monday, but that was when his quick and biting wit was most sharply honed.

Opening his desk, he spied the golf ball-embossing machine given him by Bill Cook. Pleasant memories flashed through his mind. Closing the drawer, he picked up the phone, dialed his old Hastings friend, and set up a round of golf for that afternoon. Perhaps dinner would follow, complete with reminiscence of his days as president of the Rotary International. It would be a cheery weekend, after all.[100]

XI On Monday, Kennedy surprised everyone with his calm demeanor and verbal restraint. In measured tones, he implored the jury not to be lulled into losing sight of the facts by Sigler's siren songs. "Mr. Sigler told you that defense counsel are blackening the character of his witnesses by referring to their prison records," he began, "yet, in truth, did they not blacken their own character by telling you what they are? Mr. Sigler himself, if you recall, called his witnesses professional, paid, scurvy little killers. Of course, there has been no testimony to substantiate his claim, but by reasonable inference it could be assumed that Sam Abramowitz was the killer. Is it not possible that Henry Luks and Sam Abramowitz — the Sam Abramowitz who admitted that his shoe fit the imprint of the murderer's found at the scene — could have hatched the plot themselves at O'Larry's Bar, committed the crime and, after being caught, decided to drag in their former friends who sit here as defendants? Remember, by their own testimony, when Luks arrived at O'Larry's Bar he did not join the big shots, Harry Fleisher and Myron Selik. No, he went and sat down with Sam Abramowitz. Ladies and gentlemen, I ask you, if Sam Abramowitz was willing to hire himself out to do the murder, why could he not have actually done it?"[101]

Looking consolingly at Sigler, Kennedy shrugged his shoulders and gently suggested, "You may have given immunity to the assassin. I really think you have made a mistake in this case, Kim. I really do."[102]

Returning his attention to the jurors, Kennedy pursued his litany of purported prosecution confusion and error. "Why did Sigler bring Jeanette Welker in here as a witness anyway?" he demanded in louder, more fiery tones. "Is that just an act? Mr. Sigler does keep talking about the drama of it all. Did he bring Miss Welker here simply to testify that Harry Fleisher did or did not pay her rent? What does it matter? Why did he waste our time?"[103]

Whirling to face the special prosecutor, he spat forth questions: "Who's behind this case? There's a lot of talk about a big shot politician being behind it, and if that's true, Kim, why isn't he here charged with this crime? If you have the evidence in this lawsuit, why haven't you charged that great politician not with conspiracy to kill, but charged him along with these defendants for murder?" Scornfully, he turned to the jurors and answered his queries. "You see, no matter what, Mr. Sigler feels he has to get the politicians he is going to try in later cases involved in this case in some way. Maybe he believes that it is McKay who is on trial here. I don't know. But you know that he isn't."[104]

When Kennedy concluded, Sigler addressed his adversaries in a closing statement. "On Friday, Mr. Walsh, you claimed that this trial was necessary for success in the upcoming McKay trial. Well, Mr. Walsh, I tell you to go back to Chicago where you belong and tell everyone there that we don't need this trial to convict Frank McKay. We have plenty of evidence for that trial in September to prove that McKay did certain things." Thoughtfully staring at Kennedy, he inquired: "Why do you and your co-counsel keep talking about McKay and trying to defend him? Why don't you ever say anything about Floyd Fitzsimmons or William Green who were named in the same warrant? It sure sounds like you are McKay's lawyers more than those of the defendants! But I can assure you, and the jurors, and the people of the state of Michigan, that if we had the connecting link between Frank McKay and Harry Fleisher, who got the $15,000, we wouldn't be here. We'd be in Jackson County trying a murder case!"[105]

"You think I made a mistake in this case, do you, brother?" he smiled. "Well, let me tell you, if Sammy Abramowitz is the killer, then Judge Carr, the state police, and myself are a bunch of fools, and I don't believe we are. I have made no mistakes. You can't get a witness to a conspiracy-to-murder case in a Sunday school class. Commissioner Oscar Olander and his whole team have worked day and night on this case and I commend them. Oh, no, I haven't made any mistakes, Mr. Kennedy, but you have."[106]

Pausing, he leaned on the jury box rail, and implored the jurors not to be taken in by the smoke screen blown across their eyes by defense charges of an unfair trial. "Any man who lives in this great country is entitled to a fair trial," he exclaimed patriotically, "and these defendants have been given a fair trial. Oh, the defense attorneys have made clever and skillful arguments. Their theory has been to make you believe that all the state's witnesses were liars. You must not believe that, my friends. The state's evidence is undisputed and uncontradictable." Thanking them for their attention and praising them for having the wisdom and courage to make the proper decision, he strode confidently to the prosecution table. As a reporter tritely remarked, "Well, it's all over but the shouting."[107]

XII In his charge to the jury, Judge Hatch first recapitulated the evidence presented by the state, going into each minute detail, such as in which seat the individuals sat during their automobile rides and the spying of an egg sign in front of the Earl Nice residence. He then recounted each of the journeys to Albion as related by Abramowitz, Kurner, and Luks.[108]

Reviewing the claims of the defense, the judge instructed the jurors to return separate verdicts for each alleged conspirator. Considerable time was spent in impressing the panel that it was imperative that the testimony of the main state witnesses must be weighed in light of what each had to gain through their immunity from prosecution. "Study the testimony of Abramowitz and Luks carefully," he commanded, "and give it intense consideration. You must decide whether these witnesses are trustworthy. You must consider whether the fact that they have been given immunity and that without immunity Luks would be guilty of a fourth felony and Abramowitz would be guilty of a third felony. It is proper for you to receive their testimony with utmost caution because of their interest in the outcome of this case. You must consider their motives and whether they expect leniency because of their testimony."[109]

The charge consumed one hour and thirty-six minutes, and just as the jurors were about to retire, one inquired, "Your Honor, just what is the scope of the immunity which has been granted state witnesses? I'd like to know how far it reaches. Does it apply to this case or does it apply to the murder also?"[110]

Sigler sprung to his feet, assuring the curious juror that it pertained solely to the conspiracy case. "That is not the truth and you know it," snapped Walsh. "The statute under which the immunity was granted covers all questions asked of the witnesses and, therefore, in this case it would include immunity from prosecution even for the actual murder of Senator Hooper."[111]

Cutting Sigler's retort with a brisk wave of his hand, Judge Hatch stifled further debate by informing the jury that "the immunity applies to this alleged crime and to any crimes growing out of the alleged conspiracy." He added that it was not within the jury's prerogative to consider the immunity in determining their verdicts because they were to be concerned only with the charges in the present trial. Satisfied, at 10:49 a.m. the jurors dutifully trooped single-file from the room to begin their task of meting out justice.[112]

XIII No one expected a lengthy deliberation and so, despite the return of record-breaking heat and humidity, tortured spectators stubbornly refused to leave their seats lest they either miss the jury's return or lose their valuable vantage points to other onlookers standing in the aisles. At 2:12 p.m. the jarring gong announcing the re-entry of the jury rang through the courtroom. Judge Hatch, his black robe flowing, slipped bat-like into his chair. Defendants and attorneys strode to their places. State police troopers quickly positioned themselves at their preassigned stations throughout the room. When the jurors filed in at 2:15, anxious anticipation filled the air.[113]

Judge Hatch admonished the gallery not to engage in any demonstration, "no matter what the verdict may be." Foreman George Westbrook, at 77 the eldest juror, rose and in a steady voice informed the Court that: "The jury finds all four defendants guilty as charged, Your Honor." Not a sound was heard. The defendants grinned defiantly and exchanged whispered conversation. Naomi Selik and Mrs. Sam Fleisher, sitting in the front row just behind their husbands, never altered their expressions. Neither did Senator Hooper's widow.[114]

The eerie silence was shattered by Judge Hatch thanking the jury and excusing them from further duty. One at a time, the defendants were summoned to the judge's chambers for brief interviews. Each professed that the verdict was a miscarriage of justice. This process was completed by 2:40 p.m. The attorneys remained in the chambers a few minutes longer, while their clients, with the wives of Mike Selik and Sam Fleisher, huddled in the courtroom.[115]

Judge Hatch returned to the bench at 2:45 p.m. "I suppose," he began, "that there is no use in sentencing these men separately. They were all convicted together of the same offense." The defendants came forward and stood closely together, shoulder to shoulder, before the judge.[116]

"Is there anything you wish to say before I pass sentence?" he asked. All four looked straight ahead in silence, although Harry Fleisher vigorously shook his head no.[117]

"You realize that this is a serious offense," resumed the jurist. "It carries no great penalty, but it is the sentence of this Court that you each shall serve four and a half to five years in Jackson Prison. Court is dismissed."[118]

Reporters flooded onto the floor, jostling and grabbing interviewees as fast as they could. Harry Fleisher, who was now on the threshold of Southern Michigan Prison for the first time despite more than forty arrests in the preceding twenty years, refused to comment, but his brother blubbered, "It's all wrong. It's all wrong. I'm not guilty. The jury was prejudiced by the fact that I had a prison record." Having spent fourteen of his thirty-four years in jail, Mike Selik was deep in thought, staring blankly into space, talking only occasionally to his wife. Pete Mahoney, who had no jail record, was incredulous, repeating his refrain: "I don't know how the jury found me guilty on that evidence. All I know about the case is what I read in the newspapers and what I heard here." Mrs. Hooper congratulated the prosecution staff, but when asked if the verdict was gratifying, she spoke for herself and her two sons when she sobbed poignantly, "We are not happy about anything because our Daddy isn't coming home. We need him."[119]

Most of the jurors had already escaped the clutches of the press, but one, George E. Fountain, was eager to speak. "We would have reached a verdict in five minutes," he exaggerated, "if it had not been for a holdout on Mahoney. We took three ballots on him. First we did Harry Fleisher, then Sam Fleisher, and finally Mike Selik. All of them were convicted on one ballot." Foreman Westbrook offered an enlightening mea culpa, as he blurted: "You know when that law was passed letting women be jurors, I was quite opposed to it. I might say I didn't hide my feelings either. That was some years ago, though. This is the first time I ever had any experience with women jurors and right now I think they make as competent jurors as men. In fact, they seem to have slightly better memories."[120]

Sigler was jubilant and effusive. "This case," he gushed, "meant a great deal to the people of Michigan. It is the opening wedge in the solution of the Hooper murder and a complete vindication of the witnesses for the state, particularly those who had criminal records. The verdict testified to the hard work done by the officers in this case and everyone else who had anything to do with it. We had a good judge and a sensible jury."[121]

Kennedy spoke for the defense, protesting the verdict as "one unsubstantiated by the facts." Defense counsel perfunctorily commended Judge Hatch on the way he conducted the trial, forced their clients to shake hands with Sigler, and then arranged for $15,000 bail for each pending motions for a new trial and permission to appeal the case to the supreme court.[122]

The Hooper murder conspiracy trial was over. The plotters had been found guilty. However, as the *Detroit Free Press* editorialized, the question on the lips of every Michigan resident remained unanswered: "Who did murder Hooper a few days before he was to testify against Boss Frank D. McKay?"[123]

CHAPTER SEVEN

A POLITICAL PHOENIX

I Basking in the glow of his easily achieved triumph, Sigler relished being lionized as the "hero of the probe" and mentioned as a potential 1946 gubernatorial candidate by both major parties. Before leaving on a Montana vacation with his family, he modestly brushed aside all political speculation with a breezy "I haven't the slightest ambition to run for governor." However, he added, with a twinkle in his eyes, "And I am not a Democrat."[1]

While the special prosecutor was enjoying his two-week respite, Edwin Goodwin of the *Michigan State Digest* saturated Ingham County with stories of the integrity of Sigler's next target, Frank D. McKay, and cast aspersions on the motivations of his chief legal tormentor. The August 1 issue denounced the prosecutor for granting immunity to the "probable slayers" of Hooper simply to pursue an "unfounded remote possibility" that the Grand Rapids entrepreneur was somehow implicated in the crime. "Hooper was the exact type to say money to affect horse racing legislation came 'from McKay,' because it would punish McKay for not having given Hooper $5,000 which the senator demanded ostensibly for a gift to a 'naturopathic hospital,' but which was really intended for himself," the editorial surmised. "By attributing fault to McKay, Hooper thereby could conceal and protect the REAL BRIBER, if there was one. His story would delight both paid and nonpaid political smear men and would mislead authorities and the public." Rather than slandering McKay, the real issue ought to be, Goodwin proposed, "whether Michigan is engaged in detecting or bringing to trial and convicting the killer of Hooper, or is the crime to be made merely the springboard from which to launch throughout the state and the United States repetitious defamations and detractions against an exceptional and distinguished public servant?"[2]

The following week's edition strove to deflect attention from McKay by focusing on the source of the $15,000 purportedly put up for the slaying. "Were underworld men given $15,000 by the foes of the anti-chain bank bill in an effort to buy Hooper's silence on their widespread bribery of legislators," posed the rhetorical question, "only to have the would-be assassins, Abramowitz and Luks, decide as an afterthought to substitute DEATH for BRIBERY?" To validate this hypothesis, the proposed scenario portrayed Abramowitz and Luks as crafty, clever, fearless gangsters rather than as the slow-witted, crude thugs they really were. "Certainly the bankers had no thought of murder. They knew Hooper was a grafting, money-hungry senator who could have told PLENTY about graft in banking legislation. They also knew that Hooper, to save his own neck, might have lied about the graft and told the grand jury whatever it wanted to hear. But they wanted to try to buy his silence. Even Abramowitz and Luks testified that the plan was to first try to reach Hooper with money. The bankers had a motive which others did not. But only Abramowitz and Luks had a motive for KILLING Hooper. They could retain the money, and by implicating their companions in a SO-CALLED CONSPIRACY TO MURDER, procure for themselves IMMUNITY and enjoy their super bonanza."[3] Even though this supposition was naive in its view of how a bribe was offered and ignored the fact that McKay was also a director of the state's largest chain bank, it did raise the question of whether the horse racing bill was significant enough to merit the murder of a witness.

With the stage thus editorially set, on Monday, August 27, 1945, McKay's expensive defense team of Eugene Garey of New York and William Henry Gallagher of Detroit petitioned Judge Carr for a one-year postponement and a change of venue. Further, it was Gallagher's contention that Judge Carr should disqualify himself from presiding over the trial because he had issued the warrants and thereby demonstrated a presumption of guilt. Moreover, he argued, Carr was held in such high esteem universally throughout Ingham County that no jury could be found which could give McKay his constitutionally mandated presumption of innocence.[4]

After the presentation of the petitions, McKay verbally lambasted Sigler in a hastily convened city hall press conference. "This unscrupulous prosecutor," railed the portly, bespectacled defendant, "has made a studied effort to sully and besmirch my reputation. He has made me, in the eyes of the people, a murderer, an employer of assassins, a grafter, a grand jury obstructionist, a noted corruptionist, a crooked politician who belongs in jail, a sinister politician who manipulates the affairs of this state, and a man who would stop at nothing, even murder, to gain my ends. He has inspired newspapers and radio stations to whip up a defamatory anvil chorus of prejudice against me. Sigler has only one object, and that is to get me at any price. He has used the Hooper murder conspiracy trial as a forum to pillory me, insinuating at every opportunity that there was a sinister connection between the Hooper murder and the fact that Hooper was the star witness against me at a forthcoming preliminary examination. The impression was conveyed that I was guilty of the charge against me, and, therefore, that I had Hooper killed to prevent him from testifying against me. The fact is, I had no more to do with Hooper's murder than the judge who is hearing the motion. If Sigler's inferences have any foundation in fact, why was I not made a respondent in the murder case?"[5]

"A long tirade of a panicky man who has found the strong arm of the law catching up with him," beamed Sigler as he urged his faithful followers from the press to sharpen their pencils. "We are not surprised at all," he confided. "We have been expecting it for more than a year, ever since we caught a detective slinking around grand jury headquarters. He confessed, telling us that McKay assigned him to 'get' something against Judge Carr and myself. He even told us what it was to be and why. Apparently McKay thinks he is above the law, and that anyone who has the temerity to try to bring him to justice must have political motives. However, in my book, McKay is in no different a position than anyone else who has violated the law. But if his campaign to discredit the integrity and motives of the grand jury succeeds, McKay will have accomplished a clever defense. If he gets that idea into the mind of even one juror, it will have helped him."[6]

As expected, on Friday Judge Carr ruled against both defense motions. Furthermore, the jurist announced that respondent Charles Leiter had joined Isadore Schwartz in pleading guilty to the conspiracy counts and was now willing to testify against McKay.[7]

II Defense counsel scored a major victory before the proceedings opened on Wednesday, September 5, when Circuit Judge John Simpson, who had gained dubious renown in his home county of Jackson as its "honest judge," was assigned by Judge Charles Hayden, chief of the circuit, to preside over the trial. McKay's associates viewed the selection as doubly fortuitous since it not only removed Carr, but also placed in his stead a known friend of the chief defendant.[8]

Before the jury could be impaneled, Sigler was forced to respond to another round of motions for delay and change of venue. With the slightly built jurist peering down at him through shell-rimmed glasses, the special prosecutor began the rebuttal, his voice echoing through the nearly empty, third-floor city hall courtroom at Mason, the rustic seat of Ingham County. "Your Honor, the prosecution has not entered into a conspiracy, as my learned brothers claim, to prejudice this case. Mr. Gallagher says that I have proclaimed to the world that I believe McKay is guilty of obtaining the murder of Senator Hooper. I say that when Senator Hooper was murdered, he was the only witness against McKay and his co-defendants in the horse racing bill, and I ask why it is considered improper for us to say so. Aren't the people of Michigan entitled to know the facts concerning the murder of a state senator? Is the prosecution to be condemned because we told the facts to the people of Michigan that after Hooper died the case against McKay would have to be dropped? I don't want McKay's scalp. Frank McKay means no more to me than any other respondent. My brothers ridicule Judge Carr because he said grand jury witnesses would be guarded after Hooper was murdered. Was that wrong, too?"[9]

Having evoked the names of the martyred lawmaker and a legendary local dispenser of justice, Sigler scornfully went on. "Defense counsel claim the entire case should be quashed because it is merely a rehash of the old liquor conspiracy case which was tried in federal court three years ago. Then, in the next breath, they say they haven't had long enough to prepare their case. The Great Gallagher and Broadway Garey and the rest of them were engaged in that federal case for nearly two years. If it is a rehash, why aren't they prepared?"[10]

At the conclusion of the exchange, Simpson ordered an adjournment until Thursday morning, at which time he issued a thirty-day continuance to enable him to study the defense requests.[11] For the first time since being appointed to the grand jury, Sigler's barbed eloquence had failed.

III On September 16, fate dealt Sigler a cruel setback with the death of Michigan Supreme Court Justice Howard Wiest. Speculation that Carr would be appointed to the high court swept the state, and with it went a like amount of theorizing on the future of the grand jury without his leadership.

For three days Kim Sigler uncharacteristically shunned the press as he mulled over his own destiny. He was Carr's fair-haired boy. Through sheer force of personality he had convinced the staid jurist to give him free rein. Certainly the strict, letter-of-the-law judge had not approved of his protege's unorthodox tactics to coerce witnesses into testifying, but the success they brought muted any criticism.

Carr had rewarded these legal triumphs by granting his special prosecutor authority to hold press conferences, travel, and spend grand jury funds at his own discretion.[12] Now that was all endangered. A new grand juror might curtail, or even terminate, his independence. Yet to try, in any way, to deprive his benefactor of a lifelong aspiration would be an act of selfishness too extreme even for Sigler.

As Governor Kelly pondered the potential impact on the grand jury if its chief was removed, Sigler made the task easier by ending his silence. "The grand jury," he asserted, his voice choked with emotion, "can conclude its work without Judge Carr — now. One or two years ago, I would have said no. But Judge Carr held the fort when the going was tough. He has set the pattern — laid the bricks — and from here on out it's a matter of following the form. And I know Judge Carr wouldn't leave the job if there was any question about the grand jury not being able to be carried to completion by another judge."[13] With this impetus from the special prosecutor, on September 23 the governor named Carr an associate justice. The "Sigler-Carr Era," as Lansing correspondents derisively dubbed it, was history.

IV Sigler's new boss was 41-year-old Louis E. Coash. A former Lansing municipal judge, Coash had been on the circuit court only four months when Carr, as his last official act as presiding judge of the Ingham County Circuit Court, designated him grand juror.[14]

The affable, dark-haired, moon-faced jurist, who relied more on his instincts than knowledge of the law, approached his latest task in a calm manner. Meeting with reporters, he adjusted his horn-rimmed glasses and good-naturedly confessed: "Since I am grass green about grand juries, I shall have to depend heavily upon Mr. Sigler and the members of his present staff for guidance."[15] Sigler smiled politely, confident he could mesmerize Coash just as he had done with Carr. After the conference ended, however, Sigler had to reassess his plans. Coash instructed the special prosecutor that henceforth only the grand juror would dictate policy and warned Sigler against trying to "run the damn thing without consultation." This time, Coash insisted, all press releases would have the grand juror's name first.[16] With ill-concealed indignation, Sigler assented and left with the thought that perhaps Carr's successor might prove to be an enemy not only of his, but also of the grand jury.

V On October 10, Judge Simpson set January 14, 1946 as the date for McKay's liquor conspiracy case, thereby affording Sigler an unexpected opportunity to direct personally the prosecution in the Aristocrat Club trial. Before the impaneling of a jury for that case began on October 23, attorneys representing the four mobsters convicted of conspiracy to murder Hooper each and collectively filed a petition listing forty-three improprieties serious enough to warrant a mistrial declaration. Their main contention was that the defendants were "irreparably prejudiced in the minds of the jurors by the repeated injections by Mr. Sigler of the name of Frank D. McKay and his alleged guilt in this crime, though no evidence was adduced tending to show that McKay had anything to do with the matter." In rebuttal, Sigler, who had heard the exact argument in reverse by McKay's attorneys, scoffed, "It's all part of a smokescreen to divert attention from the evidence and the jury's decision."[17]

Judge Hatch took nearly two weeks to study the trial transcript and then denied the petition. He admitted that some "minor irregularities had crept into the case," but claimed that they were "not sufficiently prejudicial to justify setting aside the jury's verdict." Regarding McKay, the judge held that while the Grand Rapids politician had not been charged as a conspirator, the evidence did show that Harry Fleisher and Mike Selik had been offered $15,000 to dispose of Senator Hooper before he could testify against "a certain politician" to the grand jury. Since that testimony was to have been against McKay, the ruling went on, it was within the prosecution's right to bring his name into the case. Expressing dissatisfaction, defense counsel informed Hatch of their intent to request the Michigan State Supreme Court to overrule his opinion.[18]

As the Pontiac trial lingered through November and into December, Sigler maintained a high profile, being photographed both at the prosecution table and, to his embarrassment, at a Detroit nightclub sipping cocktails with Victor C. Anderson while two torch singers ran their fingers under his lapels. The chagrined prosecutors charged the *Lansing State Journal* with political motives in printing a picture which, they feared, abstemious jurors might deem offensive and which might be used to the detriment of their case at the McKay trial.[19]

The highlight of the Pontiac legal circus occurred on November 28 when, for the first time in his twenty-one-year criminal career, Harry Fleisher took the stand to testify in his own behalf. Using notes prepared for him by his attorney, Edward H. Kennedy, Jr., because his memory "was not good," the mobster stated that his real name was

Fleish and that the "er" had been added by a police officer who had booked him years earlier; that he had attended school with several members of the Purple Gang, including Ray Bernstein, Harry Keywell, and Irving Keywell, but denied being a Purple himself; and that he had no involvement whatsoever in either the robbery of the Aristocrat Club or a conspiracy to murder Senator Hooper. It was to no avail, however, as once again the stories of Sam Abramowitz and Henry Luks, who had received immunity for this case also, convicted not only Harry Fleisher but also his four co-defendants, and each was sentenced to twenty-five to fifty years in prison. When Harry Fleisher, Mike Selik, and Pete Mahoney entered Jackson Prison under heavy guard on December 10, Sigler had finally achieved some satisfaction, even though he had not been able to wring from them the name of the politician who had paid the $15,000 to have the Albion senator killed.[20]

V I Tanned and fit from a two-week vacation in Florida, Sigler eagerly awaited the upcoming battle with McKay. However, four days before the trial was to commence, Edwin Goodwin and Ira H. Marmon, former head of the Michigan State Police Detective Bureau, were arrested on charges of jury tampering. The two admitted to distributing issues of the *Michigan State Digest*, containing articles praising McKay and damning Sigler to prospective jurors. Overruling Sigler's protests that the bench was playing into a cleverly conceived trap set by Garey and Gallagher to obtain their long-denied change of venue, Judge Simpson ordered the trial moved to Jackson County.[21]

Throughout the remainder of January and into February, Sigler produced a string of witnesses who claimed McKay had hired agents to represent liquor companies and then demanded a percentage of their sales commissions before recommending that their product be placed in state-licensed stores. McKay was portrayed as a behind-the-scenes political mastermind who manipulated the Liquor Control Commission like puppets.

Immediately after the prosecution rested its case at 11:37 a.m. February 6, defense counsel moved for a directed verdict of acquittal, saying that the state had failed to demonstrate either the intent or commission of a crime. Court recessed for four days to allow Simpson to examine the court reporter's notes. Upon reconvening on February 11, the judge expressed doubt as to the validity of the prosecution's case. "There is no doubt," he declared sharply, "that McKay had a right to take money from his salesmen. He could establish a sales agency for any firm and go to the state just as any other citizen in a private capacity. He, like anyone else, could hire salesmen to call on state officials and demand a commission. After all, the state is in the liquor business. You must prove, Mr. Sigler, that there was a criminal intent in his business practices. You must prove that what your witnesses claim were threats were not merely statements of fact which may have been misconstrued. You must do that or else your case must fail." No such proofs were forthcoming; hence, three days later the judge read a thirty-two-page opinion culminating in a directed verdict of innocence.[22]

During Simpson's discourse, Sigler sat slumped in his chair, his face expressionless. When the gavel fell, he rose with a shrug, and as he strode from the room remarked hollowly, "Oh, well, it was just another law suit. We'll get the next one." Angry, frustrated, and unwilling to discuss his initial grand jury setback, he made plans to set off on another Florida vacation.[23]

In contrast, an ebullient McKay was crushed by well-wishers and reporters. "I hope this is the end of my political persecution," he gushed, placing his arm around his wife. "I regard my acquittal more than a vindication of myself. It is a reflection of the judicial integrity and courage of Judge Simpson, and should be reassuring to all people to know our courts can still dispense justice unhampered by the subtle influences that were aligned against me."[24] Although grimy from battle, the veteran gladiator had unhorsed yet another white knight.

VII To compound Sigler's hostility and humiliation, before he departed on his southern journey the Michigan senate created a three-man committee chaired by Ivan A. Johnston, a long-time intraparty foe of the special prosecutor, to investigate grand jury expenditures. Judge Coash promptly pledged cooperation, but Sigler adamantly refused to share grand jury secrets, especially with members of the body that was under scrutiny. Announcing his plan to issue warrants in the anti-chain bank bill case upon his return, Sigler voiced his concern about the senate action. "It's natural, I suppose, after the results at Jackson, to expect some new opposition to the grand jury," he said philosophically. "We've had that sort of thing since its beginning. But there are certain people right now — some in the senate — who are very worried and would like to know what we are doing and going to do. Who want desperately to find out what we are working on. If they have an accounting at this time, they could find out. I oppose it for that reason, but I promise that when we are through, there will be an accounting for every dime."[25]

Within the senate chamber, a lone voice was raised in support of Sigler's stance. Murl H. DeFoe, a friend of the special prosecutor and a state witness in the liquor conspiracy trial, alleged that the investigation was "an attempt to glorify Frank D. McKay and at the same time insult Justice Leland W. Carr." The real purpose of the resolution, he contended, was designed "to weaken the grand jury and its work in the minds of the people by centering attention on the costs rather than the jury's record." His remarks were met with icy silence on both sides of the aisle.[26]

In response to a senate subpoena, Coash turned over all grand jury records but requested that Victor C. Anderson be permitted to attend committee hearings to assure the material's confidentiality. When this was refused, without comment, by Johnston, the Ingham County prosecutor snapped: "Well, the only way I know of to protect the information now under investigation is to have someone present who knows what's going on in the grand jury. I don't understand why they're afraid of me." Later that day, both Coash and Anderson telegraphed the day's events to Sigler in Miami, and he wired back that he was driving home at once because it seemed that the "senate inquiry is a deliberate attempt to sabotage the future value of the grand jury."[27]

Senator Johnston landed the initial blow when, in public session, he began calling witnesses on Wednesday, February 27. George MaDan, special auditor and accountant for the grand jury, recited that the probe had been appropriated $440,000 by the legislature, of which approximately $325,000 had been expended. Specifically, to date, Sigler had pocketed $69,565 in salary and expenses, while his chief aides, H. H. Warner and Thomas J. Bailey, had received $36,978.42 and $3,724.36, respectively. The Olds Hotel had been paid $25,361.89 for twelve rooms and other services. Continuation of the grand jury, Johnston interjected maliciously, would certainly be to the financial benefit of the prosecution staff.[28] The most shocking revelation, however, came from Detective Sergeant Leo Van Conant, who meticulously detailed from his own records how more than $8,000 had been spent to satisfy the lavish whims of Major Charles F. Hemans. As reporters scampered to snatch telephones, Johnston smugly cautioned those remaining in the near-empty chamber to keep in mind that "we are not interested in grand jury secrets, but are only concerned how the expenditures of money were made by the grand jury." With that, he adjourned the committee "for a few days."[29]

As headlines blared "HEMANS GOT $8,850 OF JURY'S FUNDS" and "FAT FEES PAID," Judge Coash, in a prepared statement, deftly deflected all criticisms toward his predecessor and the special prosecutor. "I had the assurance of both Judge Carr and Kim Sigler that all expenditures were properly within the scope of the grand jury and necessary to its investigation," he declared. "When I questioned some expenditures, I was assured they were proper. I have received only $43.22 for expenses on trips I took in behalf of the grand jury, and Prosecutor Anderson has received only $87.11 since the start of the grand jury in late 1943. Any explanation of use of funds before I became grand juror will have to come from Carr and Sigler."[30]

Anderson, who knew that the grand jury was looking into allegations that Johnston was involved in illegal gambling operations in his home county of Macomb, understood the political motivations of the committee chairman and defended Sigler, while at the same time raising a question as to the timing of the disclosures. "It is significant," he said tersely, his voice reflecting the vengeance he intended to extract, "that the senator's findings were made partially public when Mr. Sigler was on the way back to Michigan and had no opportunity to be present." The air would be cleared, he promised, when Sigler confronted the charges.[31]

On Sunday, March 3, the special prosecutor, his shock of silver hair vivid against his sun-basked face, refuted all the committee's inferences. He asserted that it was a crude attempt to smear the grand jury and himself, and that by defaming Hemans, who was to be the star witness in the anti-chain bank bill case, the committee had virtually destroyed any possibility for obtaining convictions. Once again, he insisted, "personal interests" were at work to undermine his crusade to ferret out grafters.[32]

Swept up in the maelstrom of controversy, on Monday, March 4, Coash temporarily suspended the grand jury. "I do not claim, at this time," he explained cautiously, "that any expenditures were improper or that anyone got a dime illegally, but I want to make certain to my own satisfaction that all expenses are proper, and that the state is getting its money's worth for funds expended." In response to capitol gossip that Sigler would be ousted, he said, "No one has been fired, but I cannot predict if there will be any changes in the future."[33]

With Sigler reeling, Johnston leveled his knockout punch. Noting that the special prosecutor's refusal to deny payments had been made to Hemans amounted to a tacit verification, the senator reminded the citizens that "hired testimony is un-American and smacks of fascism." Then, reading from a prepared statement, Johnston tattooed his target with a series of rapid blows. "The committee hopes," he began, "that Mr. Sigler may admit with greater frankness and less subterfuge that 'Nightshirt Charlie' Spare was reinstated on the grand jury payroll at a salary of $400 a month and expenses, which have averaged over $300 a month, under the name of Mary Duke so that the records do not disclose that a person of such ill-repute was again in the employ of the grand jury. We hope Mr. Sigler will admit that within the last six months, he has taken three vacation trips to Colorado, Nebraska, and Florida, with Kenneth Templin of the state police as his driver, and that on these trips to Nebraska and Florida he drew $4 a day from grand jury funds for living expenses. We hope he will admit he placed the late Senator Miles Callaghan on the grand jury payroll and paid him a salary in addition to his hotel bills and car storage bills while he was a witness for the grand jury. We hope Mr. Sigler will tell us why grand jury funds were used to purchase four or more scrapbooks and fifty newspaper cuts of his own photograph. It has been said that the committee has broken faith with the grand jury by revealing that Hemans was an important witness in the pending bank case. The committee asks Sigler who it was that revealed Hemans was to be a witness in the case. We did not know that fact until we learned it from Sigler's statement attacking the committee. If anyone has broken faith with the grand jury and Judge Louis E. Coash, it is the special prosecutor himself."[34]

Teetering on the brink of losing every political goal he had so painstakingly calculated for himself, Sigler played a desperate gambit. He would link Coash to the foes of the grand jury in an effort to force the jurist to remove him as prosecutor. This, in turn, would shift public sentiment back in his favor.[35] The risk was substantial, but the only alternative was oblivion.

On March 6, Sigler distributed to reporters copies of a letter he had submitted to Coash. In it, he accused the grand juror of undermining the investigation into grafting legislators and threatened to ask the Michigan State Supreme Court to assume control of the probe. "Your action suspending the grand jury investigation," the letter began, "has played directly into the hands of certain persons who want the inquiry discontinued and the grand jury wrecked. Your public utterances to the press have created and encouraged distrust in me to enemies of the grand jury." He then labeled Coash a liar for denying knowledge of Hemans and Spare being on the payroll and condemned him for "losing valuable time and causing incalculable harm" by examining expense accounts which he had previously approved.[36]

"At the beginning of your services as grand juror," the letter continued, "you started out with great enthusiasm. When pressure began to develop and you saw the possibility of criticism, your enthusiasm began to wane. For some weeks past, you have talked of little but winding up the grand jury. The members of the staff and myself have worked long hours over two years and more to expose graft and to bring about a clean and honest government in Michigan. It has been a thankless and difficult task. I sacrificed my law practice and have been away from my family and home for over two years. Your attitude has encouraged the making of baseless and slanderous statements concerning myself.... The citizens of this state have the right to expect that graft will not be tolerated. I humbly believe that I owe to the people of this state the duty of continuing the fight.... I believe it to be my duty to take such action as will salvage the grand jury. I am working on a petition to submit to the Supreme Court of this state asking it, under Section 4 of Article VII of the State Constitution, to take general superintending control of this proceeding."[37]

Sought out at his office, Coash took the news of Sigler's blast calmly. "I have not yet received the letter," he said with embarrassment, "and I will have no comment until I have read it and studied it carefully."[38]

Three days passed and the fitful special prosecutor still retained his office. Fearful that his scheme had misfired, Sigler unleashed another salvo. "The great statesmen of the senate committee," he blathered, "have been unable to find anything on me, so they've upped the ante on what they said we paid Hemans to $16,000. Handing out photostatic copies of secret grand jury records is an excellent way to help the defense in a criminal case. Their actions have now become tantamount to obstructing justice."[39]

Able to tolerate the rantings of his chief aide no longer, on March 12 Coash fired Sigler and replaced him with former Ingham County Prosecutor Richard B. Foster. "This is a move which I very much regret to make," the judge told reporters. "However, I've given the matter a great deal of consideration and feel the grand jury can do more without Sigler."[40]

"I'm not surprised at anything Judge Coash would do," stormed Sigler with feigned fury when apprised of his removal. "I'm going ahead and file my petition with the supreme court. My only aim as prosecutor was to punish the grafters and crooks. If the grand jury continues that policy, I'll be satisfied. Now, I'm going to be just another lawyer with a practice to look after in Battle Creek." Within hours he had resigned as assistant prosecutor in Ingham, Oakland, Calhoun, and Jackson counties, had sent nearly all his grand jury records, keys, and documents to the grand juror, and had closed his Lansing office.[41] All that remained was to see if his ploy would achieve the intended results or if his star was in permanent eclipse.

VIII Within forty-eight hours the answer was known. Fifteen editors of weekly rural newspapers pledged their support for a Sigler gubernatorial bid; Nieber and McCormick reaffirmed the backing of their Detroit dailies; petitions were circulated in Detroit enlisting backers from both major parties; and publications chronicled the forty-one convictions, twelve guilty pleas, and eight contempt-of-court sentences meted out by the no-nonsense Carr-Sigler team. Maintaining a perfunctory public coyness, the ex-prosecutor initially spurned the thought of public office but expressed gratification at the "tremendous amount of popular pressure" exerted on him to enter the race. Waiting a week before "answering the call of the citizens," on March 21 he announced his candidacy on the Republican ticket, pledging to continue his crusade to eradicate graft and corruption from state government.[42]

In keeping with his new populism, Sigler sought to dispel his image of lofty superiority. "People have noticed," he informed Nieber in an exclusive interview, "that my fabled wardrobe is dated. Well, let me tell you something about that. Back in 1942 I successfully defended a man who, because of his poverty, asked if a relative of his who was a tailor could pay my fee in clothing. I got twenty-one suits out of it, and I haven't bought a suit since, and I won't for some time, regardless of changing styles. My favorite, by the way, is the gray pinstripe I wore when I announced for governor." Twitting his good friend, he added with a smile, "Your story, Al, about forty-seven suits in my closet was a pretty wild guess and must have included pajama suits and union suits."[43] Candidate Sigler — hard on criminals, but a common man at heart — was being packaged for the electorate. Pearl gray topcoats with velvet collars had been replaced by conservative blue, as Sigler's quest for the White House was back on schedule.

The campaign was spirited, with Lieutenant Governor Vernon J. Brown, Detroit Mayor Edward Jeffries, and Raymond J. Kelly contesting Sigler for his party's prize. In nearly every speech, the maverick Republican played upon his sacrifices and service as grand jury prosecutor. At one stop, he philosophized to his audience: "None of you realize the terrific pressure that can be brought to bear to prevent the uncovering of graft in government. Perhaps I should be glad I'm out of a job where someone calls you on the phone in the night and says, 'Listen, cowboy, a sideswipe from a truck some dark night can take care of you.'" At another rally, he intimated that Judge Coash was aligned with the forces of evil, saying: "I was discharged from the grand jury because I was naming names." At yet another gathering, he raised the ghost of his favorite nemesis, recalling with a folksy flair: "You know, Frank McKay hired a detective to get some dirt on Judge Leland W. Carr and myself. We couldn't take a walk without being followed. We grabbed the fellow, and he was so dumb that he carried his instructions from his clients with him. McKay and his friends were moving heaven and earth to smear us."[44] Throughout Michigan, the ousted crusader made martyrdom his mantle, and he wore it with pride.

As election day neared, his adversaries used the senate committee report to try to halt Sigler's increasing popularity, but the front-runner had a biting retort for each allegation. Yes, he had taken Trooper Templin with him on his trips because he had received numerous death threats, but no tax dollars had been used for his expenses. Yes, he had hired a clipping service to preserve newspaper articles in leather scrapbooks, but it was so the grand jury staff could have ready access to what local press throughout the state was writing about their work and what prospective jurors were reading. Yes, witnesses had been paid, but that was common practice in grand juries because criminals needed incentives to squeal on their pals. As to the charge that he spent $95.00 one evening at a dinner party, he scoffed derisively: "I don't need to tell you folks that I spent the entire month of October, in fact six weeks, right in Oakland County preparing for, and trying, the case which sent five hoodlums to prison. McKay's friends in the senate want you to think I spent the state's money buying whiskey and having a good time. If any one of them had been through that ordeal, working night and day to be prepared, he would know that I didn't have any time for partying, even if I had been in the mood. You know, McKay doesn't care who is governor so long as it isn't Sigler. He's got his stooges all over the state working because he knows there won't be room in Lansing for his methods, or for anyone to cash in on influence, if I am elected."[45] It was vintage Sigler, and it fired fervor in the faithful.

Any lingering doubt as to who would oppose the Democratic nominee, former Governor Murray D. Van Wagoner, was blasted away one week before the primary when Macomb County grand juror Herman Dehnke, a political ally of Sigler, issued a warrant charging Senator Ivan Johnston with accepting bribes while serving as county prosecutor from 1939 to 1943. The ensuing stories afforded Sigler not only further credence as a prophet scorned, but also thousands of dollars of free publicity. The election of June 17 was now anti-climactic.[46]

CHAPTER EIGHT

CONVICTS AND "KITES"

I During his successful campaign against Murray Van Wagoner, Sigler assured voters that he had "a good idea who Hooper's killer was," but would not make any arrests until he possessed "all the links in the conspiracy."[1]

After his first two years as governor, however, the case remained unsolved. "Cowboy Kim" had discovered that better headlines could be achieved by delving into alleged subversive activities.[2] Michigan, like the rest of postwar America, had communist, rather than criminal, conspiracies on its collective mind.

Lack of public pronouncements belied the chief executive's continuing interest in the assassination. Upon taking office, he instructed his attorney general, Eugene F. Black, to "stay out of the Hooper case" until he was needed, because the governor considered it "his baby."[3] Detroit Police Commissioner Harry S. Toy was granted free rein by Sigler to conduct probes into all statewide criminal activities, except the Hooper murder.[4] Special Prosecutor Richard B. Foster felt that he and Judge Coash "did a lot of work on that damn Hooper case, but never got anywhere" without support from the governor's office.[5] The state police – headed by Donald S. Leonard after Sigler, as his first official act as governor, removed Olander – were stymied in their ongoing investigation into the slaying.[6] Captain Mulbar expressed his department's frustrations by complaining that, from the day of the crime, Sigler had taken "full and complete control," refusing to divulge any information garnered by his team of sleuths even though several members of the grand jury squad were Michigan State Police troopers.[7] The governor even knew that Harry Snyder, the chief witness, had met with state police officers and Sigler's chief legal advisor, Victor C. Anderson, and positively identified photographs of the two men he had seen at the site of the killing as he drove by Hooper's car.[8] Yet, to the dismay of incredulous state police detectives, the governor — who had admitted to Leonard as early as January 27, 1947 that he "could see the light regarding the Hooper murder and what really transpired" — opted for inactivity.[9]

So completely were the diligent efforts of the state police detectives kept shrouded in secrecy that Sigler could mark the third anniversary of the slaying by predicting to an unsuspecting public that someday he would solve the crime, while at the same time urging their patience because, "like many difficult murder cases, it sometimes requires a long time to fit together all of the links in the chain of evidence."[10]

Sigler's protestations notwithstanding, the "chain of evidence" was both substantial and strong. Shortly after receiving news of the killing, State Police Lieutenant Lyle Morse assigned Lieutenant Joseph Sheridan, a short, stocky ex-prize fighter who was the bureau's underworld specialist, to visit his informants in Detroit's criminal haunts. All of them told him to arrest every hoodlum who frequented O'Larry's Bar. Furthermore, the detective was tipped that not only were Harry and Sam Fleisher and Mike Selik acting jittery, but so were Ray Bernstein's brothers Joey and Abe, Charles Leiter, Isadore Schwartz, and the other mobsters referred to in their circle as "Frank McKay's gang."[11] This information was turned in to Morse and Mulbar, along with the names of several of Harry Fleisher's closest associates.[12]

When his superiors had failed to respond by late February, Sheridan submitted another statement citing the underworld's version of the crime. Mobsters were convinced that a person or group of persons who feared enormous financial losses and imprisonment ordered the senator silenced before he could testify to the grand jury. He appended a list of suspects named by his contacts. These included former Purple Gang king Ray Bernstein and his top aides Harry and Phil Keywell, all of whom were in Jackson Prison; Harry and Sam Fleisher; Mike Selik; Charles Leiter and Isadore Schwartz, former bodyguards for Frank D. McKay; and McKay himself.[13] Again, to the disgust of Sheridan, who was spending sixteen to eighteen hours a day on the case, no arrests were made.[14]

Even more distressing to Sheridan was that, after the Fleishers and Selik were taken into custody in April 1945 — along with Pete Mahoney whose name had never been mentioned by underworld sources — all further investigation into uncovering the actual perpetrators of the crime came to an abrupt halt. For more than a year, the conspiracy to murder was deemed more significant than the assassination.

IIIn November 1946, following Sigler's election as governor, Morse sent Sheridan to Detroit to pick up what should have become an ice-cold trail. Tipsters directed him to Louis Brown, a black 48-year-old recent parolee from Jackson Prison. Brown was reluctant to talk, saying: "If Raymond Bernstein or the Keywell brothers ever learned who tipped the state police off of the men that killed Senator Hooper, his life would not be worth a dime."[15] Sheridan repeatedly assured the ex-convict of around-the-clock protection and, after a series of meetings, Brown consented to tell his story in the presence of Sheridan and Dr. David Phillips, the Jackson Prison psychiatrist.[16]

On December 26, 1946, Brown made a preliminary statement. Having verified it to the best of his ability, Sheridan arranged a conference in Lansing on January 27,. 1947, between the witness and Sigler, Leonard, Anderson, Black, Phillips, Corrections Commissioner Garrett Heyns, and himself.[17] That evening, during a nearly five-hour grilling by Sigler, Brown unhesitatingly related an amazing tale of prison intrigue.[18]

According to Brown, in early December 1944, a Jackson Prison inmate group, headed by Bernstein and including several black and Jewish Detroit mobsters, was offered $15,000 to kill an unnamed prominent politician. Without asking for details, Harry Keywell told the convict emissary that the amount was at least $10,000 "too light," and Bernstein concurred. About a week later, Deputy Warden D. C. Pettit and Inspector Robert Wilson reassembled the clique and suggested that the ante would be raised. A few days passed, and then Pettit introduced "a Jew from Flint named Wake" to the prisoners. Wake showed them a photograph of Hooper and promised to pay $25,000 for the murder. The deputy warden promised Bernstein and Harry Keywell guns, a state car, a bogus set of license plates, and passage from the prison if they would accept the offer. Three days later, another gathering was called at which Wake removed $10,000 from a valise and stacked it on a table. Also present, said Brown, as a show of good faith for payment of the balance, were Warden Harry Jackson and Frank D. McKay. After the warden introduced McKay to the mobsters, the two men left. Pettit placed the money in a large envelope and entrusted it to Joe Poirier, the treasurer for inmate funds.[19]

Wake, contended Brown, said he would discover the day the intended victim was to leave Lansing and notify Pettit. The go-between stressed McKay's wealth and influence, and added that the Grand Rapids financier was relying on them to protect his gambling interests by silencing the Albion senator. Furthermore, he assured Keywell that the job could be accomplished effortlessly on a deserted highway.[20]

Notification came on January 11, 1945, but because Pettit was absent it was Warden Jackson who summoned Bernstein and Harry Keywell over the loudspeaker to his office. Jackson ordered Brown to check out civilian clothing for the two from the "dress-out shop." When the afternoon dinner bugle blared at 3:30, Bernstein and Keywell drove from the prison yard in Pettit's dark red coupe. Two and one-half hours later they returned, changed into prison garb, and, acting nervous, resumed their cell block routine duties.[21]

Sigler inquired if he knew how the crime had been committed, and Brown volunteered that he remembered how Keywell, in late January, had boasted on the smoothness of the job. Keywell explained to a band of inmates, which included Brown, that Wake followed Hooper from Lansing and, at a prearranged location, signalled to the lurking hoodlums by flashing his headlights as he passed the senator's automobile. Bernstein and Keywell pulled onto the highway, pursued Hooper, and forced his car off the road. Bernstein raced to the senator's door, opened it, shoved the terrified occcupant toward the center of the seat, grabbed him, and fired three shots into his skull. After making sure he was dead, Bernstein walked quickly back to where Keywell was waiting anxiously behind the wheel of the red coupe, and they sped back to the prison.[22]

Brown recalled that on January 12, Pettit called him into his office and gave him two fifty-dollar bills. The deputy warden congratulated him for being an excellent lookout for the group and impressed on him the necessity for continued loyalty and silence. In mid-December, Brown said, he was visited at his Detroit home by Wake, who presented the parolee another two-hundred dollars to keep his lips sealed.[23]

Brown also detailed visiting Wake's place of business and home in Flint, where he and other inmates had attended a lavish party. At this point Sheridan interrupted, noting that Brown had furnished him at their initial encounter a description of these buildings and their locations. Before going to Lansing to confer with Sigler, Brown accompanied Sheridan to Flint. Not only did he locate the sites immediately, the detective stated, but also they fit his descriptions exactly. Subsequent inquiry disclosed that the store and residence belonged to Max Davis, a prominent jeweler and reputed political ally of former Flint mayor and McKay assistant William McKeighan.[24]

When Brown concluded his story at nearly midnight, Sigler beamed, thanked him, and pledged any required police protection. Taking Leonard and the state police officers aside, the governor confided that he believed the ex-convict and urged the commissioner to proceed on the assumption that the account was valid. Leonard shortly thereafter drew up a handwritten list of immediate and secondary steps to be taken, but of his nine proposals only one, the interviewing of Ernest Henry, was acted upon.[25]

III Ernest Henry, a black inmate at Jackson Prison, was interrogated by Sheridan on April 1, April 22, and May 1, 1947, and each time he corroborated Brown's story. According to Henry, three days before the Hooper murder, Ray Bernstein asked him to purchase a pair of gloves. He did so, and delivered them to Pettit, as Bernstein had instructed. The Deputy Warden tossed him a quarter to cover the cost and warned him to forget about having bought them.[26]

On January 11, 1945, shortly after 3:00 p.m., Henry was working for Mrs. Pettit in the deputy warden's house. As he entered the kitchen to go downstairs, she stopped him with the admonition that "D. C. and the gang" were in the basement "cooking up something" and did not wish to be disturbed. Glancing into the dining room, he spied a nickel-plated .38 calibre revolver and the brown canvas gloves he had gotten for Bernstein lying on the table. While he never saw the gun or gloves again, he remembered finding two spent .38 shells in the back seat of Pettit's red coupe when he cleaned it a few days later.[27]

Asked by Sheridan who killed the senator and why, Henry responded: "Ray Bernstein told me that if Mr. Hooper testified against Frank McKay in court he, McKay, could be convicted. I am positive that Ray Bernstein made that statement to me. The true story in the prison about the Hooper murder — and the big shot inmates are positive — is that Ray Bernstein, Harry Keywell, and Phil Keywell are the killers." He added that Phil Keywell, whom he regarded as the most likely of the Purple trio to confess, had regretted the number of people who knew about the plot, saying, "If we had more time to do this job, we would change it, and do it right."[28]

Despite the sworn affidavits of Brown and Henry and urging from Sheridan and other detectives, Leonard took no further steps. Bernstein, the Keywells, Jackson, Pettit, and Max Davis — whose photograph had been positively identified by Brown as that of the man called Wake — were never questioned, and Leonard steadfastly

169

refused all requests by Sheridan that the case be submitted to a grand jury.[29]

IV Throughout the remainder of 1947 and for the next three years, the state police were subjected to a constant stream of letters, known in prison slang as "kites," from convicts claiming to possess details on the Hooper slaying. While all had a basis in fact, most were put forth primarily as a legal means to leave their cells for several days while testifying.[30]

Shortly after 8:00 p.m., August 11, 1947, a reluctant Stanley (Red) Wrobel, escorted by Joe Sheridan, entered the executive office suite in the state capitol to meet with Victor C. Anderson. A four-time offender, Wrobel was serving a life sentence for armed robbery. Casting an angry glance toward Sheridan, Wrobel prefaced his remarks by complaining that ever since March, when it had been leaked to the detective that he could shed light on the Hooper murder, he had been subjected to constant badgering. Finally, to get Sheridan to leave him alone, he agreed to testify.[31]

According to Wrobel, it was "common talk among the Jew boys in Jackson Prison that Dave Mazroff, a former Purple, had been forced to bump the senator off," receiving $11,000 for the job. In a rambling three-hour discourse, Wrobel named as co-conspirators past and present inmates Alvin "Bing" Labadie, Harold Johnson, Morris Raider, John Novinski, and Mike Biagini, as well as the madam of a Jackson bordello frequented by prison guards.[32] Subsequent quizzing of the convicts convinced Leonard and Anderson that Wrobel's accusations were "unfounded."[33]

Wrobel's name arose again on February 26, 1948 when he and Alfred Kurner escaped from the minimum security Cassidy Lake prison camp. The next day they sought refuge with *Detroit News* crime reporter Al Nieber, telling him that they had new information on the Hooper case. While secreted at the *Detroit News* office, Kurner telephoned the Detroit Michigan State Police Post demanding that Sheridan and other detectives "lay off" for thirty-six hours if they wanted to learn who killed the senator. Nieber hastily arranged a meeting for the escapees with Victor C. Anderson, but insisted that the governor's chief legal aide promise that the *News* writer would have a "scoop" on the story.[34] Upon receiving word of these events from Anderson, Governor Sigler initially told his press ally that he was certain Wrobel and Kurner would set forth "unimportant material" which would "make a good newspaper story, but whose publication might hamper the Hooper investigation."[35] To avoid embarrassment to his friend, Nieber agreed and did not publish any details of what transpired until April 2.[36]

The tale spun by Kurner was that Hooper had been slain by an inmate of Jackson Prison who had been supplied with a weapon from Harry Fleisher's arsenal at O'Larry's Bar. The convict asserted that on the afternoon of either December 27 or 28, 1944, Harry Fleisher and Mike Selik took him to their office at O'Larry's and offered him two fifty-dollar bills to deliver a box to a man who would be standing at 9:00 p.m. in front of the Regent Cafe in Jackson. Identifying the accomplice by a folded newspaper under his arm, Kurner was to ask if the food inside was good; if the response was "I don't know because I'm broke," he was to turn over the package. En route, the curious mobster opened the parcel and saw a .38 calibre police special. At the cafe, he recognized his contact as Harold Johnson, D. C. Pettit's houseboy and driver. After exchanging the code, Johnson took the box and drove away in what Kurner knew to be Pettit's maroon coupe.[37]

When asked by Anderson why he had not volunteered the information sooner, Kurner sneered that Sigler had promised him an early parole in return for his testimony in the Hooper murder conspiracy trial, but had "betrayed" him. Anticipating such treachery by the special prosecutor, Kurner had shrewdly withheld "vital information" in hopes of forcing Sigler to abide by his pledge.[38]

Kurner and Wrobel were returned to Jackson Prison and on January 6, 1949, they received an additional one to three years for breaking out of jail. At the sentencing, Kurner — who previously had been highly emotional during his court appearances — was truculent when asked by Circuit Judge James Breakey if he wished to comment, either openly or in chambers, on the Hooper matter. "I'd rather let things rest as they are," was the stony response. "I'd rather not say anything about the Hooper case. I've done enough of people's dirty washing in this state. I don't want to do any more."[39] Meanwhile, Johnson, who was serving a life sentence for kidnapping and armed robbery, denied any knowledge of the assassination and polygraph tests on him proved "inconclusive."[40] No further action was taken on Kurner's testimony.

Less than three months later, Mitchell Bonkowski, 43-year-old former houseboy of D. C. Pettit, penned a letter to State Police Captain Edward Cooper in which he claimed to have facts on the Hooper case. On March 28, 1949, detectives Murray Young and Walter Williams went to Jackson Prison to take Bonkowski's statement. The officers were told that on January 11, 1945, Bonkowski was at Pettit's house and noticed Harold Johnson drive Dave Mazroff and another former Purple, Morris Raider, from the prison in the deputy warden's dark red coupe. As they passed, he heard Mazroff snarl, "We'll get the son of a bitch." Bonkowski sheepishly confessed that he was coming forward only because, unlike other convicts, he had been offered no hush money.[41]

The following July 30, Herman "Frenchie" Faubert, who had served thirteen years of his life sentence for first degree murder, was interrogated at Jackson Prison by Joe Sheridan. The 40-year-old inmate related that several convicts, along with Harry Fleisher, Mike Selik, and Floyd Fitzsimmons, had met on January 6, 1945, to plot Hooper's death. According to Faubert, he and fellow inmate Charles Watson had been instructed by another prisoner, Raymond Fox, to obtain a .38 calibre Iver Johnson revolver from the prison arsenal and bring it to him. Fox then acquired prison guard uniforms and caps for himself, Dave Mazroff, and Morris Raider. On January 11, the three donned the uniforms and sped from the penitentiary in Pettit's automobile, which had been fitted with a fake license plate. Later that evening, the successful assassins confided to Faubert — for reasons unknown to him — the details of how Fox had slain the lawmaker in return for $15,000, which Fitzsimmons had promised Frank McKay would pay for the job.[42]

During the next three months, ten more interviews were taken with the two convicts, and in early November Detective Young requested, and received, permission to have lie detector tests conducted on Harold Johnson, Charles Watson, and D. C. Pettit. Four batteries of questions were given Johnson and three to Watson, but no indication of knowledge of, or involvement in, the Hooper murder was indicated. Pettit underwent five examinations, with "very slight" variations from normal shown on questions relating to the murder. While these were not sufficient to prove guilt, the administering officer warned in his report that the results might be misleading because "the subject is not very emotional."[43]

On November 17, the *Detroit Times* broke the Faubert-Bonkowski story. Leonard immediately admitted that the state police and Detroit authorities had spent several months investigating the accuracy of their testimony, but added that he remained skeptical, especially of Faubert's account because it had changed many times.[44] This disclaimer notwithstanding, the three Detroit dailies vied for readership with bold headlines blazing *"Hooper Death Solved."*

Both Raider and Pettit, the latter having been employed since his ouster as deputy warden in 1945 by the New York Central Railroad Company branch in Jackson, voluntarily surrendered to Detroit police when they read the *Times'* account. The former prison official dismissed the allegations as an attempt by the two convicts to win "early release...or other special favors," while Raider, still dapper and youthful at 49, exclaimed confidently: "The story is fantastic. It is ridiculous. I have nothing to hide."[45]

In late afternoon on November 17, Leonard and other police officers assembled Raider, Pettit, Bonkowski, and Faubert at Detroit Police Headquarters for interrogation. After hearing protestations of innocence from the mobster and former deputy warden, the authorities turned their attention to Bonkowski, who proceeded to contradict nearly everything he had uttered during his mid-October testimony. Initially, he had claimed to have been traveling along a dirt road delivering liquor for inmate Harold Johnson when he accidentally came upon the site of the murder just as it was being committed. He heard two shots and saw Raider and Mazroff wearing prison uniforms. Later that evening he watched Johnson sit in Pettit's basement and file serial numbers from a .38 calibre pistol and then go outside and bury it in a nearby sewer trench. At the November 17 examination, however, Bonkowski asserted that he had been part of a caravan of killers, heard three shots, made M-99 a paved thoroughfare, and had been told by Johnson that the gun had been disposed of in the ditch. Variances such as these led Leonard to jot a note to himself that Bonkowski's story was "full of crap."[46]

Faubert's tale, which was related in Pettit's presence, was a compilation of parts of his earlier versions. He claimed to have been in Pettit's basement, along with Raider and Mazroff, on January 6, 1945. At that time, Floyd Fitzsimmons told them that Pete Mahoney "couldn't do any good with Hooper to keep him from talking to the grand jury" and that Mazroff and Raider "had better try to get him to take $15,000 to keep quiet." On January 11, Faubert and Harold Johnson were at Pettit's house and witnessed Raider and Mazroff, wearing prison guard caps and jackets, drive off in Pettit's red coupe. Shortly afterward, Mazroff telephoned Johnson, who was still at Pettit's residence, and ordered him to fetch a gun hidden in the basement and bring it to him. Johnson got the weapon, picked up Faubert, and drove to the assigned rendezvous, where he delivered the pistol to Mazroff. The gangsters waited until Hooper's car passed, with Mike Selik in the passenger's seat. Raider and Mazroff raced to overtake it, while Johnson and Faubert followed closely. After Hooper's car had been forced onto the shoulder, Selik told Raider that the senator had refused the bribe. "Tell him it's his last chance!" Faubert recalled Raider yelling. When the lawmaker remained adamant, Raider sent two bullets crashing into Hooper's head. The murderous band then returned to Pettit's house where, after Faubert changed the license plate and burned the uniforms in the basement furnace, the pay-off money was split amid much gaiety and drinking.[47]

Throughout the questioning, Pettit shouted "Liar, liar – you're lying!" and requested permission to quiz Faubert. Leonard consented to the unorthodox procedure, and for nearly thirty minutes the bespectacled, gray-maned former prison official, who was reputed by convicts and police alike to be addicted to alcohol and narcotics, mercilessly assailed the unflappable witness.[48] Frustrated, Pettit roared loud enough to be heard by reporters milling in the corridor: "It seems to me that every time some convict wants to get out of the can for a while he says he knows who killed Hooper. They've been coming up with this stuff every two or three months, about this murder having been plotted out at Jackson Prison. Bonkowski alone has come up with so many stories that I don't know what he can be up to now!"[49]

Despite Leonard's weary statement that little progress had been made during the day-long grilling and that he had compiled a list of thirty-six discrepancies in the accounts of Faubert and Bonkowski, Detroit Police Commissioner Harry S. Toy pronounced that the Hooper murder had been solved and urged that warrants be issued.[50] When Leonard not only refused to seek arrests, but also declined to hold Pettit, Toy vehemently blasted the state police head, angrily telling newsmen: "If this were my case, we would have had warrants long ago, and some people who are now out of prison would be in. It's hard to understand how the state police can take the attitude they have when the lie detector tests of Pettit definitely indicated there is something for the courts here."[51] Toy further suggested that a grand jury be called by Attorney General Stephen J. Roth to investigate the recent disclosures.[52]

As the story was developing, a *Detroit Free Press* reporter telephoned the senator's widow and the next day wrote that she "had pleaded for a grand jury to expose the 'politician' who purportedly paid for the slaying of her husband," as well as reiterating her belief that the state police had denied the senator protection even though they knew his life was in danger.[53] Having perused the article, Mrs. Hooper phoned her friend George V. Mather, the editor of the *Albion Evening Recorder*, to denounce the *Free Press* account. She had never "pleaded" for a grand jury, she protested, and maintained that since that unhappy night in January "the state police have been swell to me."[54] However, she did admit readily to the accuracy of the quote regarding her continuing financial plight. "At the time Warren was killed, the newspapers said the state was going to give me five hundred dollars for his funeral and pay me his salary for two years," she bitterly recounted, "but all I got was forty-five dollars. I had to borrow the money for his funeral."[55]

To silence Toy, Leonard agreed to dig for the alleged murder weapon which Bonkowski said had been interred in a ditch on Pettit's prison farm. On November 21, Bonkowski was taken to the site to assist a work gang of twenty-two convicts in locating the revolver. Two days of sifting dirt brought forth only rusty nails, scrap metal, and the scornful observation by Bonkowski that he had never stated that there was anything buried there. "They intended to throw it in the ditch, but I don't know if it's there," he said glibly. "If they dig, they're on their own."[56]

Meanwhile, Faubert was taken by two state police troopers and an equal number of Detroit police detectives to pinpoint the spot on M-99 where he had viewed the assassination. With undisguised contempt aimed at Toy for demanding a predictable exercise in futility, Leonard announced: "Faubert didn't take them to the spot. They drove right past it to the village limit of Springport. He never did point out the spot. Faubert is an unmitigated liar."[57]

On November 24, the *Detroit Times* summed up the debacle with the headline: "Hooper Case Blows Up." Morris Raider had been released on a writ of habeas corpus, and the circuit judge who signed the order ridiculed the Detroit police for believing such a "fantastic" unsubstantiated story.[58] Moreover, Detective Sergeant Edward Johnston of the state police reported that his excavations of the three-foot-wide trench had reached a depth of nine feet along its entire forty-foot length. That nothing resembling a gun or its parts was unearthed was not unexpected, he added, since prison records showed the ditch had been unopened since 1942 – three years before the Hooper slaying.[59]

On December 13, Faubert met with Leonard, Roth, and Jackson County Prosecutor George R. Campbell and confessed that his story was "a lie from start to finish." His intention had been to try to help himself, and any other inmates who supported him, to get out of prison. "I told them," he said softly, "that we'll all hit the streets if we can put this story over." With more fear than remorse, he added: "I never even met Raider until last month in Detroit police headquarters. Now I'm going back [to Jackson Prison] for what I said, and I will pay for it with my life."[60]

Undismayed by what he perceived to be state police collusion, Toy refused to accept the admission. "I anticipated that when we left here," the Detroit Commissioner huffed. "Our officers are still convinced Faubert told the truth about the slaying to us. The only place to find the truth is in a courtroom — let a judicial body decide."[61] No further investigation was made; no harm befell the returned convicts; and the perpetrator of Michigan's most sensational murder remained a mystery.

V In the midst of investigating these "kites," the state police were faced with another dilemma. On June 14, 1948, the Michigan Supreme Court unanimously upheld the convictions of Harry and Sam Fleisher and Mike Selik for conspiracy to murder Warren G. Hooper, but reversed that of Pete Mahoney.[62] "Careful consideration has been given to numerous errors asserted by the defendants," declared the justices, "but we find no justification for reaching any other conclusion than that the defendants...were not deprived of due process of law or of their right to a fair trial in consequence of any judicial error."[63] Subsequent to this ruling, Sam Fleisher prepared to enter Jackson Prison on October 18, while his brother, Selik, and Mahoney remained free on $25,000 appeal bonds pending a decision on their request for a retrial on the Aristocrat Club case.[64]

On October 4, 1948, the State Supreme Court denied the retrial motion, and within minutes of the news reaching Detroit, Mahoney was apprehended and taken to Jackson Prison. The swift arrest was made possible by Circuit Judge George B. Hartrick, who had signed commitment papers several hours before the court decision was announced. Yet no papers were prepared for Fleisher and Selik, nor were their bonds cancelled. Both the judge and special prosecutor Louis Bebout determined to withhold action on them until the supreme court made its ruling, scheduled for October 12, on a motion on behalf of all three defendants for a new hearing on their appeal. Bebout told reporters gathered in his office: "I don't care whether Fleisher and Selik are arrested or not. If they are, all right. If not, all right. If they are given additional liberty by the supreme court, it will be much simpler if they're not in jail."[65] This scenario was ridiculed by the *Detroit News* as "Pete Mahoney Sits in Jail, But Nobody Wants Fleisher." In response to Bebout, the newspaper prophesied that "it isn't very likely they'll go walking in search of a policeman for the next few days."[66]

Not unexpectedly, by the time the court denied the motion, the two mobsters were nowhere to be found. Detroit police alerted authorities at the Canadian and Mexican borders and had special patrols stationed at international airports.[67] Informed of the escape, Governor Sigler erupted with rage. "Three years ago I predicted that cash bonds, no matter how high, would never hold Fleisher and Selik," he stormed. "The people who paid for and engineered the Hooper killing will pay any amount to protect these hoodlums. I worked hard to solve the Hooper case, but I didn't get the cooperation I asked for. I advised Judge Hartrick at the time to deny bail and let the supreme court grant it if it wished to under the circumstances. Harry Fleisher and Mike Selik would not be at large now if Judge Hartrick and the court had stuck by their guns and denied bail."[68]

Hartrick, who allegedly had been promised a seat on the state's highest tribunal by Sigler in return for imposing the 25 to 50-year sentences in the Aristocrat Club trial, held a press conference to defend his actions. "I set the cash bonds when I got the heat put on me from all directions," he explained lamely. "I was told the supreme court looked with disfavor upon judges who are so tough as not to set bond."[69] When asked where the "heat" had originated, the beleaguered jurist said: "From the state's attorneys handling appeal matters. They told me I was a heel not to set bond when a bond had already been set by Judge Hatch in the murder conspiracy case. I couldn't understand it, especially when it came from Sigler's special assistant counsel H. H. Warner."[70]

By October 23, the search for the fugitives had attained a status usually reserved, as an Associated Press writer noted, for an episode in a "low grade detective story."[71] Rumors abounded that Fleisher and Selik had been seen in San Diego, California; that they had gone to Bolivia, which had no extradition treaty with the United States; and that they had fled to Israel.[72] Amidst the confusion, Sigler announced the possibility of offering a substantial state reward for their apprehension. "Only a good taste of prison existence will lead them to talk," the governor reasoned, "and if it is money that is needed to bring about their recapture, then the state will put up the money. Solving the Hooper case is more important than the money which would be spent as a reward."[73] Emphasizing the absolute necessity to put the felons behind bars, he warned: "They wouldn't care about a few more years for additional crimes. They're both in early middle age now. Forty years in prison means that they'll never get out alive anyway. In the face of this, they wouldn't think twice about taking revenge on witnesses who have sent them to prison."[74]

Fleisher managed to evade police until January 18, 1950, when he was seized by four FBI agents as he lay shirtless on a Pompano, Florida, beach having suntan lotion rubbed on his back by a female companion. With four guns trained on him, Fleisher was stripped of his trousers, handcuffed, and searched. As he was led away through a crowd of curious onlookers, he meekly said to one of the G-men: "I guess I didn't get away with it, huh?"[75]

Questioned in Miami by Michigan State Police Detective Murray Young, the tanned fugitive, nattily attired in a blue open-necked shirt and darker blue pants, winked slyly when asked if he had been in Detroit since slipping out of that city in 1948. As to the Hooper and Aristocrat Club cases, his only reply was: "You fellows know more about this than I do. You know those two rats Abramowitz and Luks framed me."[76]

On January 22, Young accompanied Fleisher — who was manacled, bound in body chains, and had his face swathed in bandages to conceal his identity — on the airplane trip to Detroit.[77] Eight days later he appeared before Federal Judge Theodore Levin for sentencing. Looking glum and clad in a wrinkled suit and raincoat, Fleisher wearily gave his rationale for having jumped bail. "I was forced to do what I done — and that's all," he muttered. "I've been given a bad deal in my other cases and I felt that this was the logical thing to do. Not that I wanted to do it. I was forced to do it, as I got a bad deal and I thought I would do what I done."[78] Oblivious to the appeal, Levin imposed five years in federal prison at Leavenworth to be added to Fleisher's existing penalties, which brought the ex-Purple leader's minimum jail term to thirty years.[79]

VI On Friday, March 17, 1950, Commissioner Leonard met with Gordon Gillis, a private investigator who had worked for Leo Wendell on the Carr grand jury, for nearly two hours at the Statler Hotel in Washington, D.C.[80] Gillis had made a hobby of the Hooper slaying and was convinced, after many conversations with his Detroit underworld informants, that Tommy Viola was the triggerman.[81] The private eye previously had discussed his findings with Hugh Daly and Al Kaufman, *Detroit Times* correspondents in Washington, D.C. and Lansing, respectively, and Michigan State Police Captain Edward Cooper, a close friend of Kaufman.[82]

Two days later in Lansing, Kaufman was summoned to brief Leonard on the "Viola angle." The reporter also furnished the commissioner a copy of a lengthy memorandum penned by Daly supporting Gillis' allegations, as well as intimating that neither Sigler nor the state police were anxious to solve the murder.[83] Daly believed Gillis because of four circumstantial facts which could tie Viola to the crime: (1) Viola was a known gangland killer; (2) Viola admitted to being in Detroit, under the alias of Shapiro, on the day of the assassination; (3) despite operating from Peter Licavoli's ranch in Tucson, Arizona, Viola had committed at least three murders for Detroit mobsters and would have been a logical choice to do another; and (4) Viola had numerous connections with Detroit hoodlums. Those

178

points, Daly declared, should have led anyone to think it worthwhile to at least question Viola, but "not so with Sigler or the Michigan State Police."[84]

According to Daly, Gillis was interested not only in any reward money, but also in cutting a deal with Sigler to help Panhandle Eastern Pipeline, his current employer, to gain an edge on Michigan Consolidated in the state's natural gas war. With the intent of trading Hooper's killer for a business concession, Gillis had gone to H. H. Warner, one of Sigler's chief legal aides, who agreed to turn the information in to the governor and arrange for a conference with him. The meeting lasted less than twenty minutes, as Sigler dismissed Gillis' theory on the grounds that Viola was Italian. Gillis lamented that the governor kept shaking his head and repeating, "It was a Jew killing; I know it was a Jew killing."[85]

Gillis then trekked to Warren, Ohio, where Viola was awaiting trial on a murder charge, and peddled his theory to the chief of police. The chief sent two telegrams to the Michigan State Police, but when he received no reply he did not even bother to question Viola on his whereabouts on the day of the crime.[86] The erstwhile sleuth took his story next to the governor of Ohio and asked if he would be willing to extradite Viola to Michigan if he confessed to the Hooper slaying. The governor consented, but garnered no response to his offer from Michigan authorities.[87]

Gillis also maintained that a wholesale grocery vendor from Jackson witnessed the crime when he stopped his car next to Hooper's in the belief that an accident had occurred. According to Gillis, the eyewitness saw the killer come around the rear of the automobile holding a gun; he was then ordered to "get the hell on your way before something happens to you, too!" The following day the terrified salesman related his story to Sigler, who vowed to protect his identity from gangland killers, put his car under protective custody, and changed the license plate and registration so they could not be traced back to the owner by the murderers. Sigler refused to permit any officers working on the case to see the witness, Gillis contended, but they were allowed to listen through a partition while the special prosecutor interviewed him. Gillis further claimed that Viola's photograph was never shown to the witness, which led the investigator to conclude that "Sigler never wanted to find the man who murdered Hooper, and that the state police, realizing this, were never free to operate as they desired."[88]

Contrary to Gillis' allegations, the state police had considered Viola a suspect as early as January 18, 1945, when *Detroit Free Press* reporter Kenneth McCormick put forth his name because the gunman was a close friend of Charles Leiter and Isadore Schwartz, an associate of Sam Fleisher, a "McKay man," and known for the same modus operandi as in the Hooper slaying; moreover, he was 5'6" in height and wore a size six shoe.[89]

On March 23, 1950, Captain Harold Mulbar sent Leonard a letter indicating that, even though Viola's name had been one of the first considered as a probable suspect, no one but McCormick had pointed a finger of suspicion toward him. The chief of detectives added that Lieutenant Morse had "never seriously considered Tommy Viola as having participated in, or having any information of value, in connection with the murder of Senator Hooper." He concluded by stating: "The state police did not have, nor does have to this date, any information that connected Viola to the murder. There was little or nothing to talk to him about. To my knowledge, Viola has always refused to answer any questions at all."[90]

Four days later, Mulbar reported to Leonard that he had interviewed Captain Cooper, the now retired Morse, Sergeant Van Conant, and detectives Edward Johnston and Walter Williams in a vain effort to secure more information on Viola's culpability. He had also been advised by Detroit police officials to discount Viola as a suspect. "I do not eliminate in my mind Viola as one who may have been approached to commit the crime," Mulbar summarized. "To the best of my knowledge he has always been considered as a probable suspect and never completely eliminated. I have never considered him as what might be considered a 'serious suspect.' We have known since his apprehension that talking to Viola will not extract any incriminating statements from him. If he is involved in the Senator Hooper murder, the information and evidence will have to develop from some other source. As long as I had anything to do officially with the investigation, no evidence was produced to indicate Viola was involved, or to give a basis of anything to talk to him about, relative to the murder of Senator Warren G. Hooper."[91]

To clear the air, Cooper and Murray Young went to Washington, D.C. on May 4, 1950, to interrogate Gillis. He told them that while loitering in the state capitol, he had overheard the eyewitness say he saw two men standing at the murder scene. The detectives noted in their report that this was doubtful because not only had the witness, Harry Snyder, always maintained there was only one partially concealed man at the site, but also he had never undergone questioning at the capitol building. Equally erroneous was Gillis' contention that Snyder had never been shown Viola's picture; in actuality, the witness had viewed the gangster's mug shot several times, always with negative results. Also, they discovered that contrary to Gillis' allegation, the FBI had no record of Viola having been in Detroit on either January 10 or 11, 1945.[92]

Gillis eagerly volunteered his theory of the motive behind the assassination: After Hooper confronted William Green, the frightened former lawmaker had been tailed by grand jury investigators to McKay's office in Grand Rapids. McKay, doubtless surrounded by his bodyguards Leiter and Schwartz, most likely remarked that the senator would have to be removed. The two ex-Purples probably contacted Harry Fleisher, who at that time was working for Mike Rubino. The Italian mobster then urged the hiring of a fellow Italian, Viola, for the job. This scenario broke down, however, when Van Conant, who had headed the grand jury detail, could not recall assigning a tail on Green and could find nothing in Green's file to indicate a visit to McKay immediately after the Hooper encounter in Lansing.[93] As a consequence, the state police came to regard Gillis as a mere opportunist, and Viola's name never again surfaced during the probe.[94]

V II During the Gillis investigations, another more promising lead occupied state police detectives. On January 10, 1950, Murray Young and *Detroit Times* crime writer James Melton visited Naomi Selik at the United States Public Health Service Hospital in Lexington, Kentucky, where she was being treated for drug addiction. She expressed great concern when told of the effects confinement was having on Pete Mahoney's mental condition. Melton hinted that if the Hooper murder weapon could be found it might help the Detroit gambler. "The gun will never be found," she sighed dejectedly. Suddenly grabbing the reporter's arm, she pleaded: "Pete had no more to do with murdering Hooper than you, Jimmy!" She then agreed to Melton's suggestion that upon her scheduled release on July 9, she would return with the writer to Michigan to speak with Mahoney and try to convince him that his imprisonment could be shortened if he would cooperate with the state police in solving the Hooper case.[95]

Before meeting with Mrs. Selik again on May 11, Young and Melton contacted Mahoney several times, and on each occasion he adamantly rejected proposals to see her. He did evince a willingness, however, to take a polygraph test on whether he had been involved in the Hooper murder, but insisted he would not submit to queries on what he had been told by Harry Fleisher or Mike Selik.[96]

When advised of Mahoney's attitude, Naomi paused and then told Young and Melton that she thought she knew the reason for his reluctance and asked their permission to write him a note to relieve his anxieties. Melton handed her a blank check, upon which she spent more than thirty minutes composing a carefully worded, cryptic message: "Hello Pete — Hear you have a new 'butch' haircut. Bet on you it looks good. Look fellow, I am in sound physical and *mental* health. As you say, everything is provitz with me. I don't know the story there but would like to say hello to you. That's all, bub. I am still just the same as I always was and expect to be permanently. Dig? Same old Naomi. Will send you regards after I'm out."[97]

When Young left the room to obtain information on her parole conditions, she hastily confided to Melton that she knew the entire story of the murder but would not do any talking to a police officer. After receiving a pledge of confidentiality, she told Melton of a purported meeting at the Book-Cadillac Hotel in Detroit between Frank McKay, Floyd Fitzsimmons, Abe Bernstein, and Harry Fleisher, at which time money had been given to the latter to pay Hooper not to testify. Mike Selik was waiting for Fleisher outside the hotel, and the two drove away in a car "borrowed from a square [noncriminal]." When they confronted the senator, Selik shot him and kept the money.[98]

Despite her assurance that the only cause for telling the story now was to clear Mahoney, Melton surmised a stronger motive for her to finger her husband as the triggerman. Perhaps, he mused, she thought Mike was dead and this would be a means of protecting the real killer and thus keep her in the mob's good graces. Then, too, she may have heard the rumors that the FBI had been tipped to Harry Fleisher's whereabouts by Frank McKay, who had been vacationing in Florida at the time of the arrest, and this could be her way of gaining revenge against the Grand Rapids financier. Regardless, Melton felt there were at least three reasons why her account might be true: (1) Harry Snyder initially had pointed out Selik and Sam Fleisher, who easily could be mistaken for his older brother Harry, as the men he saw in the maroon automobile at the murder scene, but he was not positive enough to swear to it in open court; (2) in 1948 a Jackson Prison inmate had told Melton that he had overheard Mike Selik and Ray Bernstein talking about Hooper in early January 1945, and that Selik had said he would do the job; and (3) it was a well-known fact that Floyd Fitzsimmons had attempted to buy Hooper's silence.[99]

Having divulged her confidences to Young as soon as the two men left the hospital, Melton urged another visit to Mahoney. On the afternoon of May 15, Melton and Young spoke to the convict in a prison holding room and offered him Mrs. Selik's letter. He refused to accept it or have it read to him, vigorously protesting that he had no idea what she was up to, and did not want to know, because it could only harm his cause.[100]

On July 4, 1950, Naomi Selik was released from confinement to the custody of Young and Melton. En route to Lansing, she was questioned extensively on the Hooper slaying and gave the following recollection: On the night of the murder, at around 6:00 p.m., Mike's mother telephoned to say that she had heard on the radio that Mr. Hoover had been killed. Not knowing whether this meant the former president or the FBI director, Naomi called her husband at his Twelfth Street gambling joint to relay the news. He was very abrupt and said he was too busy to talk. A few days later, Mike received a call from Ray Bernstein's brother Abe and scurried from the apartment. When he returned after a brief absence, he rushed to his closet, removed a pair of shoes and new gray suede gloves, and began cutting them. She assisted, using shears on the gloves and a razor blade on the shoes. Pieces of the gloves were flushed down the toilet and the shoes were incinerated. Another call from Bernstein took Mike away long enough for him to go to O'Larry's Bar and come back. He shoved a roll of bills containing $5,000 at her and told her to hide it, which she did by stuffing it inside a doll. This had led her to believe that Mike and Harry Fleisher must have killed the senator and that the money represented her husband's share of the pay-off.[101]

When pressed for more details, she said that on the morning of the murder Mike and Harry had driven away in Fleisher's black Cadillac, and that she had never understood why every account referred to a maroon car at the scene. Otherwise, she simply reiterated that she assumed, based on events which had transpired shortly after the crime, that her husband and Fleisher were the murderers.[102]

Two days later, she met Mahoney in the warden's office at Jackson Prison in the presence of Corrections Commissioner Earnest C. Brooks and Detective Young, but the two spoke only in generalities because, she contended, Mahoney was "too frightened to tell her anything." She then requested permission to return to her former Detroit apartment on Boston Boulevard long enough to make contacts as to Mike's possible hiding spot. This was agreed to, with the stipulation that she furnish the state police all information she acquired.[103]

On July 12, Melton notified Captain Cooper that Naomi apparently had seen her husband as she had disappeared for twenty-four hours and returned wearing one of his rings. She also had told Melton that Mike intended to surrender within forty-eight hours to Judge Hartrick, but the deadline passed uneventfully.[104]

Melton next heard from her on July 20, when she was arrested on a drunk and disorderly charge on Boston Boulevard and sought release in his custody, which was done. Cooper concluded that her value had reached a minimum and remanded her to her parole officer in Kansas.[105]

During the last week of August, Commissioner Brooks submitted a list of six questions drawn up by Mahoney for his lie detector test. Brooks warned Young that Mahoney was insistent that nothing else be asked, and that the prisoner was so nervous that "we have got to do quite a little work to get him in the proper frame of mind before we're going to find out anything from him, if then."[106]

On September 6, Mahoney was transported to East Lansing for the polygraph examination. Three tests were conducted by Michigan State Police Sergeant Wilber H. Petermann, with the key items being: (1) Were you in Albion the day Senator Hooper was murdered? (2) Were you involved in the murder of Senator Hooper? (3) Were you in Lansing the day Senator Hooper was shot? and (4) Did you kill Senator Hooper? Petermann reported "considerable deception in the responses to the first two queries.[107]

As Mahoney shuffled from the room, he was bombarded by waiting reporters. His nerves, already frayed by the ordeal, could tolerate no more questions, and he screamed: "I'm not a policeman! I'm not here to clean up the Hooper case! I'm not a stool pigeon, and I'm not a rat! I'm just here to prove my innocence. Sure, I've heard a lot of stories, but I try to put them out of my mind."[108] Sergeant Petermann fielded inquiries with the lie that Mahoney's responses were "inconclusive because he was too nervous and excited."[109] Commissioner Brooks chimed in with his opinion that finally "the picture was opening up" on the Hooper case.[110] After they departed, the thoroughly confused media representatives were left to determine for themselves which interpretation was closest to the truth.

Mahoney returned to state police headquarters again on October 24, 1950, and March 22, 1951, for additional polygraph examinations. In each instance he was asked questions similar to those posed in previous sessions regarding his possible involvement in the slaying. As before, his responses were deemed by Petermann to indicate that Mahoney was "concealing information about the Hooper case."[111] The gambler maintained his plea of innocence, however, arguing that if he had been in Albion on the day of the crime, which he denied, then certainly he would be convicted of the murder.[112]

Knowing that only Evelyn Iris Brown had placed Mahoney in Albion on July 11, Brooks, who believed Mahoney's protestations, suggested another interview with the former tavern manager. Therefore, on the night of April 4, 1951, Brooks, Young, and Cooper called at Mrs. Brown's home in Margeno, Michigan. The passing years had strengthened her memories of the visitors to the Top Hat Tavern on that fateful wintry day. The gist of her account was recorded by Young in a report submitted to Commissioner Leonard exactly two weeks later:

Shortly after the murder she had an argument with a tavern patron and told him of seeing two suspicious men in her place on the day of the murder. A few days after the argument, Detective Sergeant Bion Hoeg called on her stating the patron had informed him of her suspicion. She informed Hoeg that she came to work at 12 noon on the day of the murder and shortly afterward two strange men came in and sat in a booth. She served them several bottles of beer, and the smaller man, about 45 years of age, only drank part of each bottle and made several trips to the men's rest room. He seemed quite nervous and kept comparing the time with a pocket watch he carried in his vest with their wall clock. She concluded from the way he looked her over that he was a ladies' man. He spoke with a decided foreign accent, and she remembered that he inquired if Albion time was the same as Lansing time. She had a very good opportunity to see his face but did not see the face of his partner as he did not look up when served.... In April of 1945, Detective Johnston called on her and asked if she would go to the Jackson Post with two other ladies to look at some suspects. At the Post she was permitted to look out a rear window through drawn venetian blinds and saw eight or nine men in a line. She was given an opportunity to see them from all angles, but when she first sighted the man she later learned to be Mahoney, she stated at once he was the same man that was in her place and said so to Captain Hansen. She states now that there is no doubt in her mind that she was, and is, absolutely certain he was the man. She was not shown a picture of this subject between the time she saw him in the tavern and when she identified him at the Jackson Post.[113]

Following Mrs. Brown's recitation, even Brooks was forced to admit that Mahoney's fate was sealed. The happy-go-lucky, two-bit gambler who loved to rub elbows with the underworld elite would never breathe the air of freedom unless he squealed. However, as

Harry Fleisher stated with admiration, Mahoney was "a swell little guy who kept his mouth shut."[114] When death stilled him in 1959, Mahoney had not violated the criminal "code of silence."

VIII

At 10:48 a.m., February 2, 1951, a telegram from Chief Inspector August W. Flath of the New York City Police Department was handed to Sergeant Thomas Grant at Michigan State Police Headquarters. His eyes widened with excitement as they scanned the message: "This Department arrested on charge of robbery one Max Green, MW, 38, 5'7", 140, black hair, brown eyes, small moustache. Fingerprint classification 13 over 14, large R numerator 00 over M, final count 19 in denominator. He is identified with your Myron Selik wanted November 4, 1948 for failing to appear for sentence. Advise if wanted and if forwarding warrant."[115] Twelve minutes later, having conferred with Detective Young and other officers, the sergeant telephoned Flath to confirm the wire's authenticity and to verify the fingerprint analysis.[116]

Virtually certain that Green was Selik, Grant phoned Leonard in Washington, D.C. The commissioner ordered that Young and another officer leave by the first available commercial flight for New York City to question and, if possible, gain custody of the captive.[117]

Late in the evening of February 2, Young huddled with Edward F. Breslin, assistant district attorney for the Bronx, and learned the details surrounding Selik's apprehension. After a $20,000 jewel and fur heist from a Bronx apartment, police put well-known "second-story men" under surveillance. They had become suspicious of Selik only when he was seen accompanying three oft-arrested burglars in their flashy automobiles. For several weeks the suspects were under twenty-four-hour-a-day observation, which led one detective to boast that "we were following them so closely we put them to bed every night and took them out again in the morning."[118] When the four were seized on February 1, Selik, wearing a $350 gold wristwatch set with twelve diamonds, begged police not to shoot him. While being frisked, Selik repeated, "I was framed," but when a pocketful of the stolen jewels were found in his custom-tailored suit, he shrugged his shoulders and said with a smile, "Well, what else can I say?"[119]

Young and Breslin interrogated the fugitive for much of the next morning. "I assure you, Mike," threatened the D.A., "we have a good case against you. If you are convicted here, I will ask for a 59 to 60-year sentence in Sing Sing for you. If you cooperate with the Michigan authorities it may be easier for you."[120]

"I can't help," came the innocent reply. "I don't know anything about the Hooper case. I was railroaded."[121]

"Well, your wife told us you could help plenty!" barked Young.

"My wife is a very imaginative woman," smiled Selik with wry nonchalance. Leaning forward he pleaded with insincerity: "I'd like to help. It would make things easier for me, but I don't know a thing."[122]

"You know something about the Hooper case," hammered Young, glaring at the smirking gangster. "You know the details we need, don't you!"[123]

"Look," Selik replied smugly, "that conviction of mine was a political affair. Look at the record. The judge that indicted us is on the supreme court now. The prosecutor got to be governor. If that wasn't political, what is?"[124]

Selik laughed that he "must have a great publicity man in Detroit" when told of stories that he had spent much of his flight in Florida and South America. He rebuffed all endeavors to have him submit to a polygraph test, and he refused to seek extradition to Michigan. Dismayed, Young wired headquarters: "We don't have a lever until he knows he's going to get a long sentence from New York. There is nothing we can do now until it goes through the next term of court."[125]

The ex-Purple did not long evade the clutches of Michigan, as an arrangement was made whereby, regardless of the outcome of his New York trial, he would be returned to Michigan to serve his remaining time. In late August 1951, Selik was brought to the federal detention center in Milan, Michigan. The following February 12, Federal Judge Arthur F. Lederle handed down an additional five years at Leavenworth to Selik for his unlawful flight.[126] Once again the dapper hoodlum would be reunited with his old pal Harry Fleisher.

IX Donald Leonard resigned as head of the state police in 1952 and made an abortive bid for the Republican gubernatorial nomination.[127] When he left office he took with him all records of investigations into the Hooper murder, thereby rendering further probing virtually impossible.[128] Equally intriguing, in light of Leonard's action, is that Frank D. McKay vigorously backed the former commissioner not only in 1952 but also in his successful primary race two years later, stating flatly that Leonard was the only hope for the state GOP.[129]

On the fifteenth anniversary of the assassination, the *Detroit News* ran the last feature story ever printed on the Hooper case. In a half-page article, complete with photographs of the principal characters, the drama was reconstructed. Its conclusion summarized the futile quest to answer the question "who paid for the slaying?" with the simple comment that "the mystery is as great today as ever."[130]

CHAPTER NINE
THE MYSTERY RESOLVED

I More than four decades have elapsed since that fateful January afternoon, and the assassination of Warren G. Hooper has been all but forgotten. When law enforcement officials are asked about the crime only the senior members reply, and then with the scant recollection that it had to do with some politician.

Despite the aura of mystery which shrouds every unsolved criminal act, this was neither a perfect crime nor a brilliantly conceived conspiracy. Although successful, in many respects it was amateurish. Thus, it not only could have been, but was, quickly deduced by several Michigan State Police detectives. Their findings, however, were ignored by their superiors, quite possibly at the urging of Kim Sigler.

The questions of who killed Senator Hooper and why are answerable once all the known facts are amassed. In defense of the police, such assembling was not possible until 1985 when a box of grand jury transcripts, believed to have been destroyed by Judge Coash with the remainder of the Ingham County grand jury records, was discovered by the Records Division of the State of Michigan Archives. This box, which may have been taken by Sigler and after his death passed to his law partner Victor C. Anderson, contained affidavits from every witness interrogated by the grand jury following Hooper's death. After the contents were examined by the Criminal Division of the Michigan Attorney General's Office, the authors of this book were graciously permitted to peruse those documents. The explosive information revealed therein, when used in conjunction with material gleaned from state police records, files spirited away by Donald S. Leonard, published accounts, government reviews, and personal interviews, spelled out the truth of the lawmaker's murder.

II The most viable method of uncovering the identity of the assassins is to demonstrate the overwhelming weaknesses of all but one of the theories put forth during the investigation. By a process of elimination the sole probable solution emerges.

During the conspiracy-to-murder hearing and trial, defense counsel contended that Sigler, in an effort to learn who funded the slaying, had granted immunity to the actual murderer and his accomplice — Sam Abramowitz and Henry Luks, respectively. Yet careful consideration of these men must discredit all such allegations of guilt.

Henry Luks wanted no part of the crime. A safecracker and armed robber who had never taken a life in the course of his illegal activities, Luks had been in an alcoholic stupor when he consented to wire Hooper's car and later to accompany Abramowitz and their employers, Harry Fleisher and Mike Selik, to Albion to "case" the job. Upon attaining temporary sobriety, he shied away — first telling Fleisher and Selik that he had been unable to acquire dynamite and then offering the falsehood that he could no longer get out of Ingham County because of difficulty with his parole officer. Henry Luks simply was not capable of premeditated murder.

Sam Abramowitz, while possessing the psychotic qualities necessary to commit the crime, would not have been able to refrain from boasting of his deed. He was an insecure, small, swaggering, belligerent man who sought desperately to move up the ladder of underworld status. Abramowitz, who wore his self-admitted total of more than one hundred arrests as a badge of honor and claimed gangland leaders Harry Fleisher and Mike Selik as personal pals, would have been compelled by his ego to leak his part in so stupendous an act because his newly acquired reputation as a triggerman rested upon the underworld's knowledge of his participation.

Egotism aside, another strong argument against Abramowitz's involvement can be made. By his own admission, Abramowitz had the opportunity to attack his intended victim, but chose not to use it. On his final journey to Albion with Sam Fleisher, he saw Hooper reclining at his desk, the back of his head clearly visible through an office window. A severe, if not mortal, wound could have been inflicted easily by a shot from their parked automobile. However, Abramowitz convinced his accomplice that such action would be too risky because he spied a woman and two small children near the senator. Certainly a dedicated assassin, worthy of the trust of the Purples, would not have wavered; he would have either lurked in ambush or massacred everyone present. The mission was too important and the stakes too high to allow chances to slip away as the deadline for the killing loomed large.

Why did Abramowitz falter? His protestations notwithstanding, it was not from compassion for the innocent bystanders but rather out of fear for his own safety. When he discovered that Sam Fleisher was carrying a concealed pistol, Abramowitz astutely theorized that once Hooper had been slain Sam Fleisher would dispose of his purported buddy during the drive back to Detroit. Sam Abramowitz may have been the coward that Kim Sigler later contended, but he was not a fool. Allowing Hooper to survive for a few days longer was Abramowitz's life insurance policy.

It is true that Abramowitz and Luks did fit the vague description given by Harry Snyder of the assassins being "a small man and a large man," and it is also accurate that Abramowitz's shoe fit the footprint found at the murder scene. Yet such general circumstantial evidence cannot offset the personality traits of these two criminals. It is inconceivable, based on known facts, that Abramowitz and Luks were involved in anything beyond the conspiracy plot to kill Hooper.

A second theory which received credence was that Harry Fleisher and Mike Selik did the job themselves after their hirelings failed. There are, however, at least two flaws in that scenario. First, its chief proponent was Naomi Selik, a drug addict and alcoholic whose veracity was questioned by all who knew her. Second, and more important, neither Fleisher nor Selik, despite their many years of crime, had ever gone past armed robbery, bootlegging, gambling, and prostitution. They were the trusted lieutenants of Ray Bernstein and the Keywells, the link between those imprisoned Purple Gang kings and those on the streets who kept their nefarious empire of crime functioning. Harry Fleisher and Mike Selik were not independent agents, but rather were intermediaries who took orders from their superiors and hired small-time hoodlums to do their bidding. They were too indispensable to be utilized as common gunmen. This was demonstrated by their refusal to accompany Abramowitz and Sam Fleisher to Albion and their lack of active participation in the Aristocrat Club heist. Despite possessing the capacity to kill, and despite fitting Snyder's description, Fleisher and Selik were second-echelon gangland organizers who never would have jeopardized their status by engaging in the slaying of a prominent politician. While certainly guilty of conspiring to kill Hooper, Fleisher stated a simple truth when he rhetorically silenced his current mistress, who had inquired if he and Selik had taken part in the murder of the senator, by asking: "Why would we get involved with something like that?"

Having eliminated Abramowitz, Luks, Fleisher, and Selik as triggermen, the remaining probable theory is that the crime was perpetrated by inmates from Jackson Prison. Many facts support this contention. First, the "inmate angle," as it was called, was believed by Attorney General John R. Dethmers, as well as by Michigan State Police Captains Edward Cooper and William Hansen, and Lieutenant Joseph Sheridan, each of whom had spent hundreds of hours investigating the murder. Second, it provides the only logical answer to Mrs. Hooper's perceptive query as to why the killers waited until her husband was almost home before attacking him. The murder site was slightly more than eighteen miles from Jackson Prison, thereby making it extremely simple for the slayers to leave the prison in midafternoon, commit the crime, and return before the evening meal rollcall. Furthermore, Snyder testified that he saw the maroon car bearing the alleged assassins speed from the scene and round a bend, presumably heading for Lansing; however, just out of Snyder's view was the junction with M-50, a paved thoroughfare leading directly to the prison, which was the actual route taken by the automobile. Third, long before Dethmers made his revelations in July 1945, it was common knowledge among convicts that special favors were being granted Purple Gang members by Jackson Prison Warden Harry Jackson and his deputy. D. C. Pettit. The latter was a frequent visitor to O'Larry's Bar, the Purple Gang hang-out owned and operated by Mike Selik's brother, Charles. By being given permission by Jackson and Pettit to use their office and home, respectively, for clandestine meetings with their free compatriots, Ray Bernstein and Harry Keywell continued to orchestrate their mob with equal, if not increased, effectiveness from within the prison. Fourth, it was a longstanding practice for convicts to bribe guards for permission to leave the prison while remaining officially "on count" (within the walls), so that they might attend local bordellos, taverns, and sporting events. Finally, those inmates illicitly departing were furnished civilian garb and state-owned automobiles, usually in return for bringing back liquor for Pettit or other official benefactors.

If this "convict killer" theory is accurate, still other questions must be answered. Why should the testimony of Alfred Kurner, Louis Brown, and Ernest Henry, the main proponents of the supposition, be trusted? The broad response is that their stories contain far too much provable evidence to be dismissed as mere "kites." More specifically, there is no doubt that Kurner told the truth concerning the role of Abramowitz and Luks in the conspiracy to murder Senator Hooper. Even Abramowitz confessed that offering to bring Kurner in on the job had been his biggest error. Moreover, neither Theodore

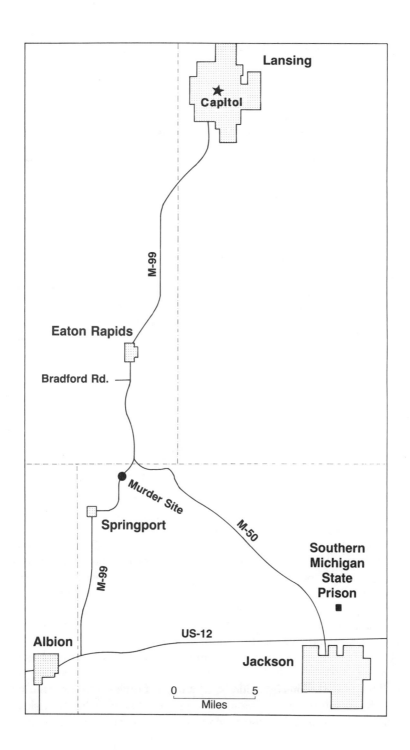

Lansing

★
Capitol

M-99

Eaton Rapids

Bradford Rd.

Murder Site

Springport

M-99

M-50

Southern
Michigan
State
Prison

US-12

Albion

Jackson

0   5
Miles

Rodgers, Maurice Walsh, nor Edward Kennedy, Jr., all experts in courtroom wiles, could undermine his credibility. Therefore, if he did not lie on that occasion, it seems highly unlikely that he would have any motive to fabricate his role in delivering the possible murder weapon to Harold Johnson, an inmate at Jackson Prison who arrived at the assigned rendezvous driving D. C. Pettit's automobile. Likewise, Louis Brown related an account which was so plausible that Sigler immediately proclaimed it to be the solution of the crime. Most significant in proving Brown's story is that there could have been virtually no way for Brown to have taken the state police directly to the Flint home and business of "John Wake" had he not been truthful in his contention that he had been there on a previous occasion. That the earlier trip was with other convicts as part of a reward for their participation in a crime appears valid, as there is little reason to suspect that Brown, a black Detroiter who had been imprisoned for several years, would have had any social motivation for frequenting the jewelry store and home of a prominent white Flint entrepreneur. Since no crime had been committed at either locale, the only conclusion must be that Brown had been invited. In addition, his story, which was corroborated by another black inmate, Ernest Henry, contains nothing which falls outside of the known time frame for the commission of the murder. Equally important, neither Brown nor Henry were blessed with the intelligence or inventiveness to concoct an elaborate lie and not be tricked into betraying themselves by trained police interrogators.

A second question which needs to be addressed is, if "John Wake" and Flint jeweler Max Davis were the same man, as Louis Brown testified when he singled out Davis' photograph as that of the man with the valise of money, why would a prominent civic leader serve as Frank McKay's bag man? If Davis was involved, the explanation could be that Davis was a political crony of former Flint Mayor William H. McKeighan, who was McKay's most faithful and trusted confidante. If asked to supply such a person, who better could McKeighan recommend than a Flint jeweler with no criminal record, who was obscure to the point of anonymity both to the residents of the city of Jackson and the inmates in its prison? Even Louis Brown had no inkling of the identity of "John Wake" until he had taken the police to the house and shop of Davis and, as a consequence, seen a picture of the jeweler which police had inserted among several mugshots shown to him.

The third obvious question is, why would Frank McKay, even if he was financing the assassination attempt on Hooper, take the risk of going to Jackson Prison and meeting with the alleged conspirators? If this visit was made, as Brown and Henry contend, it was born of extreme desperation. There is no doubt that McKay, through his bodyguards Charles Leiter and Isadore Schwartz, had access to the Purple Gang's leaders. If it is also true that Bernstein and Harry Keywell rejected the initial offer of $15,000 made by Wake as "too light" and refused to accept his assurance that the ante could be increased, the intermediary had to do something to demonstrate that the money would be forthcoming after the killing had been accomplished. In such a scenario, McKay could have been convinced of the necessity to prevail upon another of his longtime political allies, Warden Harry Jackson, to sneak him into the prison, allow him to be viewed by Bernstein, Keywell, and the other would-be conspirators amid verbal anonymity, and then be spirited away. Granted, this course would be dangerous, but certainly no more so than to permit Warren Hooper to take the stand and reveal McKay's role in legislative bribery on the anti-chain bank and horse racing bills. The trek to Jackson was risky, but without it he faced the distinct possibility of making the journey later to don prison gray.

Acceptance of the convict theory, therefore, is not only logical, but also provable. With it, both the plotting and commission of Warren Hooper's death can be reconstructed.

III During the last two weeks of November 1944, Warren Hooper testified three times before the Ingham County Grand Jury. On his final appearance, the senator was stunned when Special Prosecutor Kim Sigler brought him face to face with William Green, Floyd Fitzsimmons, and Frank McKay, and elicited from him a hesitating accusation that in 1943 the latter had offered a $500 bribe for his vote on pending horse racing legislation. Unnerved by Sigler's questionable tactic, Hooper returned to his Albion home and related the events to his wife who, with unerring, albeit brutal, frankness, predicted that his life was no longer "worth a penny."

Within a week of the Hooper-Green-McKay-Fitzsimmons confrontation, incarcerated Purple Gang kingpins Ray Bernstein, Harry Keywell, and Phil Keywell assembled a coterie of armed robbers and murderers to listen to another Jackson Prison inmate present a proposition of $15,000 for the assassination of a politician who was going to squeal to Judge Carr. Spurning further details, Harry Keywell and Bernstein refused, demanding at least an extra $10,000 before considering such an important job. The emissary departed, saying that he would relay the message to his contact. Several days later, Deputy Warden D. C. Pettit and Jackson Prison Inspector Robert Wilson instructed Bernstein to reassemble his clique. At the gathering, Pettit introduced to the predominantly black and Jewish mob "a Jew from Flint" named John Wake. The newcomer produced a photograph of the intended victim and pledged that $25,000 would be paid, but stipulated that the deed had to be accomplished before the politician took the witness stand during the second week of January. When Keywell reiterated his reservations about the financing, Wake agreed to return in four days with conclusive proof that the money would be delivered. Pettit then assured the gang leaders that he would assume responsibility for furnishing weapons, transportation, bogus license plates, and safe passage from and to the prison. When Wake next appeared, he displayed a valise containing $10,000 which he entrusted to Pettit who, in turn, deposited it in the inmates' accounts. As a further demonstration of good faith that the balance would be paid when the crime had been successfully accomplished, Wake summoned Warden Harry Jackson, who brought with him a man Wake introduced as Frank D. McKay. The two remained briefly and departed, while Wake emphasized again the importance of the job to McKay and reminded them that the Grand Rapids financier could help them in the future if they befriended him in his present hour of need.

Within seventy-two hours of this meeting, prison records indicate that Bernstein received visits from his brother Abe, Harry Fleisher, and Mike Selik. While what transpired in that closed-door conference cannot be known for certain, it can safely be assumed that it concerned Wake's proposal.

On December 23, 1944, as the wall clock in O'Larry's Bar showed nearly midnight, Henry Luks was summoned by Mike Selik to meet with Harry Fleisher in the latter's private office in the rear of the Detroit tavern. There Fleisher offered the safecracking explosives expert $5,000 to wire Senator Hooper's car. Accepting the task, the inebriated hoodlum expressed possible difficulty in procuring dynamite and was told to report back on Christmas Day. Shortly after midnight, on the morning of December 26, Luks related to Fleisher and Selik his anticipated failure, but agreed to enter into a partnership with Sam Abramowitz to do away with the senator by some other means. Around 8:00 a.m. that same frigid day, Harry Fleisher loaded Selik, Luks, and Abramowitz into his large black Cadillac and drove to Albion to case the job. Having pointed out the target's house and office, described his car, and detailed his daily routines, Fleisher headed back to Detroit, stopping off in Jackson so Luks could catch a bus to his Lansing residence.

Later in the evening of the twenty-sixth, Luks concocted a story which was related to Selik in an effort to extricate himself from any further involvement in a crime he now considered "too hot." Fleisher and Selik then entrusted the slaying to Abramowitz who, in turn, made a tentative partnership with Al Kurner to assist him in "bumping off this Albion politician before he could talk to the grand jury." Perhaps having reservations, on December 28 Abramowitz told his youthful confederate that the deal was off because his employers were going to try to gain the lawmaker's silence through bribery rather than bullets. Not coincidentally, this corresponds to the visit of Floyd Fitzsimmons, Frank McKay's ally and co-defendant in the horse racing warrant, to Hooper's senate office with a pledge of an undisclosed sum of money from "Frank" if the senator suddenly felt the need for funds to cover "legal expenses."

When word reached Fleisher that Hooper had turned down all monetary offers and insisted on testifying against his former benefactor, the mobster sent Abramowitz, in the company of Sam Fleisher, on two abortive missions of murder to Albion, the last of which occurred on January 2, 1945. When Abramowitz returned to the Purple Gang arsenal and told of his failure, Fleisher calmly dismissed him from any further role, mumbling that now he and Mike Selik would probably have to do the job themselves.

Fleisher then trekked to Jackson Prison and, doubtless with fear and chagrin, told Bernstein of what had transpired. This news probably led to a verbal lambasting of Fleisher for his inability to carry out so simple a task as murder, but it certainly convinced Bernstein that if the bargain was to be consummated, the deed would have to be done by himself. Probably warning his lackey to keep his mouth shut or he would suffer a most unpleasant fate if he ever entered the prison again, Bernstein set upon his task, knowing that the deadline hung over his head like the Sword of Damocles.

Bernstein was aware that D. C. Pettit had previously sent inmate Harold Johnson, driving the deputy warden's maroon coupe, to meet with Al Kurner and receive a .38 calibre pistol from the arsenal at O'Larry's Bar. Consequently, on January 8 he dispatched Ernest Henry, another member of his inside gang, to Jackson to purchase a pair of work gloves. Brown, who as one of Pettit's houseboys had many liberties, delivered the gloves to the deputy warden as Bernstein had instructed, and they were placed next to the revolver. Bernstein also arranged for Pettit to learn, and relay to him, the exact day and time of Hooper's departure from Lansing.

Early in the afternoon of January 11, Warden Jackson, in Pettit's absence, summoned Bernstein and Harry Keywell over the loudspeaker to his office. Jackson ordered Louis Brown to go to the prison "dress out shop" and check out civilian clothing for the two convicts. Bernstein, a convicted murderer who bore a striking physical and facial resemblance to Mike Selik, and Harry Keywell, who could have passed for Harry Fleisher's twin, then went to Pettit's house, picked up the revolver and gloves, and shortly after the 3:30 afternoon dinner bugle blared, drove away from the prison yard in the deputy warden's maroon automobile. Close behind in a red car, possibly that of Pettit's wife, came at least two other accomplices. Interestingly, all prison records for official car use for that day were found to be mysteriously missing.

Meanwhile, in Lansing, Warren Hooper was being closely observed. Both his wife and secretary, as well as several legislative colleagues and personal acquaintances, were aware that he was planning to forego the Republican state convention in Grand Rapids and the inevitable meeting with McKay that his attendance would assure, and instead to return to Albion on the afternoon of January 11. He ate a light lunch, packed his travel kit, drove from the capitol parking lot to a local hotel to conclude some osteopathic business, and then began what he expected to be a leisurely journey home.

Somewhere south of Lansing along M-99, the accomplices' car pulled in behind the senator's green Mercury and proceeded to follow at a safe distance. Keywell and Bernstein had parked on a side road, north of the intersection of M-99 and M-50. They hastily bolted on a phony license plate and waited, only to be forced to move onto the shoulder of M-99 when a snowplow operator pulled up behind them with his grader.

As the senator inexorably neared the assassins' rendezvous point, the accomplices' vehicle increased speed and passed Hooper's car. Approaching the maroon automobile driven by Keywell, the confederates signalled — probably by flashing their headlights — that the victim was in the car immediately following.

Hooper scarcely noticed the parked car until he was nearly upon it. Suddenly, it lurched into his path, forcing the senator's car into a long skid across the highway before coming to rest on the shoulder of the northbound lane. The maroon car formed the bar of a "T" blocking any attempt to escape.

Bernstein leapt from the passenger seat, rushed to the other car, opened the left front door, and seized the terrified driver by the overcoat. His hat jerked down over his eyes, Hooper was shoved to the right side of his seat, whereupon a lit cigarette fell from his trembling fingers. Gruffly yanking his prey back toward him, Bernstein pressed his gloved index finger against the trigger of the .38, launching the first of three bullets into the senator's skull.

During these few moments, the accomplices had turned to begin the drive back to the prison, while Keywell had backed his car across the road to the southbound shoulder, not knowing that he had scraped the left front fender, leaving maroon paint on the green Mercury. The mobsters must have felt incredibly fortunate, for throughout the commission of the crime no cars had passed the scene.

However, just as Bernstein released his grip on the lifeless lawmaker and stood at the door of the automobile, another car drove slowly by and its occupant, Harry Snyder, thinking that an accident might have occurred, stared across the Mercury's top directly into the eyes of the killer. As he wended methodically northward, Snyder's conscience troubled him, and he wondered if he could be of any assistance. Glancing into his rearview mirror, he saw the man at the door of the Mercury run in front of the car, across the street, and bound into the maroon coupe, which then started to pursue the passerby. Rapidly, Snyder's thoughts turned from altruism to fear for his own safety. Within seconds, he breathed a sigh of relief as he was passed by the maroon vehicle which disappeared around a curve. Snyder innocently assumed that the car was headed for Lansing, but out of his vision it veered onto M-50 and sped toward Jackson Prison.

Meanwhile, the driver of the lookout car and his companion had re-entered the penitentiary previously, parked the car, changed clothes, destroyed the license plate used on the red automobile, and occupied themselves with odd jobs while anxiously awaiting their comrades' arrival. Soon thereafter, Bernstein and Keywell drove in, still in a state of agitated euphoria over their deed. At the deputy warden's home, they donned their prison garb and prepared to slip quietly back into their daily routine. Before leaving, they handed the weapon and gloves to their accomplices to destroy as they had the license plate. The inmates deftly dismantled the revolver, disposed of the pieces in various trash receptacles, and tossed the gloves into Pettit's blazing basement furnace.

Later that evening, amid gleeful swaggering, the perpetrators told their assembled cohorts of how smoothly the killing had gone and of the wealth which now would be theirs. The murderous bargain had been fulfilled. Warren Hooper's lips had been permanently stilled by men who officially had remained "on count" as being present within the prison walls at the moment of the crime.

IV Investigating officers and the state attorney general confidently theorized that Jackson Prison inmates had committed the murder. Every denizen of Detroit's gangland haunts whispered to detectives that Harry Fleisher and Mike Selik took orders only from Ray Bernstein and the Keywell brothers, and that the solution to the slaying rested within the world's largest walled penitentiary. Despite being cognizant of these leads and putting forth a public facade of feverish sleuthing, Kim Sigler, in reality, was extremely reluctant to solve the crime. He demanded complete authority over the probe, but refused to permit questioning of Bernstein and Keywell and inspection of D. C. Pettit's automobile for scratches or missing paint. Therefore, the actual mystery surrounding the death of Warren Hooper is not so much who killed the senator, but rather why Sigler was reluctant to bring the guilty parties to justice.

The answer to this aspect of the case may be found by examining the personality traits and motives of the Battle Creek barrister. Kim Sigler was a monumentally vain man who was driven by ambitions which dared to reach as far as the White House. However, these dreams seemed destined to wither, as he had been defeated in his bids for elective office above the level of county prosecutor. Only when his honored law partner induced Ingham County Circuit Judge Leland W. Carr to select the firm's junior partner to be grand jury prosecutor did Sigler's star finally ascend.

Ingratiating himself to Carr, the brash, dynamic attorney assumed nearly despotic power in formulating the practices and direction of the grand jury probe. In this fashion, he charted a course which he believed would enable him to follow the path to political fame recently blazed by another crime-busting district attorney, Thomas E. Dewey. Unlike the New York governor, Sigler's target would not be an underworld luminary such as "Lucky" Luciano, but rather a longtime political boss. It was his destiny, Sigler once confided, to do what had repeatedly eluded federal and state prosecutors: he would send Frank D. McKay to prison.

It was this goal which led Sigler, as defense counsel at the conspiracy hearing and trial correctly noted, to be more intent on uncovering the identity of the person who financed the assassination than on disclosing the names of the assassins. In Sigler's mind, scant personal or political glory would be gained by painstakingly proving that Hooper had met his end at the hands of two mobsters already serving life sentences for murder. To do so certainly would have been an indictment of the prison system, but since the attorney general was in the process of preparing a lengthy report on abuses in the state penal institutions, Sigler would be advancing the aspirations of John Dethmers, not himself, if he demonstrated the validity of the attorney general's allegations. Moreover, there was no possible inducement Sigler could offer Bernstein and Keywell to testify against McKay. The Purple Gang leaders were serving life terms, thus the special prosecutor was powerless to either threaten them or grant immunity.

Consequently, Sigler was compelled to attempt an approach which, although the only one available, was unlikely to bring forth the desired result. One of those charged with conspiracy to murder the senator would have to be coerced into talking. If Harry Fleisher, his brother Sam, Mike Selik, or Pete Mahoney cracked, the trail of money might lead back to McKay. This strategy explains why Sigler worked so carefully with Sam Abramowitz and Henry Luks to construct an ironclad case of conspiracy against Harry Fleisher and Mike Selik, and why he granted those habitual offenders immunity from any and all involvement in the murder. It is the reason Sigler orchestrated Abramowitz's testimony so that the would-be gunman could casually insert reference to his injured arm, which led to a revelation of the roles of Harry Fleisher, Mike Selik, and Pete Mahoney in the Aristocrat Club heist. This was crucial to Sigler, because he knew that the hoodlums were not likely to break under the pressure of a $4^{1}/4$ to 5-year sentence for conspiracy to murder, but might cave in at the prospect of a 25 to 50-year stretch for armed robbery. Regardless of the methods, Sigler had to get McKay.

His scheme was foiled when the convicted co-conspirators kept silent. Sigler was then in an untenable situation. Despite his inability to link McKay conclusively to the Albion senator's death or to convict him on a liquor conspiracy charge, Sigler had retained his crusading "white knight" image with Michigan voters, and in 1946 they sent him to the governor's chair. Yet, as chief executive, he remained plagued by the spectre of the senator's murder. Hope for political advancement seemed to hinge greatly on his fulfillment of a campaign pledge to unravel the intricate web of conspiracy and unmask Warren Hooper's slayers.

Unfortunately for the new governor, such action could also prove to be his political undoing. After hearing Louis Brown's account, Sigler was positive that Bernstein and Harry Keywell were the murderers, and that they had received their pay-off money from McKay. He admitted this belief to State Police Commissioner Donald S. Leonard but declined to act on it as it did nothing to increase his odds for convicting his Grand Rapids nemesis. Long years of courtroom experience convinced him that it would be virtually impossible to get an outstate white jury to accept the word of a black armed robber from Detroit, whose testimony would be corroborated by another black convict, over that of a prominent white entrepreneur-banker-politician. Indeed, in the past McKay had glided through trials based on substantive allegations set forth by citizens whose reputations were above reproach. Louis Brown told the truth, but that would not help Sigler achieve his aim.

Lodged in a "no win" vise, Sigler chose as his avenue of escape a cover-up of the facts. From interrogations of Mrs. Hooper during the weeks immediately following the slaying, Sigler had learned what she had been told by her husband concerning his grand jury appearances. Through not-so-subtle questioning, the special prosecutor implied that if the widow did not do as he instructed, he could manufacture a very strong circumstantial case against her as an accomplice in the death of her unfaithful husband, as well as make public sordid details of the couple's marital life. She therefore consented not to be called upon in open court to detail her husband's role as one of McKay's legislative stooges or to explain why she believed that the Grand Rapids multi-millionaire had not only masterminded her husband's death, but also intended possibly to take her life as well. While governor, Sigler met with Mrs. Hooper at least twice at the capitol in the presence of Victor C. Anderson, and from the tone of the legal aide's subsequent correspondence it seems likely that the conversation included a reaffirmation by the governor that continued silence was her best assurance of safety as long as there was no way to prove McKay's complicity. It is equally conceivable that those confrontations did nothing to alter Mrs. Hooper's earlier trembling admission — "I'm afraid of you, Kim."

Similar motives dictated the intimidation of Mrs. Hooper's attorney, Theodore VanDellen, and the senator's secretary, Agnes Wickens, both of whom had related tales of Hooper's intimacy with McKay. On the stand they could have linked Hooper to McKay politically but could not have offered proof that McKay had been connected with the murder. The last thing Sigler needed was to enable defense counsel to use cross-examination to disclose the truth of Hooper's character and the methods utilized by the special prosecutor to wring information from witnesses. Everyone who had been privy to the Hooper-McKay tie had to be kept silent, by whatever means necessary, until Sigler managed to break one of the conspirators. Without that, he had no case.

When he was ousted as special prosecutor, Sigler protected his position by retaining all affidavits taken from grand jury witnesses regarding the murder — statements which Sigler had not disclosed even to the state police. During the gubernatorial race, Sigler urged his supporters at the Republican state convention to back Murl Aten for the post of auditor general, thereby elevating to statewide prominence the obscure Jackson County prosecutor who, coincidentally, was the only person with firsthand knowledge of the extent to which Sigler had misled deliberately the press and public about evidence. As governor, Sigler's first official act was to fire Oscar G. Olander. The veteran state police commissioner was highly regarded for his efficiency, but he also knew nearly as much as Sigler about the Hooper investigation. Therefore, Sigler accused him of condoning corruption in his administration and replaced him with Captain Donald S. Leonard. Shortly after this, every state police officer involved in the Hooper probe — from Chief of Detectives Harold Mulbar down to the radio dispatcher who received Floyd Modjeska's telephone call relating the discovery of the body — was recommended by Leonard, at Sigler's urging, for promotion. Everyone even remotely connected with inside knowledge of the case was now beholden to Sigler, and he expected nothing more than their silence in return.

In public, Sigler self-righteously postured that no matter how long it might take, he would bring the senator's killers to justice, but in private he realized the depth of his dilemma. Any hope of proving McKay's implication had ended with the disappearance of Harry Fleisher and Mike Selik. Knowing the identity of the triggermen brought no solace for it was useless. If he now chose to reveal their names, he would be compelled to answer a barrage of queries which would force his admission of laxity and impropriety in his handling of the case. To avoid embarrassment and political ruin, Sigler desperately hid the fact that he had deliberately permitted the assassins to remain anonymous and unpunished while he engaged in an abortive vendetta against Frank McKay.

All Sigler's dreams for greatness died when he was defeated for re-election. Six years later his life was snuffed out when the small airplane he was piloting crashed into a Battle Creek television transmission tower and burst into flames. In a twist befitting his ironic rise and fall, Sigler was fated to lie in the political coffin which he had so meticulously crafted for McKay. Unlike that of an earlier political martyr, the truth of Kim Sigler did not march onward.

EPILOGUE

SAMUEL ABRAMOWITZ was discharged April 16, 1947 from his four-year parole in Genesee County (Flint), Michigan. Both the commander of the Flint State Police Post, where he was housed during much of his parole, and his parole officer deemed Abramowitz a bad risk for discharge, but A. Ross Pascoe, Assistant Director of Corrections, and State Police Commissioner Donald S. Leonard urged his freedom "in keeping with promises made by then Commissioner Olander and Captain Mulbar years earlier in return for his testimony on the Hooper murder." (Donald S. Leonard Papers, Box 19, Bentley Historical Library, Michigan Historical Collections, the University of Michigan.) Upon his discharge, Abramowitz attempted to blackmail Governor Sigler into paying him $500 to keep his mouth shut on the truth of his testimony. In early 1950, Abramowitz signed an affidavit in Detroit for Edward H. Kennedy, Jr., Harry Fleisher's attorney, in which he accused Sigler of promising him "a check with figures a mile long" and admitted that he "knew what Sigler wanted me to say [against Fleisher, Selik, and Mahoney in the Aristocrat Club case] and I told him." Sigler's response was a disgusted, "Oh, nuts. Who's been scaring Sammy? The thing is absolutely silly and false" (*Detroit News*, 19 January 1950). The ex-convict never uttered another word against his former alleged benefactor, however, as within days of this statement Abramowitz disappeared. State police officials professed an inability to locate him and by 1952, when the FBI was finally asked to assist in the search, the trail was too cold for any hope of success. The always loquacious, heavy drinking, irresponsible Abramowitz mysteriously acquired permanent silence.

HARRY FLEISHER was paroled October 18, 1965 with the stipulation he reside in Oakland County, Michigan. After 48 months, he was discharged. Immediately, the 66-year-old ex-convict disappeared and his whereabouts have never been discovered. It was rumored in the late 1970s that he was living in Nevada and working for the notorious Licavoli family, who had been his rivals in crime during the Prohibition Era in Detroit.

SAMUEL FLEISHER served 3½ years of his conspiracy-to-murder sentence and was paroled on February 3, 1953. On January 18, 1960, at the age of 49, he was reported as being dead by the Miami, Florida, Police Department. At the time of his death he was a model citizen and president of the Carol City (Florida) Lions Club.

ALFRED KURNER, having served 6½ years for armed robbery, was paroled November 19, 1951, with the promise that he live thereafter in California. After four years on parole in Los Angeles, he was discharged and began a new life at the youthful age of 34.

HENRY LUKS was discharged from his two-year parole in Ingham County on July 16, 1945. He moved to Bay City, Michigan, changed his name to Henry Pruss, married, bought a house, and worked his way to a salaried position with Dow Chemical Company. According to state police records, he "went straight."

PETE MAHONEY had his conspiracy to murder conviction overturned by the Michigan Supreme Court, but he continued to serve time on the Aristocrat Club sentence. A model prisoner, Mahoney won the respect of both his fellow inmates and prison personnel. On June 20, 1959, he suffered a heart attack, lapsed into a coma, and died six days later at the age of 57. If he knew who killed Senator Hooper — and many people believed that he did — he never violated the underworld's "code of silence." As the banner on the wreath sent by Fleisher and Selik said, Mahoney was "a swell little guy who kept his mouth shut."

MYRON SELIK joined Harry Fleisher in jumping a $40,000 bond following their convictions in the Aristocrat Club trial. Ever dapper and brazen, Selik grew a moustache, took the name Max Green, and fled to Chicago. From there he joined a gang in New York City. In February 1951 he was arrested for participating in a Bronx apartment house robbery which netted $20,000 in furs and jewels. He was returned to Michigan where he served 4½ years on a federal sentence of unlawful flight and an additional nine years on his state offense. He was placed on a 48-month-parole in Wayne County (Detroit), Michigan on August 10, 1965 and was discharged exactly four years later. Selik, still a young man in his early 50s, dropped from sight and his whereabouts remained unknown. His wife Naomi remained in Kansas living with her parents and spending considerable time in alcohol treatment centers.

FRANK D. McKAY died January 12, 1965, at the age of 81, in Miami Beach. His covert influence on the Republican political scene in Michigan continued until the mid-1950s. He masterminded the defeat of Sigler in 1948 by urging conservative Republicans to stay away from the polls. His plans to recapture the governorship failed, however, when his candidates, including Donald S. Leonard, could not unseat the popular liberal Democrat G. Mennen Williams, whom he had helped elect in 1948. His estate, which included extensive real estate holdings in Florida and Michigan, was estimated to exceed $2,000,000. In his will, he established an annuity trust to The University of Michigan for the creation of the Frank D. and Agnes C. McKay Medical Research Foundation. In an obituary, Kenneth McCormick recalled: "He always went out of the way to tell you the good things he had done for the underprivileged and to insist on his straight-laced conduct." His papers, housed at the University of Michigan, attest to this, as they contain virtually nothing but congratulatory messages on his legal triumphs, plus letters and newspaper accounts of his philanthropic activities.

VICTOR C. ANDERSON left the grand jury to serve as Governor Sigler's chief legal advisor. He then joined Sigler and Carr in a Lansing law firm. To his death in 1982, Anderson remained convinced that McKay had brought about Hooper's murder, but that without a break from the convicted conspirators, it could not be proven in court.

MURL K. ATEN served as auditor general of Michigan from 1947 to 1951 and then made an unsuccessful bid for Congress. After leaving public service, he was a lobbyist and an attorney. He died June 15, 1971, at the age of 70.

LELAND W. CARR stepped down from the state supreme court in 1963, disappointed that President Dwight D. Eisenhower had overlooked him for a seat on the nation's highest tribunal. He continued to practice law in Lansing until his death, at the age of 85, on Memorial Day, 1969.

JOHN R. DETHMERS, having been refused renomination as attorney general by the Sigler-dominated Republican convention in 1946, resigned to assume a vacancy on the state supreme court in mid-August of that year. Capitol gossip claimed that Governor Kelly had pressured Justice Raymond Starr into resigning so that he could reward his friend Dethmers by placing him in a position in which he would be immune from Sigler's vengeance. He served on the high court until his defeat for re-election in 1970. While his twenty-five years on the bench ranked him second in longevity among supreme court members, like Carr, he always harbored a resentment that his long years of party service had not been rewarded by Eisenhower with an appointment to the United States Supreme Court. In September 1971, Dethmers suffered a stroke and, after lingering for nearly two months, died on November 1, at the age of 68.

RICHARD B. FOSTER served as grand jury prosecutor until the dissolution of that body in 1953. As of this writing, he is a senior partner in Lansing's largest law firm.

HARRY F. KELLY, having helped defeat Sigler in 1948, was narrowly defeated two years later in a bid to regain the governorship. In 1952, he was elected to the state supreme court, where he served until his retirement in 1971. On February 8, 1971, six weeks after he left the bench, he suffered a massive stroke and died, two months short of his seventy-sixth birthday.

DONALD S. LEONARD retired as State Police Commissioner in 1952 to seek the Republican gubernatorial nomination. After losing the primary, he was appointed Police Commissioner of Detroit, a post he held until 1954 when he quit to make another bid for the governor's chair. Successful in the primary, he was defeated by incumbent Democrat G. Mennen Williams in the general election. He then practiced law until 1963, when Republican Governor George Romney appointed him to the Liquor Control Commission, where he served for three years. In 1966, he was elected to the Detroit Recorder's Court, where he remained until his death in December 1976, at the age of 73.

KIM SIGLER served a turbulent two years as Governor, expending most of his energy ferreting out criminals and suspected communists in the state. His flashiness, egotism, short temper, and apparent disdain for the average citizen combined to wear thin on voters, as did his constant complaint that being governor was "a crummy job" because there were too many legal restrictions on his ability to act on issues. As his frustration mounted, he spent more time flying and less in Lansing, which made him increasingly susceptible to criticism from both conservative Republicans and Democrats. After his crushing 160,000 vote defeat in 1948, he entered into a law practice with Victor C. Anderson. While he never ran for office again, he maintained that he intended to solve the Hooper case, which would instantly put him back into the public limelight. A daring pilot who had flown as far as the southern tip of Chile and past the rim of the Arctic Circle, the 59-year-old former governor was returning to Lansing on November 30, 1953, when he crashed his plane into a recently erected, fog-shrouded television transmitter tower northwest of Battle Creek. Sigler, his longtime personal secretary Ruth Prentice, and two other passengers perished instantly in the ensuing inferno. Guy H. Jenkins, capitol correspondent for the Booth news-papers and a critic of Sigler, came forth with the most accurate description of the late governor: "Kim Sigler was one of a kind. He will always be remembered as the political skyrocket of Michigan. He went sky high, spewing brilliantly colored sparks all the way, and then quickly faded out."

CALLIENETTA HOOPER and her two sons moved to Marysville, Michigan, where she fulfilled a lifelong ambition by becoming a music teacher in that city's public school system. Embittered not only by her personal loss, but also by the refusal of the legislature to award her the Senator's salary for the rest of his unexpired term and burial expenses, she received some measure of financial solace in June 1947 when the Michigan Supreme Court, by a 5-3 vote, reversed a Calhoun County Circuit Court decision and granted her double indemnity on her husband's $10,000 life insurance policy. Ironically, the minority decision was penned by former Attorney General John R. Dethmers. Mrs. Hooper, who never remarried, retired from teaching in 1972 and continued to reside in Marysville until her death in 1986, at the age of 79. Despite telling a reporter for the *Battle Creek Enquirer* on April 15, 1980 that she would "love to have it [her husband's murder] cleared up," the authors of this book found her totally uncooperative, as she not only refused to be inter-viewed, but also returned registered correspondence unopened.

RAYMOND BERNSTEIN suffered a crippling stroke in 1963, which paralyzed his left side and impaired his speech. On January 16, 1964, having been granted a mercy parole because of his health, the Purple Gang leader ended thirty-two years behind bars. Ironi-cally, he immediately was confined again, this time to a bed at The University of Michigan Medical Center, where he died July 9, 1966. During his prison stint, Bernstein taught elementary classes to fellow inmates and was said to have given financial assistance to many con-victs and their families. In an obvious contradiction, Bernstein, who steadfastly maintained his innocence of involvement in the Col-lingwood Massacre or Purple Gang activities, told the Parole Board in 1963: "I needed correction, and I got it. I learned that crime certainly does not pay." (*DETROIT NEWS*, September 26, 1971)

HARRY KEYWELL had his life sentence commuted and left prison on October 21, 1964. After his parole expired in 1969, he married, found permanent employment, lived the life of a model citizen, and disappeared from the public and police records.

Chapter 1 - Notes

1. Karl Detzer, "The Maddest Man in Michigan," *Reader's Digest*, January 1947, 6; Michigan State Police Supplementary Report, "Ingham County Grand Jury," 27 October 1947.

2. Ibid. Those prosecuted were former Lieutenant Governor Francis Murphy and eighteen other Democrats: Charles C. Diggs, Leo J. Wilkowski, Francis Nowak, William Bradley, Stanley J. Dombrowski, Walter Stockfish, William Buckley, Ernest Nagel, Martin Kronk, Joseph Kaminski, Joseph Kowalski, Michael Clancy, Adam Sumeracki, Earl Gallagher, Edward Walsh, Henry F. Shea, D. Stephen Benzie, and Isadore Weza. The latter three were from the Upper Peninsula, while the remainder came from Detroit. Five Republicans were sentenced: Jerry T. Logie, Carl Delano, Miles Callaghan, William Green, and William C. Birk.

3. *Flint Journal*, 24 August 1943.

4. Ibid.

5. Ibid.; Don Gardner, interview with authors, 9 August 1983.

6. William P. Lovett, "One Man Grand Jury in Action," *National Municipal Review* 33 (1944): 292-94; *Flint Journal*, 14, 19 August 1943; Michigan State Police Supplementary Report, "Ingham County Grand Jury," 27 October 1947.

7. *Michigan Manual* (1945): 627; Don Gardner, interview with authors, 19 November 1982; Al Kaufman, interview with authors, 24 February 1984.

8. Al Kaufman interview, 24 February 1984.

9. Don Gardner interview, 19 November 1982.

10. *Flint Journal*, 2 September 1943; *Michigan State Digest*, 2 September 1943.

11. Michigan State Police Supplementary Report, "Ingham County Grand Jury," 27 October 1947; *Detroit Free Press*, 14 September 1943; *Flint Journal*, 27 September 1943.

12. *Flint Journal*, 26 November 1943.

13. *Detroit Free Press*, 8 December 1943; *Flint Journal*, 28 September, 8 December 1943; *Ingham County News*, 9 December 1943. The *Free Press* assertion was not without basis as on 28 September Rushton had announced "virtual completion" of the grand jury's work.

14. *Detroit Free Press*, 11 September 1943.

15. *Detroit Free Press*, 17 November 1963.

16. *Detroit Free Press*, 13 January 1965; Frank B. Woodford, *Alex J. Groesbeck* (Detroit: Wayne State University Press, 1962), 245-51. Ironically, the *Detroit Free Press*, which would be McKay's bitterest enemy, supported him in his anti-Groesbeck campaign because it believed the Governor's roadbuilding program would benefit outstate residents more than those in Detroit.

17. *Detroit Free Press*, 17 November 1963.

18. *Detroit Free Press*, 13 January 1965.

19. Ibid.; Dr. Willard B. VerMeulen interview taken by Dr. Thomas F. Soapes, 26 January 1980. Gerald R. Ford Presidential Library, Ann Arbor, Michigan. Dr. VerMeulen was a leader in the Grand Rapids "Home Front" movement which was opposed to McKay.

20. *Detroit Free Press*, 13 January 1965; *New York Times*, 13, 28 November 1940, 13 July 1941; *Newsweek*, 9 December 1940; *Michigan State Digest*, 28 May 1942. On 29 May 1942 McKay wrote H. S. Babcock, editor of the Alma, Michigan *Recorder*, "I am advised they spent between 1½ and 2 million dollars in attempting to satisfy the whims of a certain gentleman in Washington who was disappointed in a Michigan election." Four days later, he penned a note to a Grand Rapids friend, Burt Decker, in which he described his trial as a "federal farce." Frank D. McKay Papers, Michigan Historical Collections, Bentley Historical Library, The University of Michigan.

21. *Detroit Free Press*, 17 November 1963.

22. *Flint Journal*, 11 December 1943.

23. *Flint Journal*, 14 December 1943.

24. Ibid.

25. *Flint Journal*, 13 December 1943.

26. *Flint Journal*, 14 December 1943.

27. Ibid.; Biographical Sketch of Kim Sigler, 1946, Biography File, Library of Michigan, Lansing, Michigan; Richard B. Foster, interview with authors, 30 September 1982. Foster was Sigler's successor as grand jury prosecutor.

28. *Newsweek*, 24 February 1947; *Lansing State Journal*, 2 December 1953, 29 November 1963; *Grand Rapids Press*, 3 July 1954; *Detroit Free Press*, 15 February 1959; Victor C. Anderson, interview with authors, 4 June 1981. Anderson later formed a law firm with Sigler. *Detroit News*, 31 January 1944.

29. Kim Sigler to William R. Cook, 2 May 1944. Cook Papers, Michigan Historical Collections, Bentley Historical Library, The University of Michigan.

30. Kim Sigler to William R. Cook, 25 December 1943, Cook Papers. Sigler's altruism was short-lived, however, as in his 2 May 1944 letter to Cook he refers to his press conferences and completion of a series of photographic sessions with Judge Carr.

31. Kim Sigler to William R. Cook, 25 January 1944, Cook Papers.

32. Kim Sigler to William R. Cook, 9 May 1944, Cook Papers.

33. *Detroit Times*, 21 December 1943.

34. Ibid.

35. *Detroit News*, 21 December 1943.

36. *Detroit Times*, 22, 23 December 1943; *Flint Journal*, 22 December 1943; *Detroit News*, 27 December 1943; Don Gardner interview, 19 November 1982. Following Dalton's dismissal, the Office of Price Administration announced it was considering a probe to determine if the McKay trip was a violation of gas rationing laws. Also, William P. Lovett, whose complaints had launched the grand jury probe, began a series of public statements charging Rushton with trying to sabotage the grand jury to protect his friends.

37. *Detroit Times*, 21 December 1943.

38. *Detroit News*, 31 January 1944.

39. *Detroit Times*, 26 December 1943.

40. Ibid.; Don Gardner interview, 19 November 1982; Richard B. Foster interview, 30 September 1982. Both Gardner and Foster were convinced of Morris' ties to McKay, but admitted such ties were impossible to prove.

41. *Detroit News*, 4 January 1944; *Michigan State Digest*, 6 January 1944; Herbert J. Rushton to Harry F. Kelly, 26 January 1944, *Records of the Executive Office, Harry F. Kelly*, Accession 42, Box 18, Folder 17, Office of the Attorney General, Michigan State Archives, Michigan History Division.

42. Warrant, Case Number 6215, Ingham County Circuit Court, 22 January 1944, Michi-gan State Police Records; *Detroit Times*, 23 January 1944; *New York Times*, 23 Janu-ary 1944; *Ingham County News*, 27 January 1944. Those indicted were Detroit Democratic Senators Leo J. Wilkowski, Charles C. Diggs (the state's lone black law-maker), and William M. Bradley, along with Detroit Democratic Representatives Wil-liam G. Buckley, Edward J. Walsh, Joseph L. Kaminski, Stanley J. Dombrowski, Joseph J. Kowalski, Michael J. Clancy, Earl C. Gallagher, Martin A. Kronk, Ernest G. Nagel, Francis J. Nowak, Walter N. Stockfish, and Adam Sumeracki. Outstate law-makers named were Democratic Senators D. Stephen Benzie and Harry F. Shea, and Democratic Representative Isadore Weza. Republicans cited were Senators Jerry T. Logie and Miles M. Callaghan. The finance officers were Abraham Cooper (President of the Union Investment Company), Samuel Hopkins, Ernest J. Prew, and Mark Young, all of Detroit, and John Hancock and George Omacht of South Bend, Indiana.

43. *Flint Journal*, 24, 30 January 1944; *Detroit Times*, 24, 25, 30 January 1944; *Kala-mazoo Gazette*, 30 January 1944; *Report of the Michigan State Senate Investigation Sub-Committee*, 5 March 1946, Guy H. Jenkins Papers, Michigan Historical Collec-tions, Bentley Historical Library, The University of Michigan. Callaghan received pay-ments under the alias "Herb Cook."

44. *Detroit Times*, 2 February 1944; *Ingham County News*, 3 February 1944; *Michigan State Digest*, 3 February 1944.

45. *Detroit Times*, 2 February 1944; *Michigan State Digest*, 3 February 1944; *Report of the Michigan State Senate Investigation Sub-Committee*, 5 March 1946. Only Sigler's removal as special prosecutor would permanently delete Spare from the payroll.

46. *Lansing State Journal*, 28 February 1944.

47. *Detroit Free Press*, 16 March 1958.

48. Ibid.

49. *Report of the Michigan State Senate Investigation Sub-Committee*, 5 March 1946.

50. Ibid.

51. Ibid.

52. Ibid.

53. *Detroit News*, 14 August 1944; *Detroit Free Press*, 16 March 1958; Richard B. Foster interview, 30 September 1982. Mark Young and Samuel Hopkins were acquitted.

54. *Detroit Free Press*, 16 March 1958; Richard B. Foster interview, 30 September 1982. Hemans' benefactor was Charles Bohn, President of Bohn Aluminum Company and member of the Board of Directors of Michigan National Bank, the state's largest chain bank. Don Gardner interview, 19 November 1982.

55. Don Gardner interview, 19 November 1982; Al Kaufman interview, 24 February 1984.

56. *Michigan State Digest*, 15 November 1944; *Ingham County News*, 16 November 1944.

57. Confidential memo from Will Muller and Al Nieber to Jack Gaertner, 22 January 1945, Michigan State Police Records. In this memo, Sigler admitted to the newsmen that he had never anticipated that McKay might make an attempt to silence Hooper, and that was why he did not insist on an armed guard for the witness.

58. The bill was to install totalizers at the Detroit Race Course to assure honest odds and raise increased tax revenue by more efficient accounting of amounts wagered.

59. Muller-Nieber memo, 22 January 1945.

60. Eugene Black, interview with authors, 20 August 1982. Black served as Governor Sigler's attorney general and later was a justice on the Michigan Supreme Court. Richard B. Foster interview, 30 September 1982; Don Gardner interview, 19 November 1982; Al Kaufman interview, 24 February 1984. Everyone who knew Sigler claimed he had an eye on the White House.

61. Circuit Court of Ingham County Warrant Against Frank McKay, et al., 2 December 1944, Michigan State Police Records.

Chapter 2 - Notes

1. *Battle Creek Enquirer,* 11 January 1959; statement of Callienetta Hooper to Kim Sigler, Oscar G. Olander, and Harold V. Mulbar, 26 January 1945, Attorney General Records, Criminal Division, 105-07; testimony of Warren G. Hooper, *The People of the State of Michigan* v. *William J. Burns,* Docket 7723, Ingham County Circuit Court, 8 October 1943, 13-15.

2. Testimony of Warren G. Hooper, 8 October 1943, 16-18.

3. Ibid., 20; Betty Keyes, interview with authors, 16 August 1984; George V. Mather, interview with authors, 21 August 1984. (Mather was editor of the *Albion Evening News* during Hooper's years in that city, while Mrs. Keys was the Hooper's regular babysitter.) Statement of Callienetta Hooper, 26 January 1945, 58.

4. Testimony of Warren G. Hooper, 8 October 1943, 20.

5. Ibid.; George V. Mather interview, 21 August 1984. Joseph L. Hooper of Battle Creek served in the United States House of Representatives from 1927 until his death in February 1934. According to Mather, "A lot of folks thought Warren was his, the congressman's son, or something of that kind. I don't imagine Warren did much to dissociate himself with those stories. He wasn't too popular in town."

6. *Hastings Banner,* 18 January 1945.

7. Statement of Agnes Wickens to Kim Sigler, Murl K. Aten, Oscar G. Olander, William Hansen, and Lyle Morse, Attorney General Records, Criminal Division, 13 January 1945, 46-47.

8. Testimony of Warren G. Hooper, 8 October 1943, 67.

9. Ibid., 8-9.

10. Confidential memo from Will Muller and Al Nieber to Jack Gaertner, 22 January 1945, Michigan State Police Records.

11. *Detroit News,* 16 March 1946.

12. Ibid.

13. Statement of Agnes Wickens, 13 January 1945, 38.

14. Statement of Callienetta Hooper, 26 January 1945, 14, 17, 53; statement of Callienetta Hooper to Kim Sigler, Murl K. Aten, and Oscar G. Olander, 16 January 1945, Attorney General Records, Criminal Division, 2, 4, 16, 19-22, 33.

15. *Lansing State Journal,* 12, 19 January 1945; *Albion Evening Recorder,* 12 January 1945. Contrary to initial reports, these two "mysterious" men had nothing to do with the subsequent events in Hooper's life; they were minor state officials who had dealt with the senator and were being friendly.

Chapter 3 - Notes

1. Statement of Floyd Modjeska to Kim Sigler, 12 January 1945, Attorney General Records, Criminal Division (hereafter referred to as Modjeska), 6-7, 14-16; Mervyn B. Howard interview, *Lansing State Journal*, 12 January 1945.

2. Modjeska, 7; statement of Kyle Van Auker to Murl K. Aten, 12 January 1945, Attorney General Records, Criminal Division (hereafter referred to as Van Auker), 12.

3. Modjeska, 7; Howard interview, *Lansing State Journal*, 12 January 1945.

4. Howard interview, *Lansing State Journal*, 12 January 1945; statement of Mervyn B. Howard to Murl K. Aten, 12 January 1945, Attorney General Records, Criminal Division (hereafter referred to as Howard), 5.

5. Howard; Van Auker, 16; Modjeska, 12.

6. Modjeska, 8.

7. Howard interview, *Lansing State Journal*, 12 January 1945.

8. Howard, 7; Van Auker, 11; Report of Detective Bion Hoeg, 14 January 1945, Michigan State Police Records.

9. Report of Lawrence J. Baril, 12 January 1945, Michigan State Police Records; Report of Detective Bion Hoeg, 14 January 1945, Michigan State Police Records.

10. Report of Detective Bion Hoeg, 14 January 1945.

11. Modjeska, 6, 14-17; Van Auker, 13-14; Howard, 16-17; Report of Detective Bion Hoeg, 14 January 1945.

12. Modjeska, 16; Report of Detective Bion Hoeg, 14 January 1945.

13. Report of Detective Bion Hoeg, 14 January 1945.

14. Report of Detective Fred A. Van Campen, Michigan State Police Records, 11 January 1945; Report of Lawrence J. Baril, 12 January 1945.

15. Statement of Callienetta Hooper to Kim Sigler, 26 January 1945, 86.

16. Ibid.

17. Ibid., 86, 99.

18. George V. Mather, interview with authors, 21 August 1984.

19. Ibid.

20. Ibid.; statement of Callienetta Hooper, 26 January 1945.

21. Mather interview, 21 August 1984.

22. *Detroit Times*, 13 January 1945.

23. Ibid.

24. Ibid.

25. Ibid.; *Detroit News*, 12 January 1945.

26. *Detroit Times*, 13 January 1945.

27. Ibid.

28. *Detroit News*, 12 January 1945.

29. Ibid.; *Detroit Times*, 13 January 1945.

30. *Detroit News*, 12 January 1945.

31. *Lansing State Journal*, 12 January 1945.

32. Ibid.

33. *Detroit Times*, 13 January 1945.

34. Ibid.

35. *Albion Evening Recorder*, 24 July 1945; *Detroit Free Press*, 24, 25 July 1945; *Flint Journal*, 24 July 1945.

36. *Detroit News*, 13 January 1945; *Albion Evening Recorder*, 13 January 1945.

37. *Flint Journal*, 15 January 1945; *Detroit News*, 16 January 1945.

38. *Flint Journal*, 12 January 1945.

39. *Detroit Times*, 15 January 1945.

40. *Lansing State Journal*, 13 January 1945.

41. *Flint Journal*, 15 January 1945; *Detroit News*, 16 January 1945.

42. *Detroit Free Press*, 16 January 1945; *Flint Journal*, 16 January 1945.

43. *Detroit News*, 16 January 1945.

44. *Detroit Free Press*, 16 January 1945.

45. *Detroit Free Press*, 17 January 1945.

46. Ibid.

47. *Detroit News*, 18 March 1957.

48. *New York Times*, 13 January 1945.

49. *Detroit Free Press*, 13 January 1945; *Detroit Times*, 15 January 1945.

50. *Detroit Times*, 15 January 1945.

51. Ibid.

52. *Chicago Herald American*, 12 January 1945; *Detroit News*, 13 January 1945.

53. Report of Trooper Larry Stackable and Detective Wesley R. Jones, 13 January 1945, Michigan State Police Records.

54. *Detroit Times*, 13, 15 January 1945; *Detroit News*, 13 January 1945; statement of Callienetta Hooper to Kim Sigler, Murl K. Aten, and Oscar G. Olander, 16 January 1945, Attorney General Records, Criminal Division, 35-39.

55. *Detroit Times*, 15 January 1945.

56. Report of Trooper Adrian Wentzel, 15 January 1945, Michigan State Police Records.

57. Ibid.; *Detroit News*, 13 January 1945; *Detroit Times*, 13 January 1945.

58. *Detroit News*, 13 January 1945; *Detroit Free Press*, 14 January 1945; *Detroit Times*, 14, 15 January 1945. After the Mymachod story was printed, Mrs. Hooper told Sigler that she had been mistaken earlier, and that she now believed the voice on the day of the murder was not the same. "It was more smooth and cultured," she said adamantly on 26 January (statement of Callienetta Hooper to Kim Sigler, et al., 26 January 1945, Attorney General Records, Criminal Division, 89).

59. *Flint Journal*, 13 January 1945; *Battle Creek Enquirer*, 13 January 1945.

60. *Battle Creek Enquirer*, 13 January 1945; *Detroit News*, 13 January 1945.

61. *Detroit News*, 13 January 1945; *Flint Journal*, 13 January 1945.

62. *Battle Creek Enquirer*, 13 January 1945.

63. Statement of Harry Snyder to Kim Sigler, Murl Aten, Oscar G. Olander, Harold V. Mulbar, William Hansen, and Lyle Morse, 13 January 1945, Donald S. Leonard Papers, Box 19, Michigan Historical Collections, Bentley Historical Library, The University of Michigan, 1, 5, 6, 7, 10.

64. Ibid., 7-15.

65. Ibid., 21.

66. Ibid., 16-19.

67. Ibid., 22. Snyder later identified the man as Bernstein.

68. *Detroit News*, 13, 15, 16 January 1945; *Battle Creek Enquirer*, 13 January 1945; *Chicago Herald American*, 14 January 1945; *Flint Journal*, 14 January 1945; *Detroit Free Press*, 15 January 1945.

69. *Detroit News*, 13 January 1945.

70. *Detroit Free Press*, 14 January 1945.

71. Statement of William Bracey to Murl K. Aten, 15 January 1945, Attorney General Records, Criminal Division, 7-10.

72. Ibid., 10-12. Bracey was mistaken as to the sex of the larger person.

73. *Michigan Manual* (1949): 626.

74. Statement of William Bracey, 15 January 1945, 12.

75. Ibid., 13-16.

76. *Detroit Free Press*, 14 January 1945. McCormick revealed the extent of his intimacy with Sigler in a *Free Press* article, 2 December 1953: "I first met Sigler on December 13, 1943 after he had accepted his assignment as special graft grand jury prosecutor.... For nearly three years we had our meals together. We took long walks at night to talk over progress of the grand jury. I got to know Kim as few persons have."

77. *Albion Evening Recorder*, 15 January 1945; *Detroit Times*, 16 January 1945.

78. *Michigan State Digest*, 16 October 1946; *Michigan Manual* (1951-1952): 88, 439.

Chapter 4 - Notes

1. *Lansing State Journal*, 16 January 1945; *Detroit Times*, 16 January 1945; *Detroit News*, 16 January 1945.

2. *Detroit News*, 16 January 1945.

3. Ibid.; *Detroit Times*, 16 January 1945.

4. *Albion Evening Recorder*, 16 January 1945.

5. *Lansing State Journal*, 16 January 1945.

6. Statement of Callienetta Hooper to Kim Sigler, Murl K. Aten, and Oscar G. Olander, 16 January 1945, Attorney General Records, Criminal Division, 2-6.

7. Ibid., 7.

8. Ibid.

9. Ibid., 8.

10. Ibid.; *Detroit News*, 12 January 1945; *Lansing State Journal*, 13 January 1945.

11. Statement of Callienetta Hooper, 16 January 1945, 9.

12. Ibid.

13. Statement of Theodore Van Dellen to Kim Sigler, 15 January 1945, Attorney General Records, Criminal Division, 31-32.

14. Ibid., 32.

15. Ibid., 30.

16. Statement of Callienetta Hooper, 16 January 1945, 10-11.

17. Ibid.

18. Ibid., 12-18.

19. Ibid., 20-21.

20. Ibid., 22; Betty Keys, interview with authors, 16 August 1984; George V. Mather, interview with authors, 21 August 1984.

21. Statement of Callienetta Hooper, 16 January 1945, 23.

22. Ibid.

23. Ibid., 26-27.

24. Ibid., 27-28.

25. Statement of Agnes Wickens to Kim Sigler, Murl Aten, Oscar G. Olander, William Hansen, and Lyle Morse, 13 January 1945, Attorney General Records, Criminal Division, 43-49; Calhoun County Tax Records, City of Albion, Waldo Library, Western Michigan University, 327:241; 339:241; 350:241.

26. Statement of Callienetta Hooper, 16 January 1945, 33-36.

27. Ibid., 49.

28. Ibid., 41, 50-54.

29. Ibid., 56-57, 61.

30. Ibid., 62-64.

31. Ibid., 65-68.

32. Statement of Charles Cobb to Kim Sigler and Murl Aten, 16 January 1945, Attorney General Records, Criminal Division, 2-4.

33. Ibid., 4-10.

34. Report of Detective Vincent Neering, 2 March 1945, Michigan State Police Records; statement of Callienetta Hooper, 26 January 1945, 56. According to Mrs. Hooper, Wickens owned 200 shares, the same number as Mrs. Hooper, of stock in the J. W. Brandt Co., which put out Kirn's Tea Wheeler's and Sedelixir. Senator Hooper, who had purchased the company from former state representative Robert Baldwin in late December 1942, retained the remaining 600 shares. The company had been manufacturing patent medicines in Albion for eighty years (*Albion Evening Recorder*, 1 January 1943).

35. Report of Detectives Vincent Neering and Edward Johnston, 3 March 1945, Michigan State Police Records.

36. Ibid.; Report of Trooper Russell Kitzinger, 13 January 1945, Michigan State Police Records. Morehouse, however, was ordered by the trooper "not to touch another thing in the office."

37. Report of Lieutenant Bion Hoeg, 9 March 1945, Michigan State Police Records.

38. Report of Lieutenant William Watkins, 16 January 1945, Michigan State Police Records. Several months later, the alleged victim told state police that when she removed her jacket Hooper had remarked, "Oh, do I affect you like that?" which was the extent of his improper behavior (report of Lieutenant Bion Hoeg, 9 March 1945).

39. *Lansing State Journal*, 19 January 1945.

40. *Lansing State Journal*, 18 January 1945; *Detroit News*, 19 January 1945; Report of Detective Sergeant Harry Biggs, 17 January 1945, Michigan State Police Records; Report of Trooper Adrian Wentzel, 23 January 1945, Michigan State Police Records.

41. *Detroit News*, 13 January 1945.

42. *Albion Evening Recorder*, 3, 4 June 1936.

43. *Detroit News*, 13 January 1945.

44. *Albion Evening Recorder*, 13 January 1945. Subsequent interrogation of several witnesses revealed that some believed the man in Albion was Louis Fleisher, who was serving a prison sentence at Alcatraz, which may account for Hansen's statement (Report of Trooper Adrian Wentzel, 15 January 1945, Michigan State Police Records).

45. *Detroit Times*, 3 September 1945.

46. Report of Detective Harry Biggs, 17 January 1945.

47. Statement of Stella Kalenchick to Murl Aten, 19 January 1945, Attorney General Records, Criminal Division, 10-12, 15-16.

48. Ibid., 13-14.

49. Ibid., 34.

50. Report of Lieutenant Wilber Petermann, 19 January 1945, Michigan State Police Records.

51. *Lansing State Journal*, 19 January 1945; *Detroit Times*, 20 January 1945; *Detroit Free Press*, 20 January 1945. Rosenberg was arrested more than thirty times in Detroit between 1915-1943.

52. *Detroit Times*, 20 January 1945.

53. Ibid.

54. *Flint Journal*, 24 January 1945.

55. Ibid.

56. *Lansing State Journal*, 22 January 1945; *Detroit Free Press*, 25 January 1945.

57. *Detroit Free Press*, 25 January 1945.

58. Report of Detective Harry Biggs, 17 January 1945, Michigan State Police Records. In a subsequent report dated 27 January 1945, Detective Neering said Moore told him the Hoopers had not had intercourse for two years. The senator complained about his wife's constant "bitching" about money, and Moore added that Mrs. Hooper begged for a raise for her husband every time she saw a member of the Osteopathic Society.

59. Report of Detective Vincent Neering, 24 January 1945.

60. Statement of Callienetta Hooper, 26 January 1945, 2-6.

61. Ibid., 11-17.

62. Ibid., 19-21.

63. Ibid., 26-27.

64. *Wayne County Democrat*, 20 January 1945, Frank D. McKay Papers, Michigan Historical Collections, Bentley Historical Library, The University of Michigan.

65. Statement of Callienetta Hooper, 26 January 1945, 38-39.

66. Ibid., 46-54.

67. Ibid., 56-59.

68. Ibid., 60-64.

69. Ibid., 65-66

70. Ibid., 68-69.

71. Ibid., 69.

72. Ibid., 90-91.

73. Ibid., 91-92.

74. Ibid., 97.

75. Ibid., 98.

76. *Detroit News*, 28 January 1945.

77. Ibid.

Chapter 5 - Notes

1. Statement of Agnes Wickens to Kim Sigler, 13 January 1945, Attorney General Records, Criminal Division, 53; statement of Callienetta Hooper to Kim Sigler, 16 January 1945, Attorney General Records, Criminal Division, 53; statement of Callienetta Hooper to Kim Sigler, 26 January 1945, Attorney General Records, Criminal Division, 92-93.

2. *Michigan State Digest*, 25 April 1945.

3. *Detroit Times*, 18 January 1945; *Detroit Free Press*, 18 January 1945.

4. *Detroit Free Press*, 18, 29 January 1945.

5. *Albion Evening Recorder*, 29 January 1945.

6. Ibid.

7. *Detroit Times*, 30 January 1945; *Detroit Free Press*, 30 January 1945.

8. *Detroit Times*, 30 January 1945.

9. The People of the State of Michigan v. Floyd Fitzsimmons, Docket 8019, Ingham County Circuit Court, Mason, Michigan, 1945.

10. *Detroit Times*, 1 February 1945.

11. *Detroit Free Press*, 2 February 1945; *Albion Evening Recorder*, 2 February 1945.

12. *Flint Journal*, 2 February 1945.

13. *Albion Evening Recorder*, 3 April 1945.

14. *Michigan State Digest*, 11 April 1945.

15. *Report of the State Senate Investigating Committee on Ingham County Grand Jury Expenses*, Guy H. Jenkins Papers, Michigan Historical Collections, Bentley Historical Library, The University of Michigan.

16. *Flint Journal*, 11 April 1945; *Jackson Citizen Patriot*, 11, 12 April 1945.

17. Report of Lieutenant W. H. Petermann, 17 April 1945, Michigan State Police Records.

18. Ibid.

19. Reports of Detective Sergeant Joseph Priestas, Detective Sergeant Edward C. Johnston, and Corporal Vincent Neering, 20 April 1945, Michigan State Police Records.

20. *Battle Creek Enquirer*, 20 April 1945; *Flint Journal*, 20 April 1945; *Detroit Times*, 21 April 1945.

21. *Flint Journal*, 21 April 1945; *Detroit Free Press*, 22 April 1945.

22. *Flint Journal*, 21 April 1945.

23. *Detroit Times*, 22 April 1945.

24. *Flint Journal*, 22 April 1945.

25. Report of Trooper C. E. Miller, 25 April 1945, Michigan State Police Records.

26. *Detroit Times*, 21 April 1945.

27. *Detroit Times*, 24 April 1945; *Michigan State Digest*, 25 April 1945. It is interesting that a clipping of the *Michigan State Digest* article on Fleisher's refusal to leave jail was preserved in one of Frank D. McKay's personal scrapbooks.

28. *Flint Journal*, 29 April 1945.

29. *Detroit Times*, 3 May 1945.

30. *Jackson Citizen Patriot*, 1 May 1945; *Michigan State Digest*, 2 May 1945.

31. *Detroit Times*, 3 May 1945.

32. *Detroit Free Press*, 11 July 1945.

33. *Detroit Times*, 6 May 1945; *Flint Journal*, 6 May 1945.

34. Al Kaufman, interview with authors, 20 February 1984.

35. *Detroit Times*, 6 May 1945.

36. Report of Detective Sergeant Edward C. Johnston, 7 May 1945, Michigan State Police Records.

37. *Detroit Free Press*, 7 September 1945.

38. *Flint Journal*, 11 May 1945; *Albion Evening Recorder*, 11 May 1945; *Detroit Times*, 12 May 1945; *Detroit Free Press*, 12 May 1945; transcript of the Examination of Harry Fleisher, et al., 11-15 May 1945, conducted before the Honorable William H. Bibbings, Justice of the Peace in and for the County of Calhoun, State of Michigan, at the Circuit Court Rooms, City Hall, Battle Creek, Michigan (hereafter referred to as Examination Transcript), 5-8.

39. Examination Transcript, 12-14.

40. Ibid., 15-16.

41. Ibid., 17-18.

42. Ibid., 19, 21.

43. Ibid., 22-23.

44. Will Mueller-Al Nieber Supplemental Report, 23 April 1945, Michigan State Police Records. Leo Wendell was the founder and sole member of the Detroit-based "public relations" firm of Wendell, Walsh, & Brown. A two-fisted, top secret information gatherer, the mysterious sleuth had earned a reputation for efficiency while working for the United States Army Intelligence Service, the Alcohol Enforcement Bureau of

the United States government, and several Michigan grand juries. On the strength of his past record, Wendell was hired by Judge Carr but was removed by Sigler when the special prosecutor learned that the investigator's methods of acquiring information included dangling recalcitrant witnesses by their heels from upper story hotel windows. Michigan State Police Supplementary Report, "Ingham County Grand Jury," 27 October 1947; *Detroit Times*, 12 July 1945; Don Gardner, interview with authors, 9 August 1983.

45. *Detroit Free Press*, 12 May 1945.

46. *Battle Creek Enquirer*, 12 May 1945; *Albion Evening Recorder*, 12 May 1945; *Detroit News*, 14 November 1951; Examination Transcript, 29-30.

47. Examination Transcript, 33-37.

48. Ibid., 39-41.

49. Ibid., 41-43.

50. Ibid., 43-45.

51. Ibid., 45.

52. Ibid., 45-49; *Detroit Free Press*, 12 May 1945; *Battle Creek Enquirer*, 12 May 1945; *Albion Evening Recorder*, 12 May 1945; *Flint Journal*, 12 May 1945.

53. Examination Transcript, 52-80.

54. Ibid., 82-91; *Detroit Free Press*, 12 May 1945; *Battle Creek Enquirer*, 12 May 1945.

55. Examination Transcript, 94, 97, 99-100.

56. Ibid., 100-102.

57. Ibid., 102-3; *Detroit Free Press*, 12 May 1945; *Battle Creek Enquirer*, 12 May 1945; *Albion Evening Recorder*, 12 May 1945.

58. Examination Transcript, 105-7.

59. Ibid., 108-10.

60. Ibid., 115-16.

61. Ibid., 117-18.

62. Ibid., 119-22.

63. Ibid., 122-23.

64. Ibid., 123-25; *Detroit Free Press*, 12 May 1945; *Battle Creek Enquirer*, 12 May 1945; *Flint Journal*, 12 May 1945.

65. Examination Transcript, 130-31; testimony of Henry Luks, 18 April 1945, Donald S. Leonard Papers, Box 19, Michigan Historical Collections, Bentley Historical Library, The University of Michigan, 2-4, 16, 17; *Detroit Times*, 13 May 1945; *Detroit Free Press*, 13 May 1945.

66. Examination Transcript, 131-35.

67. Ibid., 137-39.

68. Ibid., 140-46.

69. Ibid., 146-47.

70. Ibid., 148-52.

71. Ibid., 152-53.

72. *Detroit Free Press*, 13 May 1945; *Detroit Times*, 13 May 1945. During cross-examination, however, the question was never asked and McKay's name remained, unchallenged, as the only potential financial backer of the plot.

73. Examination Transcript, 153-56.

74. *Battle Creek Enquirer*, 13 May 1945.

75. *Flint Journal*, 13 May 1945; *Detroit Times*, 13 May 1945.

76. Examination Transcript, 157-63; *Detroit Times*, 13, 14 May 1945; *Albion Evening Recorder*, 14 May 1945.

77. Examination Transcript, 165-67.

78. Ibid., 167-69.

79. Ibid., 171-72.

80. Ibid., 178-83. This version of Luks' story is in complete accord with the official state police transcript of the confrontation between the two gangsters. Testimony of Henry Luks, 17 April 1945, Donald S. Leonard Papers, Box 19.

81. Examination Transcript, 184-86.

82. Ibid., 190-91.

83. Ibid., 197, 200, 202-3.

84. Ibid., 208-10.

85. Ibid., 210-12.

86. Report of Detective Vincent Neering, 10 April 1945, Michigan State Police Records; *Battle Creek Enquirer*, 14 May 1945; *Albion Evening Recorder*, 14 May 1945; Examination Transcript, 272-73.

87. Examination Transcript, 214-17. The attorney was Louis McGregor, who served as an appeals court judge for Michigan during the 1960s and 1970s. Report of Parole Officer Clare Spears, 30 March 1945, Michigan State Police Records. Spears concluded that many of Abramowitz's problems stemmed from an unhappy childhood during which he ran away from home several times.

88. Examination Transcript, 214. Report of Parole Officer Clare Spears, 30 March 1945; *Detroit Free Press*, 13 May 1945.

89. Examination Transcript, 225-42.

90. Ibid., 244-56.

91. Ibid., 256-59.

92. *Detroit Times*, 15 May 1945.

93. Examination Transcript, 260-66. Abramowitz had told the same story to Murl Aten and the state police. Statement of Sam Abramowitz at Jackson State Police Post, 19 April 1945, Michigan State Police Records, 56-57.

94. Examination Transcript, 267-92.

95. Ibid., 294.

96. Ibid., 294-95; *Battle Creek Enquirer*, 14 May 1945; *Albion Evening Recorder*, 14 May 1945; *Detroit Times*, 15 May 1945.

97. Examination Transcript, 295.

98. Ibid., 310-12.

99. Ibid., 319, 321.

100. Ibid., 327-28.

101. Ibid., 334-35.

102. Ibid., 336.

103. Ibid., 337-55.

104. Ibid., 355-58.

105. Ibid., 359-401.

106. Ibid., 401-2, 407.

107. Ibid., 409-10.

108. Ibid., 410.

109. Ibid., 411.

110. Ibid., 414-18.

111. Ibid., 418-22; *Battle Creek Enquirer*, 15 May 1945.

112. Examination Transcript, 422-26.

113. Ibid., 427.

114. Ibid., 428.

115. Ibid.

116. Ibid., 430-31.

117. *Battle Creek Enquirer*, 15 May 1945.

118. Ibid.; *Michigan State Digest*, 16 May 1945.

119. *Flint Journal*, 17 May 1945.

120. *Battle Creek Enquirer*, 17 May 1945.

121. Ibid.

122. *Flint Journal*, 22 May 1945; *Battle Creek Enquirer*, 22 May 1945.

Chapter 6 - Notes

1. *Detroit Free Press*, 7, 8 June 1945; *Detroit Times*, 8 June 1945. The legislators were Republican State Senator Jerry T. Logie and Democratic State Senator Charles C. Diggs.

2. Warrant of Ingham County Circuit Court against Frank D. McKay, et al., 16 June 1945, Michigan State Police Records; *Detroit Times*, 17 June 1945; *Detroit Free Press*, 17 June 1945.

3. Examination Transcript, 361-77; *Flint Journal*, 10 June 1945; *Detroit Times*, 10 June 1945; *Albion Evening Recorder*, 11 June 1945.

4. *Flint Journal*, 10 June 1945; *Detroit Times*, 10 June 1945. The nearly three hundred page transcript of the Aristocrat Club hearing before Circuit Judge Frank L. Doty, with Sigler as special prosecutor, is in the Michigan State Police files on the Hooper murder.

5. *Albion Evening Recorder*, 11, 14 June 1945; *Detroit Times*, 15 June 1945.

6. *Michigan State Digest*, 13 June 1945.

7. *Michigan State Digest*, 20 June 1945.

8. Ibid.

9. *Grand Rapids Press*, 4 July 1945; *Flint Journal*, 4 July 1945.

10. *Flint Journal*, 4 July 1945.

11. *Grand Rapids Press*, 4 July 1945.

12. *Battle Creek Enquirer*, 13 July 1945.

13. Ibid.

14. *Battle Creek Enquirer*, 15 July 1945.

15. *Battle Creek Enquirer*, 16 July 1945; *Flint Journal*, 16 July 1945.

16. *Flint Journal*, 16 July 1945; Proceedings for a Motion on Continuance before the Honorable Blaine W. Hatch, 16 July 1945, included in People of the State of Michigan v. Harry Fleisher, Peter Mahoney, Myron Selik, and Samuel Fleisher, 37th Judicial Circuit, Calhoun County Michigan, File 15-64, Docket 43436 (hereafter referred to as Trial Transcript).

17. Ibid.; *Battle Creek Enquirer*, 16 July 1945.

18. Trial Transcript, 1; *Battle Creek Enquirer*, 17 July 1945.

19. *Battle Creek Enquirer*, 17 July 1945.

20. Ibid.; *Albion Evening Recorder*, 17 July 1945; *Detroit Free Press*, 18 July 1945.

21. *Flint Journal*, 18 July 1945; *Detroit Free Press*, 18 July 1945; *Battle Creek Enquirer*, 18 July 1945.

22. *Detroit Free Press*, 18 July 1945.

23. *Flint Journal*, 18 July 1945.

24. Ibid.

25. Ibid.

26. Ibid.

27. *Michigan State Digest*, 18 July 1945.

28. *Battle Creek Enquirer*, 18 July 1945; *Detroit Free Press*, 18 July 1945.

29. Trial Transcript, 1-13, 18-21.

30. Ibid., 23-24.

31. Ibid., 24-28.

32. Ibid., 28-29.

33. Ibid., 30-31.

34. Ibid., E-H.

35. Ibid., 42-51.

36. Ibid., 51-52.

37. Ibid., 54-55.

38. *Battle Creek Enquirer*, 19 July 1945. The insurance company claimed that if the defendants had premeditated the senator's murder, it could not be considered accidental.

39. Trial Transcript, 56.

40. Ibid., 60-62.

41. Ibid., 62-65.

42. Ibid., 66-76.

43. Ibid., 76.

44. Ibid., 77-80.

45. Ibid., 81.

46. Ibid., 82-104.

47. Ibid., 107-16.

48. Ibid., 117-26.

49. Ibid., 127-35.

50. Ibid., 136-41.

51. Ibid., 142-44.

52. Ibid., 145.

53. Ibid., 146.

54. Ibid., 146-47.

55. Ibid., 148-49.

56. Ibid., 151-53.

57. Ibid., 156.

58. *Flint Journal*, 24 July 1945; Don Gardner, interview with authors, 19 November 1982.

59. *Flint Journal*, 24 July 1945; *Albion Evening Recorder*, 24 July 1945; *Detroit Free Press*, 25 July 1945.

60. *Albion Evening Recorder*, 24 July 1945; *Flint Journal*, 24 July 1945; *Detroit Free Press*, 24-25 July 1945.

61. *Flint Journal*, 24 July 1945; *Detroit Free Press*, 25 July 1945.

62. Ibid.

63. Ibid.; Don Gardner interview, 19 November 1982.

64. Trial Transcript, 176-77.

65. Ibid., 178-82; *Battle Creek Enquirer*, 25 July 1945.

66. *Battle Creek Enquirer*, 25 July 1945; Trial Transcript, 183-84.

67. Trial Transcript, 187-88.

68. Ibid., 189-93; *Michigan State Digest*, 25 July 1945; *Detroit Free Press*, 26 July 1945; *New York Times*, 26 July 1945.

69. *Battle Creek Enquirer*, 26 July 1945; Trial Transcript, 195-97.

70. Trial Transcript, 197-99.

71. Ibid., 200-201;

72. Ibid., 201-3; *Flint Journal*, 26 July 1945.

73. *Flint Journal*, 26 July 1945; *Detroit Free Press*, 26, 27 July 1945.

74. *New York Times*, 26 July 1945; *Detroit Free Press*, 26 July 1945.

75. *Battle Creek Enquirer*, 25 July 1945.

76. Ibid.; *Flint Journal*, 25 July 1945; *Detroit Free Press*, 25 July 1945; Trial Transcript, 157-58.

77. Trial Transcript, 159-61.

78. Ibid., 161-66.

79. Ibid., 169-76; *Battle Creek Enquirer*, 25 July 1945; *Detroit Free Press*, 25 July 1945.

80. Trial Transcript, 203; *Albion Evening Recorder*, 26 July 1945.

81. Trial Transcript, 204-8.

82. Ibid., 209-15.

83. Ibid., 216-26.

84. Ibid., 226-27; *Battle Creek Enquirer*, 27 July 1945.

85. *Battle Creek Enquirer*, 27 July 1945; Trial Transcript, 228-29.

86. *Battle Creek Enquirer*, 27 July 1945.

87. *Battle Creek Enquirer*, 28 July 1945; *Detroit Free Press*, 28 July 1945.

88. *Detroit Free Press*, 28 July 1945; *Battle Creek Enquirer*, 28 July 1945.

89. *Battle Creek Enquirer*, 28 July 1945; *Detroit Free Press*, 28 July 1945.

90. *Detroit Free Press*, 28 July 1945; *Battle Creek Enquirer*, 28 July 1945; *Detroit Times*, 30 July 1945.

91. *Battle Creek Enquirer*, 28 July 1945.

92. Ibid.

93. *Battle Creek Enquirer*, 29 July 1945.

94. Ibid.

95. *Battle Creek Enquirer*, 28 July 1945.

96. *Battle Creek Enquirer*, 29 July 1945; *Detroit Times*, 30 July 1945.

97. *Battle Creek Enquirer*, 28 July 1945.

98. Ibid., *Detroit Times*, 30 July 1945.

99. *Battle Creek Enquirer*, 28 July 1945; *Detroit Times*, 30 July 1945.

100. Kim Sigler to William Cook, 31 July 1945, Cook Papers, Michigan Historical Collections, Bentley Historical Library, The University of Michigan.

101. *Detroit Free Press*, 31 July 1945; *Battle Creek Enquirer*, 31 July 1945.

102. *Battle Creek Enquirer*, 31 July 1945; *Detroit Free Press*, 31 July 1945.

103. *Battle Creek Enquirer*, 31 July 1945.

104. Ibid., *Flint Journal*, 31 July 1945.

105. *Battle Creek Enquirer*, 31 July 1945.

106. Ibid.; Trial Transcript, 233-37.

107. *Albion Evening Recorder*, 31 July 1945; *Detroit Free Press*, 31 July 1945.

108. Trial Transcript, 238-40, 255-58; *Battle Creek Enquirer*, 31 July 1945.

109. *Battle Creek Enquirer*, 31 July 1945; Trial Transcript, 258-60; *Detroit Times*, 1 August 1945.

110. Trial Transcript, 280; *Battle Creek Enquirer*, 31 July 1945; *Flint Journal*, 31 July 1945; *Detroit Times*, 1 August 1945.

111. Trial Transcript, 281; *Battle Creek Enquirer*, 31 July 1945; *Flint Journal*, 31 July 1945; *Detroit Times*, 1 August 1945; *Detroit Free Press*, 1 August 1945.

112. Trial Transcript, 281; *Battle Creek Enquirer*, 31 July 1945.

113. *Battle Creek Enquirer*, 1 August 1945.

114. Ibid.; Trial Transcript, 281.

115. *Detroit Free Press*, 1 August 1945; *Battle Creek Enquirer*, 1 August 1945.

116. *Battle Creek Enquirer*, 1 August 1945.

117. Ibid.; *Detroit Times*, 2 August 1945.

118. *Battle Creek Enquirer*, 1 August 1945.

119. *Detroit Free Press*, 1 August 1945.

120. *Battle Creek Enquirer*, 1 August 1945.

121. Ibid.; *Detroit Free Press*, 1 August 1945; *Flint Journal*, 1 August 1945.

122. *Flint Journal*, 1 August 1945; *Detroit Free Press*, 1 August 1945; *Lansing State Journal*, 1 August 1945.

123. *Detroit Free Press*, 1 August 1945.

Chapter 7 - Notes

1. *Detroit Free Press*, 19, 26 August 1945. Earlier in his career Sigler had been a Democrat, serving three terms as Barry County prosecutor and making an unsuccessful bid in 1928 for attorney general.

2. *Michigan State Digest*, 1 August 1945. While there is no substantiation to this charge, it is doubtful whether Hooper would have possessed the courage necessary to confront his benefactor with a demand for money to maintain silence.

3. *Michigan State Digest*, 8 August 1945.

4. *Grand Rapids Press*, 27 August 1945.

5. Ibid.; *Detroit Free Press*, 28 August 1945.

6. *Grand Rapids Press*, 28 August 1945; *Detroit Free Press*, 29 August 1945.

7. *Detroit Free Press*, 1, 2 September 1945; *Detroit Times*, 1, 2, 3 September 1945; *Grand Rapids Press*, 1 September 1945. Leiter had been a member of the Sugar House and Purple gangs with Harry Fleisher and Mike Selik. A reputed paid gunman, Leiter was questioned repeatedly – to no avail – concerning the Hooper slaying.

8. *Detroit Free Press*, 6 September 1945; *Battle Creek Enquirer*, 7 February 1946; Don Gardner, interview with authors, 19 November 1982. Don Gardner of the *Detroit Times* went so far as to say that Simpson was "a good old boy" who was "a good friend of Frank McKay and a lot of newspaper guys in Lansing."

9. *Michigan State Digest*, 5 September 1945; *Grand Rapids Press*, 6 September 1945; *Detroit Free Press*, 6 September 1945; *Albion Evening Recorder*, 6 September 1945.

10. *Detroit Free Press*, 6 September 1945; *Grand Rapids Press*, 6 September 1945.

11. *Detroit Times*, 8 September 1945; *Detroit Free Press*, 8 September 1945.

12. Don Gardner interview, 19 November 1982; Al Kaufman, interview with authors, 24 February 1984; Richard B. Foster, interview with authors, 30 September 1982; Marvin J. Salmon, interview with authors, 14 October 1982. Salmon was a former Ingham County assistant prosecutor under Victor C. Anderson and later served as circuit

judge for that county. For a brief period he shared a Lansing law office with Charles F. Hemans.

13. *Albion Evening Recorder*, 20 September 1945; *Grand Rapids Press*, 21 September 1945; *Michigan State Digest*, 26 September 1945; *Hastings Banner*, 27 September 1945.

14. *Detroit Times*, 26 September 1945.

15. Ibid.; *Michigan State Digest*, 26 September 1945; Richard B. Foster interview, 30 September 1982; Marvin J. Salmon interview, 14 October 1982.

16. Richard B. Foster interview, 30 September 1982; Marvin J. Salmon interview, 14 October 1982; Al Kaufman interview, 24 February 1984..

17. *Michigan State Digest*, 17 October 1945; *Albion Evening Recorder*, 18 October 1945.

18. *Battle Creek Enquirer*, 29 October 1945; *Albion Evening Recorder*, 30 October 1945; *Michigan State Digest*, 31 October 1945.

19. *Michigan State Digest*, 7, 21 November 1945.

20. *Detroit News*, 29 November, 11 December 1945; *Detroit Times*, 29, 30 November, 9, 10 December 1945; *Pontiac Press*, 29, 30 November, 11 December 1945.

21. *Grand Rapids Press*, 10 January 1946; *Detroit Free Press*, 11 January 1946; *Battle Creek Enquirer*, 14 January 1946; The People of the State of Michigan v. Frank D. McKay, et al., Docket 8165, Ingham County Circuit Court, Mason, Michigan, 1946.

22. *Battle Creek Enquirer*, 6, 11, 14 February 1946; *Lansing State Journal*, 14 February 1946.

23. *Battle Creek Enquirer*, 14 February 1946.

24. *Lansing State Journal*, 14 February 1946. In private, McKay was much more critical, especially of Carr. He wrote a friend: "The thing that made me maddest of all about the trial was the fact that Judge Carr indicted me for bribery when it now appears, and he knew it at the time, that he did not have one single bit of evidence or testimony to substantiate such a charge, and after I was smeared in the newspapers throughout the state and considerable prejudice built up against me, then they decide to withdraw the charge of bribery. This, in my opinion, was very unfair on the part of Judge Carr, and it's my opinion that he walked over my dead body to get a seat on the Supreme Court. He will never enjoy it." Frank D. McKay to J. B. Whilley, 18 February 1946, Frank D. McKay Papers, Michigan Historical Collections, Bentley Historical Library, The University of Michigan.

25. *Battle Creek Enquirer*, 15, 16 February 1946.

26. *Battle Creek Enquirer*, 19 February 1946.

27. *Battle Creek Enquirer*, 26 February 1946; *Michigan State Digest*, 27 February 1946.

28. *Lansing State Journal*, 27 February 1946; *Detroit News*, 28 February 1946.

29. *Lansing State Journal*, 27 February 1946; *Detroit News*, 28 February 1946.

30. *Detroit News*, 28 February 1946.

31. Ibid.

32. *Flint Journal*, 4 March 1946.

33. *Flint Journal*, 5 March 1946.

34. Ibid.; *Battle Creek Enquirer*, 5 March 1946.

35. Don Gardner interview, 19 November 1982; Al Kaufman interview, 24 February 1984.

36. *Battle Creek Enquirer*, 6 March 1946.

37. *Detroit News*, 7 March 1946.

38. *Battle Creek Enquirer*, 6 March 1946.

39. *Flint Journal*, 10 March 1946.

40. *Flint Journal*, 12 March 1946.

41. Ibid.; *Detroit News*, 13 March 1946.

42. *Flint Journal*, 13 March 1946; *Hastings Banner*, 14 March 1946; *Battle Creek Enquirer*, 14, 21 March 1946.

43. *Detroit News*, 23 March 1946; *Battle Creek Enquirer*, 25 March 1946. Despite his new image, relatives recall that Sigler played the role of "big shot" even within his family and that his egocentrism was everpresent. Janet Pierson, a great-niece of Sigler, interview with authors, 10 May 1982.

44. *Detroit News*, 27 April, 21 May 1946; *Michigan State Digest*, 8 May 1946.

45. *Flint Journal*, 4, 8 June 1946; *Battle Creek Enquirer*, 5 June 1946.

46. *Battle Creek Enquirer*, 13, 14 June 1946. Sigler outpolled his nearest competitor, Vernon J. Brown, by 50,000 votes, and three times as many Republicans voted for governor as did Democrats. *Time*, 1 July 1946. Despite a lengthy investigation and trial, Senator Johnston was never convicted on any of the gambling allegations.

Chapter 8 - Notes

1. *Battle Creek Enquirer*, 24 August 1946. Sigler defeated Van Wagoner by a 335,000 vote margin.

2. *Newsweek*, 24 February 1947, 28.

3. Eugene F. Black, interview with authors, 20 August 1982. Black, known as an outspoken political maverick, had a political falling-out with Sigler. After leaving the attorney general's office in 1949, Black became first a Democrat and then an Independent, and served on the Michigan State Supreme Court from 1956 to 1973.

4. It was Toy's understanding that he could look into all crimes, including the Hooper murder, but he discovered that Sigler was denying him access to all information concerning that case. Only after Sigler left office did Toy become actively involved in the investigation. Telegram, Harry S. Toy to Victor C. Anderson, 27 February 1948, *Records of the Executive Office, Kim Sigler*, Accession 43, Record Group 43, Box 67, Folder 3, Michigan State Archives, Michigan History Division; *Detroit News*, 21 November 1949.

5. Richard B. Foster, interview with authors, 30 September 1982.

6. *Battle Creek Enquirer*, 3 January 1947; *Detroit News*, 4 January 1947; *Kalamazoo Gazette*, 7 January 1947. Not only did Sigler oust Olander who knew more about the Hooper case than anyone except the governor himself, but also within four months the new commissioner, Donald S. Leonard, who reputedly had political ties to Frank McKay, promoted Mulbar, Hansen, Morse, Cooper, Van Conant, and Baril — all of whom possessed intimate knowledge of the Hooper probe. Thus, all the high ranking officers involved in the Hooper inquiry were rewarded and their loyalty to both the commissioner and the governor was solidified. *Lansing State Journal*, 4 April 1947.

7. Harold V. Mulbar to Donald S. Leonard, 13 December 1949, Donald S. Leonard Papers, Box 19, Michigan Historical Collections, Bentley Historical Library, The University of Michigan.

8. Report of Lieutenant Joseph Sheridan, 7 April 1948, Michigan State Police Records.

9. Ibid.

10. *Lansing State Journal*, 11 January 1948.

11. Report of Lieutenant Joseph Sheridan, 7 April 1948, Michigan State Police Records.

12. Ibid.

13. Ibid.

14. Ibid.

15. Ibid.

16. Ibid.

17. Ibid.

18. Ibid.

19. Statement of Louis Brown, Inmate #48529-J, 27 January 1947, to Kim Sigler, Victor C. Anderson, Eugene Black, Garrett Heyns, A. Ross Pascoe, Donald S. Leonard, Joseph Sheridan, William Williams, Murray Young, Dr. David Phillips, and Philip Collins, Leonard Papers, Box 19.

20. Ibid.

21. Ibid.

22. Ibid.

23. Ibid.

24. Ibid.; Report of Lieutenant Joseph Sheridan, 7 April 1948, Michigan State Police Records.

25. Statement of Louis Brown, 27 January 1947; handwritten notes initialed by Donald S. Leonard, Leonard Papers, Box 19.

26. Statements of Ernest Henry, Inmate #13172-J, taken in the office of Circuit Judge James Breakey, Ypsilanti, Michigan, 1, 22 April and 1 May 1947, Leonard Papers, Box 19.

27. Ibid.

28. Ibid.

29. Report of Lieutenant Joseph Sheridan, 7 April 1948, Michigan State Police Records; handwritten notes of Donald S. Leonard, Leonard Papers, Box 19.

30. Richard B. Foster interview, 30 September 1982.

31. Statement of Stanley Wrobel to Victor C. Anderson, 11 August 1947, Leonard Papers, Box 19.

32. Ibid.

33. Report of Detectives Walter Williams and Murray Young, 21 August 1947, Leonard Papers, Box 19.

34. Report of Lieutenants Edward Cooper and Joseph Sheridan, 1 March 1948, Leonard Papers, Box 19.

35. *Detroit News*, 1 March 1948.

36. *Detroit News*, 2 April 1948.

37. Ibid.; Report of Detectives Walter B. Williams and Murray Young, 13 April 1948, Leonard Papers, Box 19.

38. *Detroit News*, 2 April 1948.

39. *Detroit News*, 7 January 1949.

40. Statement of Harold Johnson to Detective Murray Young, 21 November 1949, Leonard Papers, Box 19.

41. Report of Murray Young and Walter Williams to Lieutenant Edward Cooper, 3 April 1949, Leonard Papers, Box 19.

42. Statement of Herman Faubert, Inmate #38923-J, to Joseph Sheridan, 30 July 1949, Leonard Papers, Box 19.

43. Report of Sergeant Wilber H. Petermann to Donald S. Leonard, 4 November 1949, Leonard Papers, Box 19.

44. *Detroit Times*, 17 November 1949.

45. *Detroit Times*, 18 November 1949; *Flint Journal*, 20 November 1949; statement of Morris Raider to Donald S. Leonard, et al., 17 November 1949, Leonard Papers, Box 19.

46. Statement of Morris Raider to Donald S. Leonard, et al., 17 November 1949, Leonard Papers, Box 19; statement of D. C. Pettit to Donald S. Leonard, et al., 17 November 1949, Leonard Papers, Box 19; statement of Mitchell Bonkowski to Donald S. Leonard, et al., 17 November 1949, Leonard Papers, Box 19; Donald S. Leonard handwritten notes, Leonard Papers, Box 19.

47. Statement of Herman Faubert to Donald S. Leonard, et al., 17 November 1949, Leonard Papers, Box 19. David Mazroff, a former Purple Gang member, was in Florida, but Leonard did not think enough of the statements of Faubert and Bonkowski to request his arrest and return for questioning. Interestingly, for more than two years previous to this, Mazroff had been acting as a paid informant for State Police Detective Captain Edward Johnston. Edward Johnston to Donald S. Leonard, 14 August 1947, Donald S. Leonard Papers, Box 19.

48. *Detroit Times*, 18 November 1949; report of Joseph Sheridan, 11 September 1947, Leonard Papers, Box 19; statement of D. C. Pettit to Donald S. Leonard, et al., 17 November 1949, Leonard Papers, Box 19.

49. *Detroit Times*, 18 November 1949.

50. List of discrepancies in statements made by Herman Faubert and Mitchell Bonkowski in connection with the Senator Hooper case, Leonard Papers, Box 19; *Detroit Times*, 18 November 1949; *Flint Journal*, 21 November 1949.

51. *Detroit Times*, 19 November 1949; *Flint Journal*, 21 November 1949; *Albion Evening Recorder*, 21 November 1949.

52. *Albion Evening Recorder*, 21 November 1949.

53. *Detroit Free Press*, 21 November 1949.

54. *Albion Evening Recorder*, 21 November 1949.

55. Ibid.; *Detroit Free Press*, 21 November 1949. Mrs. Hooper wrote Sigler on 1 July 1948, "Once again I am begging and this seems to be a primary role in my life since the death of Warren," Kim Sigler, Records of the Executive Office, Accession 43, Record Group 43, Box 62, Folder 7, Grand Jury, State Archives, Michigan History Division.

56. *Detroit Times*, 21, 22, 23 November 1949.

57. *Flint Journal*, 21 November 1949.

58. *Detroit Times*, 24 November 1949.

59. Ibid.

60. *Detroit News*, 15 December 1949.

61. Ibid.

62. *Detroit News*, 14 June 1948; *Detroit Free Press*, 15 June 1948. Justices Carr and Dethmers abstained from the deliberations.

63. *Detroit News*, 14 June 1948.

64. Jackson Prison Records, Michigan Department of Corrections; *Detroit News*, 7 October 1948.

65. *Detroit News*, 7 October 1948.

66. Ibid.

67. *Detroit News*, 17 October 1948.

68. Ibid.

69. Ibid.

70. Ibid.; Warner later joined Victor C. Anderson as a member of Governor Sigler's legal staff.

71. *Lansing State Journal*, 23 October 1948.

72. *Detroit News*, 21 October 1948.

73. Ibid.; the state legislature refused to post a reward on the grounds that the issuance of a federal fugitive warrant was sufficient.

74. Ibid.

75. *Detroit News*, 19 January 1950. Fleisher's companion was Bernice Jackson, a plump, 31-year-old blonde Detroit prostitute who had been with him throughout his flight.

76. *Detroit Times*, 20 January 1950.

77. *Detroit News*, 23 January 1950.

78. *Detroit Times*, 30 January 1950; *Detroit News*, 30 January 1950.

79. *Detroit Times*, 30 January 1950.

80. Donald S. Leonard, notes, 18 March 1950, Leonard Papers, Box 19.

81. Ibid.; Hugh Daly memorandum to James Melton, March 1950, Leonard Papers, Box 19.

82. Donald S. Leonard, notes, 18 March 1950, Leonard Papers, Box 19; Al Kaufman, interview with authors, 24 February 1948.

83. Donald S. Leonard, notes, 20 March 1950, Leonard Papers, Box 19.

84. Hugh Daly memorandum to James Melton, March 1950, Leonard Papers, Box 19.

85. Ibid.

86. Ibid.

87. Ibid.

88. Ibid.

89. Captain Harold V. Mulbar memorandum, 18 January 1945, Leonard Papers, Box 19; Sergeant Leo Van Conant to Oscar G. Olander, 18 January 1945, Leonard Papers, Box 19; Captain Harold V. Mulbar to Donald S. Leonard, 23 March 1950, Leonard Papers, Box 19.

90. Captain Harold V. Mulbar to Donald S.Leonard, 23 March 1950, Leonard Papers, Box 19.

91. Captain Harold V. Mulbar to Donald S. Leonard, 27 March 1950, Leonard Papers, Box 19.

92. Gordon Gillis interview, 4 May 1950, Leonard Papers, Box 19.

93. Ibid.

94. Ibid.

95. Report of Murray Young to Donald S. Leonard, 12 January 1950, Leonard Papers, Box 19.

96. Report of Murray Young to Donald S. Leonard, 18 May 1950, Leonard Papers, Box 19.

97. Ibid. She was paroled to her parents in Council Grove, Kansas.

98. Ibid.

99. Ibid.

100. Ibid.

101. Report of Murray Young to Donald S. Leonard, 2 August 1950, Leonard Papers, Box 19.

102. Ibid.

103. Ibid.

104. Report of Edward Cooper to Donald S. Leonard, 24 July 1950, Leonard Papers, Box 19.

105. Ibid.

106. Earnest C. Brooks to Murray Young, 29 August 1950, Michigan State Police Records. Mahoney's list of questions were: (1) Were you in Albion? (2) Did you kill Hooper? (3) Was your car used by those who killed Hooper? (4) Did you give Harry Fleisher your car to use for the Hooper murder? (5) Did you give a gun to those who killed Hooper? and (6) Did you get rid of the gun that was used to kill Hooper? Ibid.

107. Report of Sergeant W. H. Petermann, 6 September 1950, Leonard Papers, Box 19.

108. *Detroit News*, 7 September 1950.

109. Ibid.

110. Ibid.

111. *Detroit News*, 24 October 1950; Report of Sergeant W. H. Petermann, 22 March 1951, Leonard Papers, Box 19.

112. Report of Murray Young to Donald S. Leonard, 18 April 1951, Leonard Papers, Box 19.

113. Ibid.

114. *Detroit Free Press*, 27 June 1959.

115. Sergeant Thomas Grant to Donald S. Leonard, 2 February 1951, Leonard Papers, Box 19.

116. Ibid.

117. Ibid.

118. *Detroit Times*, 2, 3 February 1951.

119. *Detroit Times*, 2 February 1951; *Detroit News*, 4, 5 February 1951.

120. *Detroit News*, 3 February 1951; Sergeant Thomas Grant to Donald S. Leonard, 3 February 1951, Leonard Papers, Box 19.

121. *Detroit News*, 3 February 1951.

122. Ibid.

123. Ibid.

124. Ibid.

125. Ibid.; Lieutenant Leo Van Conant to Donald S. Leonard, 5 February 1951, Leonard Papers, Box 19.

126. *Detroit News*, 13 February 1952.

127. Leonard was defeated in the primary by Michigan Secretary of State Fred Alger, Jr., scion of one of Michigan's most powerful Republican families. Leonard subsequently was appointed police commissioner of Detroit.

128. When the authors interviewed a state police information officer in 1984, she was unaware that there had been any investigations after the first week of January 1947, because there were no records in their files.

129. *Grand Rapids Press*, 10 October 1953.

130. *Detroit News*, 10 January 1960.

BIBLIOGRAPHIC NOTE

The investigation into the murder of State Senator Warren G. Hooper took us down many paths, some of which led to open doors and others into brick walls. In this respect, we doubtless relived both the exhilaration and frustration experienced by law enforcement agents as they sifted through evidence. Ironically, one of our greatest advantages — the passage of time, which permits reflection — also proved to be one of our biggest disadvantages, as many of those most knowledgeable about the case had long since died.

Individual personalities and their idiosyncrasies were revealed to us through interviews with persons familiar with the main characters involved in the grand jury era. Former political correspondents Don Gardner and Al Kaufman, former Ingham County prosecutor Victor C. Anderson, retired Ingham County Circuit Judge Marvin Salmon, grand jury special prosecutor Richard B. Foster, and ex-Michigan Supreme Court Justice Eugene F. Black introduced us to the private sides of Kim Sigler, Leland W. Carr, Louis Coash, John Simpson, Herbert Rushton, Frank D. McKay, and others who passed through the Lansing scene. Betty Keyes, a lifelong Albion resident who had earned money in her youth babysitting for the Hoopers, not only shared her recollections, but also introduced us to several other persons who recalled the Hoopers and the time in the 1930s when the Purple Gang used Albion as a base of operation. Gertrude Ludwick, who worked in the Ingham County Clerk's office during the 1940s, recounted the excitement generated by the grand jury trials and helped us locate trial transcripts. George V. Mather, longtime editor of the *Albion Evening Recorder*, vividly described the evening of the crime and his ride with Mrs. Hooper to identify the Senator's body. Without their aid, our story would have been much less human and more encyclopedic.

Of course, not all of our overtures were met with gracious acceptance. Former Governor Murray D. Van Wagoner would not speak with us because, as he stated in his letter of refusal, he "was not aware of any corruption in the Michigan legislature" during the 1940s. Since his lieutenant governor had been indicted for taking bribes, his rationale seemed dubious, but Van Wagoner remained adamant. Likewise, reporter Kenneth McCormick, a Sigler confidante, and former state police trooper Kenneth Templin, who was Sigler's chauffeur, did not respond to our attempts to interview them. Most recalcitrant, however, was Callienetta Hooper. Despite oft repeated claims that she sought the solution to her husband's killing, Mrs. Hooper not only refused to reply to letters or speak over the telephone, but she would not accept registered mail in which we explained our findings and requested the opportunity to hear her perspectives. The unexplained, and unexpected, lack of cooperation from the senator's widow was, perhaps, our most significant disappointment.

Another invaluable source of material was the Michigan State Police records of the murder. Colonel Gerald Hough and his staff afforded us every courtesy and made their entire case file open to us. Included were statements by Sam Abramowitz and Henry Luks, as well as everyone questioned concerning the slaying. Photographs, detective reports, and correspondence were put at our disposal. Of particular interest is that the State Police records only went through 1946. The reason for that, as we discovered, was that Commissioner Donald S. Leonard, who served from 1947 to 1952, took all the files on the Hooper killing compiled during his tenure with him when he left office. This action made further probing into the case virtually impossible. Only after his death in 1976 did the missing material reappear, as his family donated his papers to the Michigan Historical Collections of The University of Michigan. Therefore, we were able to do what previously had eluded both researchers and the police: view the complete set of State Police documents on the Hooper assassination.

Other pieces of the puzzle fell into place through persual of the transcripts of the preliminary examination and trial of those charged with conspiracy to murder Senator Hooper. Finding these proved to be a more formidable task than we anticipated, as no one seemed to have any idea where they might be located in the unlikely case that they still existed. Our persistence finally was rewarded when a member of the Calhoun County Clerk's office unearthed a microfilm copy of not only the examination and trial, but also of the material filed by defense attorneys in their appeals.

The most informative personal papers were found in the Michigan Historical Collections of The University of Michigan. Among the most useful were those of Donald S. Leonard; Murl F. DeFoe, an ardent Sigler supporter in the state senate; William Cook, editor of the *Hastings Banner* and early political mentor of Kim Sigler; Attorney General John R. Dethmers; and Booth Newspapers Lansing correspondent Guy H. Jenkins, a political foe of Sigler. Unfortunately, the Frank D. McKay collection was of little value as it contained mostly letters of praise for his civic contributions while revealing nothing about his decades of political activism.

Among government documents housed in the Michigan History Division of the State Archives, the most informative were the Records of the Executive Office, Records of the Attorney General-Criminal Law Division, and Records of the Auditor General. Included in these records were letters between Harry F. Kelly, Herbert Rushton, and Leland W. Carr concerning the operation of the grand jury as well as the complete audit of grand jury expenditures.

Published materials, especially newspapers, were extremely helpful. Especially useful were the three Detroit dailies — the *Free Press, News,* and *Times* — because they assigned staff writers to cover every aspect of the investigation and subsequent trials. Other dailies which utilized staff coverage were the *Battle Creek Enquirer, Jackson Citizen Patriot, Grand Rapids Press, Albion Evening Recorder, Lansing State Journal,* and *Chicago Herald-American.* Wire service accounts, supplemented by editorial comment, were selected from the *Flint Journal, Kalamazoo Gazette, Ontonagon Herald,* and *Port Huron Times Herald.* These newspapers were chosen because of their circulation and geographic representation. The Aristocrat Club trial received extensive coverage in the *Pontiac Press.* Kim Sigler was lionized in his hometown *Hastings Banner,* while his arch-foe Frank D. McKay was defended vigorously by the *Michigan State Digest.* All the reporters took pride in their accuracy, and when published accounts are compared to the court transcripts, their claims are proven true. Reading the daily newspaper was, in fact, the next best thing to being in the courthouse.

Newspaper stories also provided details unavailable in court transcripts. Reporters detailed everything from the temperature to the clothing of the attorneys and juries to the behavior of the gallery to the facial expressions of witnesses. No movement or sound seemed too insignificant to be mentioned. Consequently, these word pictures, when used in conjunction with photographs and trial records, enabled us to reconstruct courtroom scenes in minute detail.

Despite this vast store of material, the story still lacked an essential, but seemingly unobtainable, element: transcripts of interviews taken by Sigler and his staff immediately following the murder. However, all grand jury material had been classified top secret and had never been made public. Moreover, after the conclusion of the grand jury, Judge Coash was reputed to have personally destroyed all the records.

In early 1986 we were notified by the State Archives that a box of grand jury records had been found among their unprocessed materials, but before we could examine it, it had to be turned over to the Criminal Division of the Attorney General's office. After going over the contents, Mr. Robert Ianni of the Criminal Division, permitted us to peruse the materials at his office. By what can be explained only as pure luck, we found ourselves looking at the sworn statements of the men who found Hooper's body, witnesses who saw the assassins' automobile, Hooper's secretary and family attorney, and others. Most important, however, were the lengthy statements made by Mrs. Hooper during her two grillings by Sigler.

These documents, which were never intended to become public, revealed the ruthlessness of Sigler, his motives for not cooperating fully with the state police, and the degree of misinformation he deliberately fed the press concerning the true identity of the murderers. The gaps in the murder probe were now filled. We were able not only to answer, to our satisfaction, the question of who killed Hooper and why, but also to explain how Sigler had placed himself in a position where he neither would nor could reveal the identity of the assassins without doing himself irreparable political damage. The story of one of Michigan's most famous crimes was ready to be told.